STELLER'S ISLAND

STELLER'S ISLAND

Adventures of a Pioneer Naturalist in Alaska

DEAN LITTLEPAGE

THE MOUNTAINEERS BOOKS

THE MOUNTAINEERS BOOKS
*is the nonprofit publishing arm of The Mountaineers Club, an organization
founded in 1906 and dedicated to the exploration, preservation, and
enjoyment of outdoor and wilderness areas.*

1001 SW Klickitat Way, Suite 201, Seattle, WA 98134

First edition, 2006

Manufactured in the United States of America

Acquiring Editor: Kate Rogers
Project Editor: Christine Hosler
Copy Editor: Alice Copp Smith
Cover, Book Design, and Layout: Mayumi Thompson
Cartographer: Linda M. Feltner
Illustrator: Judy Shimono

Cover image: *Off Mount Desert Island* by Fitz Hugh Lane. © Brooklyn Museum
of Art/Corbis
Frontispiece: *Steller's jay (Cyanocitta stelleri)*

Library of Congress Cataloging-in-Publication Data
Littlepage, Dean.
  Steller's island : adventures of a pioneer naturalist in Alaska /
Dean Littlepage.—1st ed.
       p. cm.
  Includes bibliographical references and index.
  ISBN 1-59485-057-7 (pbk.)
  1. Steller, Georg Wilhelm, 1709-1746. 2. Naturalists—Alaska—Biography. 3.
Explorers—Alaska—Biography. 4. Kamchatskaia ekspeditsiia (2nd : 1733-1743)
5. Natural history—Alaska. 6. Alaska—Discovery and exploration. I. Title.
  QH31.S65L58 2007
  508.092—dc22
  [B]
                                        2006025399

I would not exchange the experience of nature I had on this miserable voyage for any amount of money.

—Georg Steller, letter to Johann Gmelin

Contents

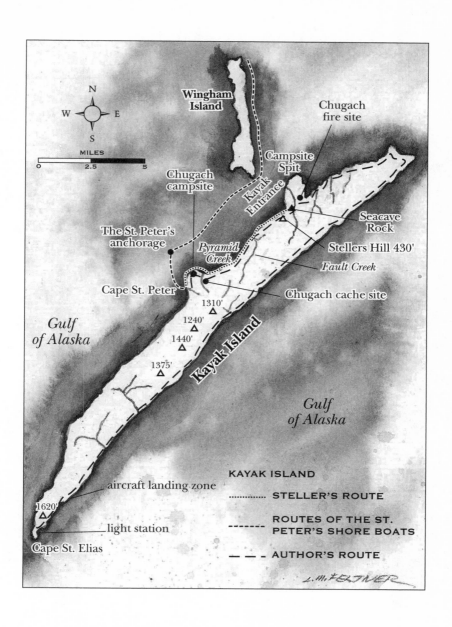

N
W   E
S

MILES
0   2.5   5

Wingham Island

Chugach fire site

Campsite Spit

Chugach campsite

Kayak Entrance

The St. Peter's anchorage

Seacave Rock

Pyramid Creek

Stellers Hill 430'

Fault Creek

Cape St. Peter

Chugach cache site

1310'

Gulf of Alaska

1240'

1440'

Kayak Island

1375'

Gulf of Alaska

KAYAK ISLAND

aircraft landing zone

STELLER'S ROUTE

1620'

ROUTES OF THE ST. PETER'S SHORE BOATS

light station

AUTHOR'S ROUTE

Cape St. Elias

L. M. FELTNER

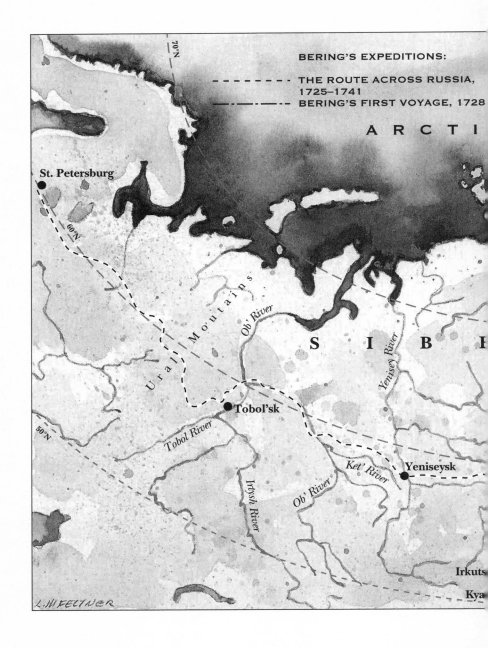

BERING'S EXPEDITIONS:

– – – – – – – – THE ROUTE ACROSS RUSSIA,
1725–1741
—·—·—·— BERING'S FIRST VOYAGE, 1728

A R C T I

St. Petersburg

S   I   B

Ural Moutains

Ob' River

Yenisey River

Tobol'sk

Tobol River

Irtysh River

Ob' River

Ket' River

Yeniseysk

50°N

60°N

70°N

Irkuts

Kya

L.W. FELTNER

MILES
0 100 200 300 400 500

N
W E
S

ALASKA

O C E A N

East
Cape

Diomede
Islands

St.
Lawrence
Island

Bering
Sea

Anadyr River

Kolyma River

Lena River

Aldan River

Yudoma
River

Urak
River

Yakutsk

Okhotsk

I A

Kamchatka

Avacha
Bay

Sea of
Okhotsk

Bol'sheretsk
Cape
Lopatka

50° N

Amur River

Sakhalin
Island

Kuril Islands

70° N

60° N

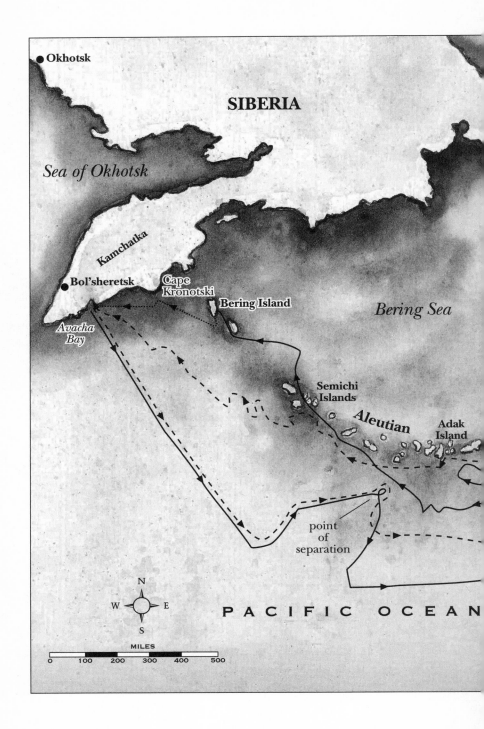

Okhotsk

SIBERIA

Sea of Okhotsk

Kamchatka

Bol'sheretsk

Cape
Kronotski

Bering Island

Bering Sea

Avacha
Bay

Semichi
Islands

Aleutian

Adak
Island

point
of
separation

N
W   E
S

PACIFIC OCEAN

MILES

0   100   200   300   400   500

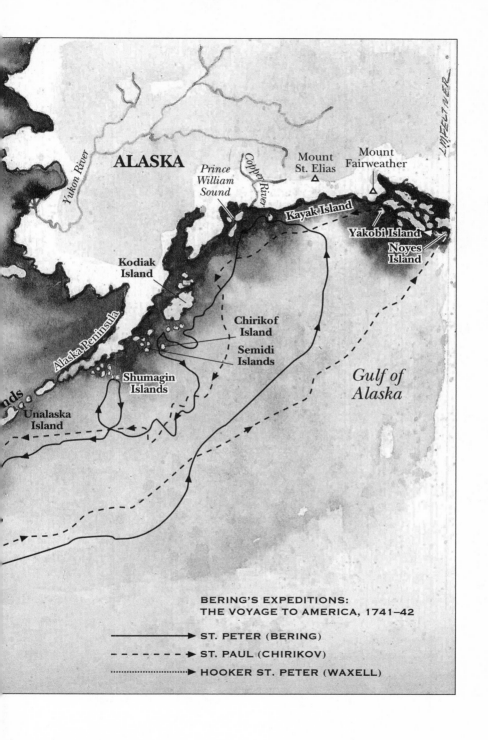

ALASKA

Yukon River

Prince
William
Sound

Copper River

Mount
St. Elias

Mount
Fairweather

Kayak Island

Yakobi Island

Noyes
Island

Kodiak
Island

Alaska Peninsula

Chirikof
Island

Semidi
Islands

Gulf of
Alaska

Shumagin
Islands

Unalaska
Island

nds

BERING'S EXPEDITIONS:
THE VOYAGE TO AMERICA, 1741–42

→ ST. PETER (BERING)

- - - → ST. PAUL (CHIRIKOV)

········→ HOOKER ST. PETER (WAXELL)

Key People on Vitus Bering's Second Kamchatka Expedition

THE AMERICAN EXPEDITION, ON THE ST. PETER:

Vitus Bering, Danish captain of the *St. Peter;* commander of the
Second Kamchatka Expedition

Sven Waxell, Bering's Swedish first lieutenant

Sofron Khitrovo, Bering's second lieutenant, a Russian

Georg Steller, German physician and naturalist; Russian Academy
of Sciences adjunct

Friedrich Plenisner, German surveyor and artist; Steller's friend

Thomas Lepekhin, Steller's Russian assistant

Andreas Hesselberg, first mate and navigator, a 70-year-old German
or Swede

Kharlam Yushin, second mate and keeper of the ship's log, a
Russian

Johan Sind, junior officer, a German

Dmitry Ovtsyn, Russian sailor, a demoted lieutenant; special
assistant to Bering

Nils Jansen, lead boatswain, a Norwegian

Aleksei Ivanov, assistant boatswain, a Russian

Boris Roselius, ship's constable, a Dane

Matthias Betge, Swedish assistant surgeon

Sava Starodubtsov, Russian journeyman carpenter

Nikita Shumagin, Russian sailor

Andrei Tretyakov, Russian army grenadier

Aleksei Chirikov, captain of the *St. Paul,* a Russian

Ivan Yelagin, Russian second mate and navigator

Louis de l'Isle de la Croyère, French geographer and
    astronomer with the Academy of Sciences

Avraam Dementiev, lead boatswain, a Russian

Sidor Savelev, Russian assistant boatswain

Martin Spangberg, Danish captain of the voyage to the Kuril Islands
    and Japan

Johann Gmelin, lead Russian Academy of Sciences biologist, a
    German

Gerhard Müller, lead Academy historian and archivist, a German

Stepan Krashenninikov, Russian student assistant with the Academy

Andrei Krasilnikov, Russian assistant to Louis de l'Isle de la Croyère

Chronology: Steller and the Voyage to America

1709   *March 10:* Georg Wilhelm Steller is born in the Free City of Windsheim (now part of Germany).

1728   Vitus Bering discovers the strait, now Bering Strait, between Asia and North America.

1729   Steller begins his study of theology at the University of Wittenberg.

1731   Enrolls at the University of Halle, studying theology, medicine, and biology.

1732   Bering leaves St. Petersburg, Russia, on his second expedition to eastern Siberia and beyond.

1734   Steller passes an examination in Berlin qualifying him as professor of botany. Arrives in St. Petersburg and finds work in the city's botanical garden.

1737   Appointed adjunct professor of natural history in Russia's Academy of Sciences, assigned to Bering's expedition. Marries Brigitta von Böchler.

1738   Leaves St. Petersburg for Siberia to join the expedition; he and Brigitta separate in Moscow.

1739   *January:* Meets the Academy's Gmelin and Müller in Yeniseysk, Siberia.

         July: Explores Lake Baikal and the Barguzin Mountains.

1740   *August:* Arrives on the Sea of Okhotsk coast; meets Bering for the first time.

September: Arrives in Bol'sheretsk, Kamchatka.

1741   *March:* Joins Bering for the voyage to America in Avacha Bay, Kamchatka.

June: Bering's ship the *St. Peter* and its sister ship, the *St. Paul,* set sail. Two weeks into the voyage, the ships separate in a fog.

July: Steller lands on Kayak Island; his exploration of the island marks the first scientific discoveries in western North America.

August: Bering's crew makes landfall in the Shumagin Islands.

September: After meeting Aleuts in the Shumagins, Steller writes the first detailed account of Alaska's Native people.

November: Suffering from a scurvy epidemic, the crew anchors the storm-battered ship off Bering Island. Led by Steller, they prepare to spend the winter on the island. A storm drives the ship onto the beach and destroys the hull.

December: Bering dies.

1742   *January:* The scurvy epidemic abates after thirty-two deaths.

July: Steller dissects a sea cow and drafts the only written account of the living animal.

August: The forty-six survivors sail away from the island in a small "hooker" built from the wreckage of the ship. Thirteen days later they land in Kamchatka.

1743   Steller completes his journal of the voyage.

1746   *November 12:* Steller dies of a sudden illness in western Siberia.

1751   *De Bestiis Marinis* (*The Beasts of the Sea*) is published in St. Petersburg.

Steller's "Beasts of the Sea"

All are marine mammals that inhabit (or, in the case of the Steller's sea cow, formerly inhabited) the arc of the North Pacific from Japan to California.

Sea otter *(Enhydra lutris):* A coastal sea mammal with the thickest fur of any animal on earth; related to the river otter and the mink; feeds on shellfish and fish.

Steller sea lion *(Eumotopias jubatus,* formerly *Eumotopias stelleri):* A large sea lion, related to seals and fur seals; feeds on fish and squid; spends much of the year on coastal rocks and islands.

Northern fur seal *(Callorhinus ursinus):* A bearlike, fish-eating seal with a thick fur, closely related to Steller and other sea lions; migrates long distances and spends much of the year at sea.

Steller's sea cow *(Hydrodamalis gigas,* formerly *Rhytina stelleri):* A coastal, kelp-grazing sea mammal, a relative of the manatees and dugongs; extinct by 1768.

Steller's sea-eagle *(Haliaeetus pelagicus)*

No one who has studied the life of the land doubts
that the vast ocean is full of unknown creatures.

—Steller, *The Beasts of the Sea*

A calm summer afternoon is unfolding in the dripping waterfront village of Cordova, Alaska. Things are not always so calm here; since my
last visit, the unfortunately named Whirlwind Laundromat, formerly
a fixture on Cordova's main drag, was torn apart in a Pacific storm.
A few rainsqualls blew through town this morning, but the skies are
clearing now as my friend Phil North and I hop into a small Cessna
and buckle up for takeoff from Cordova's airstrip. After a few minutes
of checking gauges and warming up the engine, pilot Steve Ranney
lifts the plane off the runway for the 60-mile flight to Kayak Island,
birthplace of science in western North America.

Phil and I are headed to the island to retrace the route of Georg
Steller, he of Steller's jay and the Steller sea lion, Steller's sea-eagle,
and the extinct Steller's sea cow. Steller was the first naturalist to visit
North America's Pacific Coast, and Kayak Island was the first American landfall of the grueling ten-year expedition that brought Steller
to this coast in 1741—an expedition captained by Vitus Bering, the
Bering of the Bering Sea and Bering Strait.

We have eight days' worth of food and gear with us and, weather
permitting, intend to cover most of the shoreline of the island, which
measures roughly twenty miles long and one to two miles wide. We'll
spend most of our time near the two capes that figured prominently

in the expedition: Cape St. Elias, at the south end of the island, the point of land Steller first sighted, and Cape St. Peter, on the west coast, where Steller first landed and science began on the American side of the Pacific. The plan is to set up a base camp at St. Peter and spend several days at the end of the trip exploring the country where Steller walked, to see the places where he formed his first impressions of a land new to science, and to tease out what his journey can tell us about the land and the oceans today.

Tall, dark-bearded Phil is an aquatic ecologist, a practical sort of scientist with a rare combination of intelligence and resourcefulness. A field biologist for many years, he spends much of his time in an office these days, but he still loves to explore a new valley, mountain, or island and figure out its plant and animal personality. Kayak Island, we were happy to learn, is a great destination for this kind of trip. Lying in a transition between the life zones of Southcentral and Southeast Alaska, on an exposed coast, and set out from the coastal mountains, the island is a biological melting pot, the home of an outrageous array of creatures. Steller was the first to prove it; he identified no fewer than 140 types of plants in six hours on the island's west coast.

I come to Kayak Island and Steller's story as a writer, historian, and naturalist, much less versed in hard science than Phil but no less fascinated with the North Pacific. This ocean has drawn me back many times since I first launched a kayak into saltwater many years ago. Nowhere else is there anything like the life of the northern seas: seabirds by the thousands rafting on the water and nesting on rocky headlands; the surreal, alien life of the intertidal zone; and the huge numbers of salmon that gather for spawning runs up their natal streams.

Above all, however, the North Pacific coast is about marine mammals. In my kayak wanderings I've paddled silently to the edges of ice floes where harbor seals lay sleeping; floated through a sea otter nursery of a hundred mothers with their pups on their chests; slipped by sleeping otters, the animals wrapped in brown leaves of kelp while they dozed; drifted past scores of sea lions resting on haulout rocks; traveled with a trio of juvenile sea lions that frolicked around me for hours as I paddled along the shoreline of Prince William Sound; chanced on a pod of orcas at close range and studied a dead, beached orca at much closer range; and met the eye of a great, barnacled gray whale that rose straight out of the sea, in a boiling of water, to stare at me in my kayak from three feet away.

The mammals put me on Steller's trail. Who was this naturalist of long ago who has had his name attached to so many of the creatures of the North Pacific? The trail led first to Steller's journal of his trip to America, and then to his largely forgotten manuscript *The Beasts of the Sea,* the first scientific account of the mammals of the North Pacific. The swath of Steller's influence, it turned out, went far beyond science and pure knowledge: he and the other members of his expedition spread the word of the North Pacific's rich web of life across Asia and Europe, kicking off a rush to cash in on the life of the sea. The North Pacific has never been the same.

Inevitably, Steller's trail led to Kayak Island. Now, taking off from Cordova, packed into the Cessna with our gear lashed down behind us, we're less than an hour's flight from the island. It took Steller's expedition nine years to get there, so our trip hardly registers on the scale of his journey. The island, however, is not all that different today from what it was like in Steller's time and before. Taking the long view, the only people with any real presence on Kayak Island have been Alaska Native hunting parties, and there have been precious few of them in the last century or so. Only in the last few of the island's heartbeats have other Europeans followed Steller there: a handful of explorers, a few lighthouse keepers, and lately, the odd beachcomber, hiker, hunter, or weather refugee. The talk of the coffeehouse in Cordova this morning was the lone boater who, steering his small powerboat south, landed on Kayak Island after a pummeling in high winds and heavy seas, and was forced to wait out the blow for several days before escaping.

South of Cordova now, the Cessna floats over the 1,100-square-mile Copper River Delta, the biggest wetland on the Pacific Coast and a rest and feeding stop for millions of migrating shorebirds and waterfowl. Even from a thousand feet up, the delta sprawls over our field of view in a mosaic of greens, browns, grays, and blues. We pass over thickets of willow and alder, patches of dark-green spruce, marshes, mud flats, ponds sprinkled at random on the landscape—each with its own miniature pair of white swans—and veins of water in winding sloughs and slow-moving streams. Most of the streams are plugged at some point by beaver dams, which show from this altitude as tiny

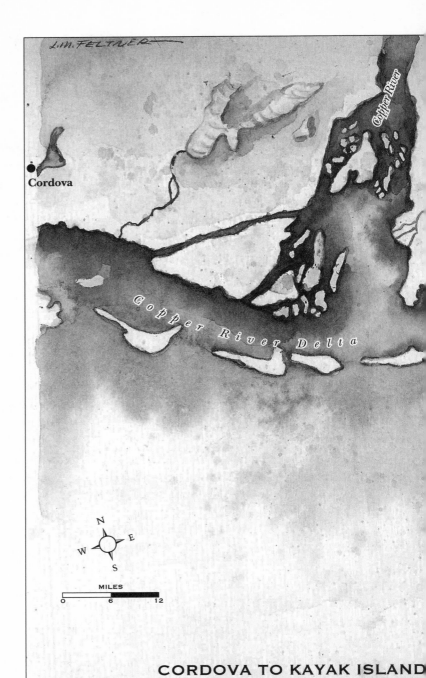

L.M. FELTNER

Copper River

Cordova

Copper River Delta

N
W E
S

MILES
0   6   12

CORDOVA TO KAYAK ISLAND

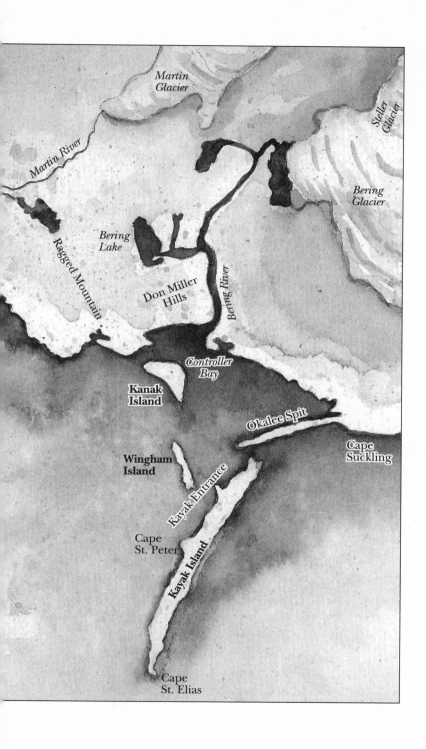

Martin
Glacier

Steller
Glacier

Martin River

Bering
Glacier

Ragged Mountain

Bering
Lake

Don Miller
Hills

Bering River

Controller
Bay

Kanak
Island

Okalee Spit

Cape
Suckling

Wingham
Island

Kayak Entrance

Cape
St. Peter

Kayak Island

Cape
St. Elias

bundles of sticks across slim trickles of water, like the twig dams the kids of suburbia build in street gutters. Toward the ocean, the colors fade to pastel—brown silt bars, gray sea—and rows of waves are breaking over long, soft beaches.

The delta's green drops behind us, and now Steve has us over the river, gray-brown and cloudy, chopped into channels by countless silt bars and islands. In another minute we're over the true mouth, all water, the whole expanse nearly ten miles wide. The Copper, one of the great rivers of Alaska, is very much a watercourse created by glaciers. After roaring out of the icy mass of Mount Wrangell several hundred miles to the north, it collects rivers and streams from four great mountain ranges, all of them heavily glaciated, on its way to the sea. The rock flour the ice grinds out of the mountains ends up here, at the mouth of the river, building new land out into the Gulf of Alaska. The silt below us is deep enough to bury a sixty-story building.

Beyond the river, we glide along the edge of Ragged Mountain, a giant dorsal fin rising out of flat terrain. Another minute, and the ocean opens beneath us. Out the window to the left is Kayak Island's neighbor, Wingham Island. Beyond is Controller Bay, a shallow bay that encloses the mouth of the Bering River, which drains a section of the wild, glaciated St. Elias Range. The range is obscured by fog and clouds today, but the map shows, back among the high peaks and glaciers, several names from Steller's expedition: Steller Glacier, Bering Glacier, and on knife-edged Waxell Ridge, rising above the rivers of ice, a 10,617-foot peak called Mount Steller.

On Wingham Island's rugged west coast, kittiwakes are circling a towering green sea stack that plunges into a foamy blue sea. The Cessna turns east and tops out over the island, and a view opens across the summit of Wingham to Cape St. Peter, the westernmost point of Kayak Island, with its oddly regular, parallel lines of tide-washed reef rock. We pass over the reef, and Steve brings us down onto the sandy beach in the bight south of the cape, the same beach where Georg Steller landed in a small boat in 1741.

Phil and I pile out of the plane with two heavy dry bags of supplies we're caching here for the base camp we'll occupy in a few days. We cross a small creek and push through a band of brushy alders at the back of the beach, to the first big Sitka spruce with stout limbs. We hang our bags high in the tree, out of reach of any bears that might wander by. Then we hike back to the plane, and we're off for Cape St. Elias.

Back in the air again, we spot a brown bear ambling along the coast between the two capes, precisely the reason we hung our supplies in the spruce. In a few minutes the Cessna swings around the white granite cliffs of Cape St. Elias, a bare rock face that plunges a third of a vertical mile to a narrow strip of gentle terrain along the coast. Nestled at the base of the cliffs below us, in a thick, green swath of brush 80 feet above the sea, is a covey of red roofs, the buildings that make up the Cape St. Elias lighthouse station. The lighthouse, vintage 1916 and a bit dilapidated now, has been unstaffed and automated since the 1970s.

St. Elias stands tall as the highest point on the island. The cape and its outlying cohort Pinnacle Rock, a 500-foot pyramid of the same white rock as the cape, are the last points of land off the Gulf of Alaska coast for 6,000 miles. If you sailed away on a roughly southwest course from here, your next landfall, if you happened to miss the tiny atolls of Micronesia, would be Papua New Guinea or eastern Australia.

This thumb of land was the first point on the island Steller and Bering sighted. Bering named it for the Russian Orthodox Church's St. Elias, and the name stuck to both the cape and the mainland mountains behind the island, one of the world's great alpine ranges. Bering named the cape, not the island; it was another set of Russian explorers, forty years later, who recorded *Kayak Island* on their chart after learning the name from the Chugach, the Native people of this part of the coast.

The island is clearly kayak-shaped—long and narrow, with a sharp "bow" at Cape St. Elias. The shape is easy to pick out on a map, and it would certainly have been obvious even without a map to the Chugach, who lived here seasonally and used kayaks for fishing and marine-mammal hunting. And, as I see now from the plane, the kayak connection also has a vertical expression, one that may have had special significance for the Chugach: the vertical walls of the cape mimic the tall, piercing prow of their traditional kayak, slicing through the waves as it aims the island-kayak south into the open sea.

Pilot Steve steers us east around the kayak-bow cape and then north toward our drop-off point, a skinny strip of beach on the east side of the island. Putting the Cessna into a set of aerial switchbacks, he lowers us gently toward the earth. He aims for two orange buoys that mark the landing zone on a stretch of shale beach, and quickly the plane's wheels are rolling to a stop. We unload our packs, drag them clear of the plane, and wave to Steve that we're out of his way. The Cessna revs up, lifts off the beach, and disappears in the direction of Cordova.

As the drone of the plane fades, the wildness of the place settles over us, and our senses begin to fine-tune to the subtler cues of the landscape. For weeks before the trip I studied maps of the island, willing the winding contour lines, green shading of forests, blue creek courses, and triangles of peaks and offshore rocks to conjure a three-dimensional image of the land in my mind's eye. Now the physical reality of the island begins to blend with the account in Steller's journal. For the next eight days, we'll be immersed in the life of this wild island and the story of Steller, his journey, and the creatures of the ocean that he introduced to the world.

Bering's ship, the *St. Peter*

CAPE ST. ELIAS

The mountains were so lofty we could see them quite clearly
at sea at a [great] distance. . . . I do not remember seeing a
higher mountain range in all of Siberia and Kamchatka.

—Steller, *Journal*

Just off the southern Alaska coast, 200 miles east of Anchorage, a
lanky island knifes out into the Pacific, intercepting the sea currents
that sweep north and west along the coast in a great gyre from Asia.
Kayak Island is locally famous for a beach that catches nearly every
piece of debris that drifts by. It's also famous for a party of explorers
it caught more than 250 years ago: a Russian expedition that brought
western North America its first naturalist.

It was the summer of 1741. The British still ruled the future
United States of America. Thomas Jefferson, Meriwether Lewis, and
William Clark had not been born, and the Lewis and Clark Expedition was still sixty years in the future. No European knew the shape
of North America's North Pacific coastline, but that was about to
change. The expedition's ship *St. Peter* dropped anchor off Kayak

Island, and a German naturalist, squeezed tightly against the rail, breathed in the view of dense forests against a background of great icy peaks like gulps of oxygen for his soul. After being cooped up on the small, crowded ship for nearly seven weeks since sailing away from Asia, searching for the coast of America but never sighting so much as a speck of land, thirty-two-year-old Georg Steller was finally going to set foot on terra firma again.

Steller had vaulted wall after wall of obstacles to get this far. He was near the bottom of the pecking order in the Russian Academy of Sciences, but he had managed to outlast all his "superiors" over the course of a long, hard trek across Asia. The expedition—formally known as the Second Kamchatka Expedition—had devoured nearly a decade since its sendoff from the Russian capital of St. Petersburg in 1732.

The other Academy scientists had traveled in style, with a safari of field chefs, crates of fine food and wine, a library, and cartloads of instruments, but they had given up on the expedition in the wilderness of Siberia. Steller had pressed on, traveling like a backpacker with just a plate, pot, and cup for a kitchen and some blankets and a pocket-knife as his personal gear. A huge contrast to the other scientists of the time, Steller was the John Muir of his century, a naturalist of wild country who did without the usual comforts, traveling light and exploring vast stretches of territory. He scandalized other scientists by refusing to wear a powdered wig, but the academic look meant nothing to Vitus Bering, the commander of the expedition to find the unknown coast of America. When Steller arrived in Kamchatka, at the far end of Asia, Bering invited him to join the voyage, and Steller accepted.

Bering, a Dane sailing for Russia, was leading a foray to explore all of northeastern Asia and find and chart America's northwestern coast. On the maps of the day, that coast was a blank space north of Cape Blanco, in what is now southern Oregon; to the south, Spanish mariners had traced the coastline, but no scientist had landed on that coast or explored any part of it. Bering's crew, with thousands of laborers pressed into service along the way, had hauled the expedition's food, supplies, tons of iron, shipbuilding tools, cannon, guns and ammunition, trade goods, and nautical and scientific equipment across Asia by wagon, sled, horseback, backpack, and boat and had then built Bering's ship, as well as its sister ship the *St. Paul,* on the shore of the Sea of Okhotsk, in eastern Siberia. By the time Bering and Steller reached Kayak Island, they had 9,000 miles behind them, 7,000 overland and 2,000 at sea, dwarfing Lewis and Clark's much later expedition to the same Northwest Coast.

As the *St. Peter* lay off Kayak Island, Steller's excitement grew as he packed his things to go ashore, but Bering would not let him leave the ship; the captain, worried about how late in the season the voyage was running, wanted to sail as soon as possible. Steller objected, and Bering relented, sending him to the island in a shore boat with a small party of sailors under orders to fill the ship's water barrels. An hour later, Steller jumped out of the boat and landed on North American sand, the first scientist to set foot anywhere on the western half of the continent.

He had to work quickly. Bering had threatened to leave him there if he failed to return to the landing in a few hours, so Steller dashed off along the coastline, plucking and identifying plants as he went. In the first few miles of his ramble he found a camp and cache left by the Native people of the coast. The people had to be nearby; the trail that led to the cache was clumsily hidden with a few branches, probably by someone who had left in a hurry only a few minutes before. But Bering was in a hurry himself, so Steller had to cut his exploration short and rush back to the boat.

In the short time Bering had given him, Steller pulled together the raw material for the first account of the life of western North America, a catalog of the plants of Kayak Island. From the camp and cache, he deduced enough about indigenous life to write the first description of the Northwest Coast's Native people. He also scribbled into his notes his theory that America's Native people must have migrated from Asia; it was the first expression of a theory that is universally accepted today. He also set down a word-picture of the black-crested, cobalt-blue bird so familiar today to the people of the Pacific Coast and the western mountains, the bird we call Steller's jay.

In addition to the jay and other "charismatic" animals that bear his name—a sea lion, an eider, an eagle, and the sea cow—Steller wrote first descriptions of hundreds of the plants and animals of northeastern Asia and western North America, including several later mistakenly attributed to Meriwether Lewis. Today Steller turns up as well in the names of less charismatic creatures such as shellfish and plants.

Steller was the first to tell the story of the North Pacific's marine mammals. This ocean is their nirvana, home to more than thirty species of the animals, and the cradle of evolution of sea otters, sea lions, and fur seals. It is the only place in which a sirenian, a manatee-like animal, evolved to live in a cold ocean, and Steller was the only scientist to observe and describe the creature before hunters wiped out the species. Steller's paper *The Beasts of the Sea* describes this extinct sea cow—now called Steller's sea cow—and the sea otter, the Steller sea lion, and the northern fur seal, as Steller experienced them, here in marine mammal heaven.

In late June, more than 250 years after Steller walked the shoreline of Kayak Island, a much humbler expedition has just landed on the island, two miles north of Cape St. Elias, the first point of land on the island Bering and Steller sighted. Ecologist Phil North and I are looking around, getting our bearings. From where we're standing, on a narrow strip of shale beach, barely long and wide enough to land a plane, set in the middle of an expansive band of dead-level reef-rock, we can see the nearest breakers pounding the rocky edge of the reef several hundred yards away.

As we witnessed on our flight, the island is still nearly as wild as it was in Steller's day, but now we see that it isn't a wilderness frozen in time. Back toward the island proper, two beach lines stand out in the distance, a quarter-mile or more away. The one nearer us is an active beach, exposed to the ocean and backed by a log-strewn storm berm, while farther back a terrace grown up in an even-aged stand of young spruces stands high and dry, cut off from the sea. The spruce-covered terrace was the active beach before Alaska's great earthquake of 1964. Kayak Island rose ten feet in the earthquake; the reef where we're standing was well under the sea before then.

The story of the reef today, however, is the amazing collection of flotsam that has come to rest here. We spot colors not found in nature—the fluorescent green of a plastic bottle, the baby-blue of a chunk of styrofoam—and a scattering of ship bumpers and buoys, sheets of plywood and insulation, and plastic laundry baskets. More exotic are a blue plastic case with red Korean characters, empty Japanese whiskey bottles, and a striking red log with a delicious, musty scent lying back in the jumble of tree trunks on the storm berm. The log, a western red-cedar, grows nowhere near here; the closest source is a good 500 miles to the south. Out toward the water, a computer monitor sits upright on the reef, the screen slightly scratched from its time in the surf but otherwise intact, as if you could sit down in front of it and log on.

Of more interest to two hikers are the dark-blue cylinders of rolled-up, inflatable campers' sleeping pads, of a French brand called L'Aventurier, and, yes, the pads have definitely had an adventure at sea. Phil rummages through them, finding most either saturated with seawater through an open air valve, ripped on the rocks, or covered with sticky tar. We're believers now in the tales we've heard about this side of the island; this is the Mother of All Catch-Beaches.

The Kayak Island catch-beach is what it is because of ocean currents. The sea spits up its contents here, onto an east-facing beach on a west coast, because of the peculiarities of the sea currents along the Alaska coast. Picture an object—say, a rubber ducky bathtub toy— dropped over the side of a boat in the middle of the North Pacific at about latitude 50°. The prevailing west winds that drive ocean circulation at this latitude would carry it toward the American coast on the east-running Subarctic Current. Before it reached the coast, the floating duck would probably catch the Alaska Current, a sweeping saltwater river that flows north and west, parallel to the Alaska coastline, in an immense semicircle from northern British Columbia, along the Southeast and Southcentral Alaska coasts, and eventually out the Aleutian Island chain, where it is known as the Alaska Stream.

Now imagine that same rubber duck floating north and west on the Alaska Current, a few miles off the Gulf of Alaska coast and south of the mouth of the Copper River. It's humming along, ready to shoot to the west along the coastline outside Prince William Sound, but, ahead, there's an island that bulges out into the current like a jetty in a harbor, clearly in the way. On a westerly swell the duck rides up into the shallows, runs into the surf, washes up on Kayak Island's east beach, and settles in with all the other junk.

And, in fact, a 1992 spill of a shipping container of bathtub toys— red beavers, blue turtles, green frogs and, yes, yellow ducks—was a

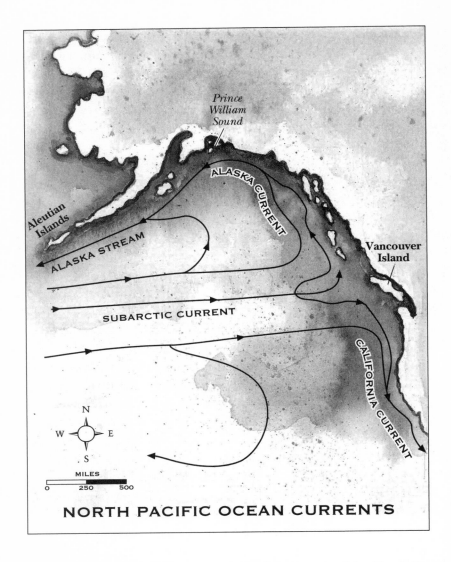

Prince
William
Sound

ALASKA CURRENT

Aleutian
Islands

ALASKA STREAM

SUBARCTIC CURRENT

Vancouver
Island

CALIFORNIA CURRENT

N

W · E

S

MILES

0   250   500

NORTH PACIFIC OCEAN CURRENTS

big help to oceanographers in mapping the currents of the North Pacific. The currents, the ocean's "sea winds," are a mosaic of saltwater streams, gyres, and eddies—and a conveyer belt that drives debris to Kayak Island, creates a tasty buffet of fish for marine mammals, and helped bring Steller here in 1741.

A few minutes of flotsam exploring is enough; Phil and I hoist our packs and hike south toward Cape St. Elias. An eagle chirrups at us from its perch high on the bluff as we round the next point, where we strike a stretch of rocky beach beneath the granite face of Cape St. Elias. Horizontal and vertical fracture lines lace the white cliffs, the pattern of a giant's fishing net hung over the cape to dry. Clumps of monkeyflowers anchor themselves at the base of the wall under small trickles of moisture working down the cliff rock. The trickles gather into small, fresh streams of water and gurgle into the tide between desk-size boulders.

We hop from boulder to boulder, over chunks of conglomerate, silty sedimentary rocks with fossilized worm tracks, and a slice of shale with a foot-long fossil fern. Here and there we have to meander around great whitish gray boulders that are exfoliating in pieces like dinosaur eggs hatching in a Lost World movie. The boulder-eggs are eroding out of the cliff face, apparently hurtling down to the beach now and then. We spot one near the top, hanging halfway out of the wall, and hope that this isn't its time to come crashing down as we walk underneath.

Now we turn the corner of the cape and take in the scene at the end of the island. The pyramid of Pinnacle Rock protrudes into the blue-gray, high-cloudy sky, and its glaucous-winged gull rookery peals with the maniacal laughter of hundreds of mad-scientist birds, all wedged onto tiny ledges on the rock face. Above the din of the gulls we can make out the roaring bedlam of the sea lion haulout on the boulders beyond the pinnacle.

Steller didn't mention a sea lion haulout at Cape St. Elias in his journal, but he spotted whales, harbor seals, and rafts of otters from the western shoreline of Kayak Island. Later, when the expedition had to pass a winter stranded in the western Aleutians, he would spend several months studying and writing about sea mammals.

After Steller, everything would change, both for the animals and for the indigenous people of the coast who subsisted on them. And hundreds of years later, Kayak Island, science's first landfall on North America's Pacific Coast, would play a pivotal role in the fate of the animals Steller first studied and described. A story that began here, one summer more than 250 years ago, would ripple out into Steller's "vast oceans" and across time from his era to our own.

Steller's jay *(Cyanocitta stelleri)*

BLUE JAYS AND CHOCOLATE

*This bird alone sufficiently convinced me that we were
really in America.*

—Steller, *Journal*

Steller's discoveries and the European opening of the North Pacific were built on a mountain of iron, vodka, and human suffering.

Imagine it this way: to trek overland as far as Bering's expedition did across northern Europe and Asia to reach Russia's Pacific Coast, you would have to hike the north-south length of California, Oregon, and Washington in triplicate. If you started hiking in the south, in the desert on the Mexican border, you would walk north to Canada, then turn around and hike back to Mexico, and turn north once more, finally finishing the trip in the fir forest of the Canadian border country. To carry the sheer weight Bering's men had to haul—literally a million pounds of everything from food and drink to anchors and cannon—you would need to recruit twenty thousand of your closest friends with backpacks to go with you . . . assuming you could find a backpack big enough to carry a cannon.

Bering, however, started with a mere five hundred men, engaged another five hundred soldiers from outposts in Siberia, and impressed into service about two thousand Siberian exiles and Native people along the route—the same way the English Navy filled out its ships with sailors at the time. To move the million pounds of cargo, the expedition team cleared trails, slapped together bridges, and built rivergoing rafts and boats. They ran rivers great and small, and hauled boats and baggage upstream on others, fighting swift currents as they went. They led pack strings of hundreds of horses and teams of reindeer sleds, dragged heavy sleds themselves, and, finally, at the end of the journey, commandeered four thousand sled dogs and several hundred Native laborers for the last leg of the trek to the Pacific. Besides the physical labor, Bering and his lieutenants spent their energy arguing and horse trading (again, literally) to wheedle supplies and transport help out of reluctant Russian bureaucrats in the tiny outposts on the way east.

The route Bering took across Russia was anything but a straight line. Only their first few hundred miles east of St. Petersburg followed a well-traveled road. For the rest of the 7,000-mile journey to the Pacific, the route was off the beaten path, up and down rivers and over portages and mountains, taking in long stretches of three of the world's longest rivers: the Ob', the Yenisey, and the Lena.

Once across the Ural Mountains, Bering and his men entered Siberia and Asia, leaving Europe behind and beginning a 2,000-mile stretch of the expedition through the valleys of the Ob' and its tributaries: down the Tobol River to Tobol'sk, the only city of any size in Siberia at the time, then down the Irtysh to the Ob', up the Ob' and the Ket', to a portage that led to the Yenisey.

From there they ascended the Yenisey and the Angara, lining and portaging up the upper Angara and then crossing an 80-mile portage to the Lena. Next they traveled 1,500 miles down the Lena, a leg of the journey that by itself was almost as long as a float down North America's Yukon River. Past the remote post at Yakutsk, they left the Lena, turning up the Aldan River and then the Yudoma River, fighting the current all the way. When the water grew too shallow to float, they abandoned their boats and cut overland across a 100-mile mountain portage to the Urak River, where they built another flotilla of boats.

They ran wildly down the rocky, swift-running Urak to the coast of the Sea of Okhotsk, where Bering set up a shipbuilding camp. Next, in ships built on the Okhotsk coast over the course of nearly two years, they sailed 600 sea miles to the west coast of Kamchatka, the California-size peninsula at the far edge of the Russian empire. The final leg, to Avacha Bay on Kamchatka's east coast, was one of the most difficult: either a dangerous sea voyage around Cape Lopatka, Kamchatka's southern tip, or a 140-mile overland crossing of the cold spine of mountains along the crest of the peninsula.

And, remarkably, this was the *second* time Bering had pushed his way across Asia. On his first trip, an expedition that had begun in 1725, it had been even worse. The route then was essentially untracked wilderness beyond the post at Yakutsk; this time, Bering knew the best combination of routes, but he had much more equipment to transport, more people to organize, and much more ambitious objectives to fulfill.

On the first expedition, Bering's goal had been to find out whether Asia and America joined at the far northern reaches of the two continents. From his deathbed, Tsar Peter the Great had written very simple orders for Bering: to build one or two decked boats somewhere on the coast of eastern Siberia, to sail north along the Asian coast and see whether it joined America, and if he found the American coast, to follow it, chart it, and return.

It was Peter's final act in his drive to Europeanize his feudal empire, which when his reign began was still looking toward the Asia of Genghis Khan. The greatest physical symbol of his westernization campaign was Russia's new capital on the Baltic Sea at St. Petersburg. It was a city of canals and palaces built on pilings in the wetlands at the mouth of the Neva River, a new capital built to replace Moscow as Russia's leading city.

In 1717 Peter had visited Paris to meet with France's scientific academy. One of the great geographical questions of the day was whether or not an arctic sea passage existed between the Atlantic and the Pacific, a route across the top of Europe and Asia to Japan. If it existed, a northern sea passage would cut travel time from Europe to Japan, as one optimist of the era estimated, from the usual eight months around Africa's Cape of Good Hope to six weeks via the Arctic

Ocean. A key issue was whether Asia joined America in the far North; the question of whether sea ice conditions would allow passage, obviously a major concern, would be moot if the two continents joined and there was no sea route at all.

In Paris, French scientists asked Peter to allow their explorers to look into the geography of that part of the world, but Peter refused. He decided he would do it himself; exploring and mapping the far northern Pacific would bring European-style scientific achievement to Russia, but, more important, it would help him lay claim to any lands Russians discovered in that part of the Pacific, and to the eastern entrance to the arctic sea passage if it existed.

Peter's orders in hand, Bering had worked with his two lieutenants, the Dane Martin Spangberg and the Russian Aleksei Chirikov, to organize his first expedition to Asia. The initial wave of the expedition, a convoy of twenty-six men and twenty-five wagonloads of supplies, pulled out of St. Petersburg in January 1725, four days before Peter died.

It took Bering and his crew more than three years to launch into the North Pacific. In July 1728 they sailed away from Asia in the *St. Gavriel,* a ship they had built on the eastern, Pacific coast of Kamchatka. Running north off the coast of Siberia in near-constant sea fog, Bering passed a prominent cape that fell away to the west, now called East Cape. The wide-open sea ahead seemed to indicate that there was no land to the north, and therefore no land connection between Asia and America.

For most of his career with the Russian Navy, Bering had been a transport ship captain, an able mariner whose job it was to bring crew and cargo home safely. Now, falling back on that experience, he cautiously decided to bring the ship around and return to Kamchatka. They returned in September, having sighted and named two islands in the strait, now known as Bering Strait, that they had sailed through: St. Lawrence Island and "St. Diomede," the western of the two Diomede Islands, now called Big Diomede. In good weather, the Alaska coastline is visible from the Diomedes; the enveloping sea fog was apparently all that had prevented Bering from sighting the American mainland.

Back in St. Petersburg, Bering's report on the voyage was not well received. His critics thought the expedition had proven nothing; he had not sighted the American mainland and had no way of knowing whether there was a connection between the two continents farther to the north than he had sailed. Bering replied with a proposal for a second, more ambitious expedition, one that would map three huge regions: the coastline of the Siberian Arctic, the western North Pacific south to Japan, and the coastline of northwestern North America.

Two years later, his proposal came back to him as orders for another expedition, the Second Kamchatka Expedition. Bering would be receiving a promotion to "captain-commander," but the scope of the expedition he was to lead was far greater than his already ambitious plan. He was to conduct the triple expedition he had proposed, to the Siberian Arctic, Japan, and America; he was also to find an easier land route to Kamchatka, prospect for minerals everywhere he went, establish schools, ports, docks, lighthouses, and ironworks in various places, and start a cattle-raising project to feed the Russians in eastern Siberia.

There was one other detail. While Bering had been away, Peter's widow and successor Catherine had followed through on her late husband's plan to found a Russian Academy of Sciences, more or less a copy of the French academy. It was well established now, staffed mainly with German, Swiss, and French scientists, and its leaders had managed to squeeze their own agenda into Bering's orders as well. The Russian Academy would be mounting, with Bering's full logistical support, a scientific exploration of all of northern Asia.

The Academy's role in the second expedition would ultimately be Steller's wedge into the North Pacific. But the landfall on Kayak Island was still a decade away, when, after Catherine's death, newly crowned Empress Anna approved all the additions to Bering's proposal and gave the Second Kamchatka Expedition a royal push, sending Bering off with a detailed set of instructions late in 1732. As nineteenth-century Bering biographer Peter Lauridsen described the countdown to the expedition, Anna and her inner circle saw Bering's expedition as a path to glory and lost all sense of proportion:

> *They had at their disposal an academy of science, a fleet, and the resources of a mighty empire. The sacrifice of a few thousand lives troubled them but little, and they exerted themselves to make the enterprise as large and sensational as possible.*

Anna had put Bering in charge of one of the most ambitious explorations in history. It was as if Thomas Jefferson had told Lewis and Clark not just to trace the Missouri River and find out whether there was a practical water route to the Pacific, but also to map all the rivers and mountains of western North America, build forts and trading posts in every major valley, write an encyclopedia of the West's plants, animals, and minerals, do a comprehensive inventory of gold and silver prospects, and build a ship, sail to Hawaii, and chart the coastlines of all the islands.

The scientific corps of Bering's Second Kamchatka Expedition set out from St. Petersburg late in 1733. It was not a modest entourage: there were thirty people including field chefs, a library of several hundred books, kegs of wine, crates of fine food, nine cartloads of scientific instruments, and the two hundred horses it took to move all the people, supplies, and equipment. Georg Steller joined the expedition late, leaving St. Petersburg in January of 1738, more than four years behind the other scientists. Traveling light and covering ground quickly, he caught up with the professors in early 1739 in Yeniseysk, a village on the Yenisey River, where they were wintering.

Steller spent a few weeks in Yeniseysk with the two leaders of the Academy corps, both fellow Germans: biologist Johann Gmelin and historian Gerhard Müller. Gmelin and Müller had traveled as far east as Yakutsk, but a fire had destroyed all of Gmelin's collections and Müller had fallen seriously ill, so they had retreated to Yeniseysk to recover and make new plans. They had sent a Russian student assistant, Stepan Krashenninikov, ahead to Kamchatka to find quarters for them and to set up the logistics for their travel and work there. But now, soured on the harsh life of the expedition, Gmelin and Müller were quick to take Steller up on his offer to continue to the Pacific alone.

In March, while the professors huddled in front of a fireplace, Steller left Yeniseysk and traveled 800 miles over the late-winter snow to the town of Irkutsk, near the shore of Siberia's great Lake Baikal. Irkutsk was booming with the explosion of trade with China along the Mongolian border, but all the food, horses, and dogs in town were not enough to meet the demands of the Second Kamchatka Expedition.

Steller, as a scientist outside the naval command, was last in line, and he would have to wait his turn for provisions and horses.

Spring came and, not wanting to waste any time when there was new country to explore, Steller sailed a small wooden boat north on Lake Baikal toward the Barguzin Range, a mostly unexplored range of mountains east of the lake. He and two companions landed at the mouth of the Barguzin River, 250 miles north of Irkutsk, and ascended the river on foot to a small Russian outpost, where they set up a base camp. Steller spent two glorious months hiking in the mountains and collecting plants and animals. (Collecting and comparing specimens, as John James Audubon famously did later with the birds of North America, was the way biologists from Steller to Audubon and beyond studied and made sense of the natural world.) He wandered high above his camp among endless alpine lakes, peaks, and meadows, reveling in the long views and the wealth of wildflowers in the high country.

In the Barguzin Range, Steller struck up a friendship of sorts with a deer. The tamed animal followed him on his rambles around the country and, at one point, helped Steller with his research. Steller had found what he thought was a new species of yellow-flowering rhododendron, and as he examined it his deer companion ate a dozen of the leaves. The deer then began to stagger and jerk its head from side to side, apparently poisoned by the rhododendron. It toppled over into a stupor and for four hours lay on the ground, occasionally shuddering in convulsions. The deer eventually woke and recovered, and Steller added toxicity to his list of the plant's qualities.

When Steller discovered a new species of wheatgrass, he noticed a brown liquid oozing from the plant that looked something like the "manna" of a European ash, a liquid that was then used as a laxative. He squeezed some of the honey-thick fluid into his tea, drank it down, and waited for the results. When nothing happened, he jotted into his notes that the wheatgrass manna was not the same as the ash.

He gathered a small collection of birds and, with his microscope, studied the tiny insects that lived in the birds' feathers. He field-improvised a preservation technique for the insects, placing them between ultra-thin flakes of mica, the light, glasslike mineral found in granite; mica cleaves easily into thin sheets that Steller used in the same way modern biologists use glass slides. Unlike glass, mica is absorbent, so the sheets would have taken up any moisture left on the insects that might have caused them to decompose. The mica technique worked so well that more than seventy years later, a laboratory biologist who studied Steller's insects for the first time since they came out of the Barguzin Range found them perfectly preserved.

Steller returned to Irkutsk in mid-September, full of excitement over the new country, the freshwater seals he had observed in Lake Baikal, a full thousand miles from the ocean, and the hordes of plants and animals he had found that he considered new to European science. In November, Steller wrote Gmelin with a list of a dozen papers he had in progress, based on or inspired by his Baikal rambles: an eighty-page portfolio of 1,100 plants of the region, 500 or so new to science; a catalog of plant seeds; a natural history of 60 birds; a description of dozens of types of fish found in Lake Baikal and its tributary rivers; a description of 100 insects; a paper on the minerals of Baikal; a travelogue; a topography, description, and history of Irkutsk and Baikal; a paper on botanical medicine; a vocabulary of two local Native languages; a description of central Siberia's Native people; and a dictionary of natural history.

Steller was in naturalist heaven, living a biological frontier dream. This was Central Asia, a completely different world from the Europe where he had studied. In school in Germany, Steller had drifted from theology to medicine, and through medicine to biology. (Medical training in Europe in the eighteenth century included botany, since a doctor's remedies came from plants, and zoology, because anatomy was taught through the dissection of animals.)

Steller had grown up in a Lutheran tradition with a strong sense of social justice. While he studied theology at the University of Wittenberg, he worked part-time as a teacher in an orphanage run by the university. In 1731 he enrolled at the University of Halle, where he studied medicine and biology and lectured in botany. After three years, unhappy with what he saw as petty academic bickering at the university, he left for Berlin, where on the recommendation of his sponsor and major professor, Friedrich Hoffman, he took and passed an examination that qualified him as a full professor of botany. But there were no university positions open in botany in Germany, and he decided that Russia, with its new Academy of Sciences, was the place to go to find opportunities in his field.

Steller's meager savings wouldn't cover the sea passage to St. Petersburg, not to mention living expenses while he looked for work, so he settled on a more circuitous route to the city. Russia had troops in Poland, fighting in what was called the War of the Polish Succession, a complicated conflict over who would succeed the recently deceased Polish king. The Russian army, chronically short of doctors in peacetime, was desperate for them during the war, and Steller left for Poland in the fall of 1734 to offer his services, thinking that a stint as a Russian army doctor would lead him in the right direction. A Russian general immediately put him to work caring for some of the hundreds of wounded and sick soldiers under his command.

After only a few weeks of field medicine, Steller was appointed in November as the doctor in charge of a transport ship carrying the wounded and sick back to St. Petersburg. Caught in a winter storm, the ship ran onto a reef on the Baltic coast, and the passengers were about to abandon ship when the sea lifted the ship off the rocks and floated them free. It was the first time, but not the last, that Steller would be involved in a near-disaster at sea.

Once in St. Petersburg, he made his way to the "apothecary garden," a botanical garden that functioned as the city's pharmacy. The accounts diverge at this point, but somehow Steller found work there cataloging plant collections for Johann Amman, a Swiss scientist who had recently taken a position as botanist at the Academy of Sciences. Then Steller met the head of the Russian Orthodox Church, Archbishop Feophan Prokopovich, and Prokopovich invited Steller to move into his household. One account holds that chance meetings led to both Steller's job at the garden and his new home with the archbishop, but more likely Steller relied on a recommendation from his former professor, Friedrich Hoffman, who was an honorary member of the Russian Academy of Sciences himself.

Three years later, in 1737, with recommendations from Amman and Prokopovich, Steller secured the job of his dreams as an adjunct professor of natural history and mineralogy with the Academy. It was an appointment that included a trip to Siberia to join Bering's second expedition.

While he was in St. Petersburg, Steller had met Daniel Messerschmidt, a German who knew more about Siberia than anyone else in the city. Messerschmidt had traveled through western Siberia for seven years in the 1720s, and Steller learned from him a great deal about the land across the Urals.

After Messerschmidt had come back from Siberia, he had met and married a much younger woman, Brigitta von Böchler. The years in Siberia, though, had broken Messerschmidt's health, and he died in 1735. Brigitta and Steller subsequently fell in love, and he tried to convince her to join him in Siberia. Although reluctant—she had barely survived a shipwreck a few years earlier, knew from Messerschmidt how difficult and dangerous it was to travel in Siberia, and had a young daughter to consider—she eventually agreed. A few weeks before Steller was to leave for Siberia, they married and started preparing for the long journey.

They left St. Petersburg together early in 1738, but when they reached Moscow, Brigitta changed her mind and told Steller she was staying in Europe. Steller, heartbroken, went on alone. It was a while before he was able to write to a friend: "I have entirely forgotten her and fallen in love with Nature."

Now here he was, back in Irkutsk from his Lake Baikal rambles, barely thirty years old, with 500 new plants to his credit. He had used all the paper he could find in Irkutsk pressing his plant collection into a portfolio, so in December he left for Kyakhta, a trading village on the Mongolian border, to buy Chinese paper. The 650-mile round trip by dog team, during the darkest and coldest days of the winter, took him two months. Soon after returning to Irkutsk with his precious paper, Steller packed his Baikal collections, sent them to St. Petersburg, and prepared to leave for Kamchatka.

But shipping his collections directly to St. Petersburg bypassed the scientific corps's Gmelin, who considered himself Steller's superior. Steller's understanding was different; he was only an adjunct professor, true, but his contract was with the Academy in the capital, specifically for scientific studies in eastern Asia, and he thought he was more or less an equal of Gmelin's, not a subordinate.

Gmelin, however, was offended by what he considered a breach of academic protocol. He was also annoyed, probably legitimately, that some of the "discoveries" Steller claimed were in fact plants already known to science, including some first described by Gmelin himself. Steller, Gmelin must have thought, seemed to consider everything new to him as also new to science. So, when the pack train with Steller's collections came through the village where Gmelin was staying, he intercepted them, opened the sealed packages, and threw out everything he considered unimportant or a duplicate of what he had already collected. Then, intent on teaching the upstart adjunct a lesson, he sent Steller an angry message to abandon his plans for Kamchatka and go to the Russian Arctic instead.

Steller's response was to ignore Gmelin's demand and circumvent him. He sent a nineteen-page letter to the head of the Academy in St. Petersburg, outlining his plans for his investigations in eastern Siberia, and left for Kamchatka.

He traveled by sled until the spring thaw of 1740, and then had to wait for the Lena River to break up before he could continue. Once the river was open, he floated the 1,300 downriver miles to Yakutsk in a boat one of Bering's earlier detachments had built. Yakutsk, a village of five hundred small houses and cabins, had been Bering's headquarters for three years during the early stages of the expedition, but by now the captain-commander was at Okhotsk, building the ships that would take him and his expedition to America. Steller stopped in Yakutsk only long enough to hire horses before setting off on the long mountain portage to Okhotsk over the Dzhugdzur Range.

Steller was about halfway across when Martin Spangberg, hurrying over the mountains to see Bering before he sailed for Kamchatka, caught up with him. Spangberg had completed a voyage to Japan the year before; overcoming a gauntlet of obstacles—storms, fog, treacherous sea currents, and a strange sickness that had broken out aboard his ship—he had mapped the Kuril Islands, the chain of fifty-six island-volcanoes that stretches between Kamchatka and Japan. After returning to Okhotsk, he had started out for St. Petersburg, planning to meet with the city's scientists and geographers about his discoveries. Unknown to him, a Siberian bureaucrat, an old enemy of Spangberg's, had challenged his results in a letter to the Russian Senate. A messenger from the Admiralty, the Russian Navy's central command, had met Spangberg on the Lena River with orders to go back to Okhotsk and *repeat the voyage.*

Hearing Spangberg's stories of his voyage as they rode across the mountains, Steller decided that he wanted to join Spangberg's second journey to the Kurils and Japan. But when they arrived in Okhotsk in August, Steller met Bering, and Bering described the plans for the American leg of the Second Kamchatka Expedition, which Bering was calling the American Expedition. It sounded to Steller like a voyage with more potential for pioneering biology, and he began to think of trying to join Bering.

Steller arranged to travel from Okhotsk to Kamchatka on one of Bering's ships. It would be a few weeks, however, before the expedition sailed, so he set out to explore the country around Okhotsk. He observed the great runs of Pacific salmon, seeing tiny streams near the village literally choked with spawning fish; his notes on these salmon and others he studied in Asia would become the basis for their scientific names. East of Okhotsk, he tasted a few bites of the white, buttery clay that the Native people of the area boiled with reindeer milk into a pudding. He saw for the first time the giant thickets of cow-parsnip, the tall, ubiquitous perennial of the subarctic Pacific coast that the Native people picked and processed to make a sweetener and an alcoholic drink—a plant widely known in Alaska today by a Russian common name, *pootchski*.

While in Okhotsk, Steller also met Friedrich Plenisner, a fellow German and a surveyor and draftsman, who would become Steller's best friend as the expedition unfolded. And, before leaving the village, Steller sent a gracious letter of apology to Johann Gmelin about their quarrel. It was a good thing, since they would never see each other again.

In early September the American Expedition was ready to move on to Kamchatka. Bering had sent an advance party ahead to the Pacific side of the peninsula to build a new port village in the near-perfect harbor at Avacha Bay. They named the village Petropavlovsk, meaning "the harbor of St. Peter and St. Paul," which were the names of the two ships Bering would be taking to find America.

Steller left Okhotsk for Kamchatka on the ship *Nadezhda* ("Hope"), but the ship's skipper, a Russian named Sofron Khitrovo, turned out to be hopeless as a pilot. Hauling a two-year supply of freshly baked sea biscuits, Khitrovo ran aground on a sandbar before they were even out of the Okhotsk harbor. Seawater poured into the hold, soaking and

Cow-parsnip *(Heracleum lanatum)*

ruining most of the expedition's sea biscuits. It was a major disaster, and Steller openly criticized Khitrovo for it.

After repairs, the *Nadezhda* crossed the Sea of Okhotsk in a flotilla with the *St. Peter* and the *St. Paul.* They landed at Bol'sheretsk, a village on the west coast of Kamchatka, and Steller disembarked. The ships continued south to round Cape Lopatka, the southernmost point of Kamchatka, hurrying to reach Avacha Bay before winter set in. Khitrovo, however, still with a heavy load of supplies in the *Nadezhda,* nearly ran onto the rocks at the cape and turned back to Bol'sheretsk.

Khitrovo's two mishaps came close to sinking the entire expedition. A lot of the expedition's supplies were still on the wrong side of the peninsula, and now Bering had to find another way to get them to Avacha. The Russian commander at Bol'sheretsk put his forty-five soldiers to work on the problem, and they fanned out to the villages of the indigenous Itelmen people on a mission to find sled dogs and drivers to lug the supplies overland to the Pacific. They conscripted Itelmen and their dogs from hundreds of miles around for the job, and throughout the winter convoys of heavily loaded cargo sleds, one after the other, left Bol'sheretsk for the run over the mountains to Kamchatka's east coast.

Well before their conscription for Bering's expedition, the Itelmen had had little use for the foreign presence in their territory; Russian fur traders had attacked and robbed them and forced them into service continually over the previous half-century. They had fought the Russians sporadically; on two occasions, in 1707 and 1731, they had staged uprisings and burned Russian outposts to the ground. Now some of the Itelmen rebelled against the Russian soldiers working for Bering, killing seven of them. The Russians retaliated by trapping the presumed rebels in their semi-subterranean homes and dropping grenades down the smoke holes.

Steller was sympathetic to the plight of the Itelmen. (Later, in Avacha, he complained to Bering about how harshly his men treated them.) Over the fall and winter of 1740–41 he came to know the Itelmen on their own terms, in a way Bering and the other members of the expedition never did, as he studied their hunting and fishing skills, their songs and dances, and their family and village life. He organized a village school in Bol'sheretsk for their children, and he became godfather to an Itelmen boy.

Steller's other agenda over the winter was learning more about Kamchatka. In January he led an expedition by dog team south to Cape Lopatka, covering hundreds of miles of raw country in the deep-freeze of a Siberian winter. He appointed himself supervisor of Stepan Krashenninikov, the student assistant Gmelin and Müller of the scientific corps had sent to Kamchatka in 1737. Krashenninikov had turned out to be an able scientist himself; he had spent the past three years traveling solo through the wilds of Kamchatka, studying the Native people and the peninsula's plants, animals, volcanoes, and hot springs. His notes from his wilderness adventures would eventually become the first well-known book about Kamchatka.

Now that Steller was here, however, Krashenninikov's work was done; Steller ordered him back to central Siberia. Some historians see a selfish motive in Steller's order, speculating that he may have seen the experienced Krashenninikov as a rival candidate for the job as scientist on the American Expedition.

In February a letter arrived from Bering, asking Steller to meet with him at Avacha Bay. Steller was sure Bering was considering including him on the voyage to America. Hitching up a dog team again, he left for the Pacific, crashing through Kamchatka's trackless willow jungles, sharp branches tearing at his eyes, his sled breaking through thin ice into running streams again and again. A blizzard forced him to hole up under his overturned sled until it blew itself out.

But ten days after leaving Bol'sheretsk, Steller arrived in Petropavlovsk, where sawdust was still fresh on the snow from the building of the village. The settlement consisted of a small hive of log cabins, a storehouse, a barracks, a small church, and a wharf. The sod houses of the conscripted Itelmen stood off to one side.

Steller immediately went to the officers' quarters to meet with Bering. The captain-commander greeted him and laid out the plan for the expedition. Bering wanted someone qualified to report on America's potential mineral wealth, to make observations at sea that would help Bering decide how far and in what direction land lay, and to write descriptions of any new peoples they might meet. Steller, Bering knew, would be capable in all these roles, and he invited Steller to join the expedition.

Steller negotiated with Bering, explaining that his contract with the Academy stressed discovering and recording the entire range of natural history, and that he would need to continue that work with the help and support of the crew. Bering agreed. There would be room on the ship for Steller to bring one assistant along, and, Bering told him, he could also count on help from surveyor and draftsman Friedrich Plenisner.

There was one more problem. Khitrovo, the Russian lieutenant who had ruined the expedition's sea biscuits, had taken Steller's criticism of his ship-handling skills very personally and had reacted angrily. Bering had reassigned Khitrovo as second lieutenant on the

St. Peter, the ship Steller would be sailing on, so now Steller and Khitrovo, not exactly the best of friends, were going to be confined on a ship together for months. To allay Steller's concern about Khitrovo, Bering called a council of his officers, and all of them, including Khitrovo, signed an agreement approving Steller's appointment.

Steller was going to America.

On May 4, 1741, Bering called a sea council in Avacha to decide on the expedition's course to America. As strange as it sounds for an autocratic nation like eighteenth-century Russia, the Russian Navy made important decisions by a more or less democratic council, most often a committee of officers. Steller, as a junior member of the expedition, was not on Bering's invitation list for the May 4 council; the group consisted of Captain Aleksei Chirikov of the *St. Paul* (Bering's lieutenant on his first expedition, now promoted), Bering's first lieutenant Sven Waxell, the few other senior naval officers assigned to the two ships, and the expedition's official geographer, Louis de l'Isle de la Croyère.

The main topic on the agenda was a map that de la Croyère had brought with him—the only depiction of the North Pacific available to the council to help them set a course for the voyage. The map was a family project, a product of one of Europe's most renowned academic families, the three brothers de l'Isle. Their reputation was based mostly on the work of the eldest brother, Guillaume, who had been the geographer of the French court twenty years earlier. The map was Guillaume's work from 1714, with 1731 revisions by the middle brother, Joseph-Nicolas.

De la Croyère, the youngest of the brothers (he went by his mother's maiden name), was simply the courier of the map. Brother Joseph-Nicolas, the Russian Academy's head geographer and astronomer, had landed Louis his job as a junior professor there. De la Croyère, however, was apparently not the brightest of lights in the academic world. Bering biographer Peter Lauridsen called him "an amiable good-for-nothing," and a Russian assistant on the expedition, Andrei Krasilnikov, had done most of de la Croyère's work for him so far.

The de l'Isle map was a very sketchy basis for informing a decision on the route of the voyage. It shows nothing of North America's west coast north of "Cap Blanc" and "C Mendocin," today's Cape Blanco of southern Oregon and Cape Mendocino of northern California. A blank space trails off north and west from there to a more or less correctly drawn Russian east coast. Southwest of Kamchatka are "Empire du Japon," more or less resembling Honshu, the largest Japanese island, and "Terre de Jeso," apparently representing the Japanese island of Hokkaido. The map shows nothing resembling the Kuril Islands.

But the most relevant features for the sea council to examine were two vaguely drawn lands in the Pacific to the southeast of Kamchatka: "Terre de la Compagnie"—"Company Land," after the Dutch East India Company—and "Terre Vue par Dom J. de Gama," a land supposedly seen by a mystery mariner named Juan de Gama and generally known as "De Gama Land." Company Land and De Gama Land are each shown with an indeterminate coastline trailing off in the direction of America.

Both Company Land and De Gama Land were pure fantasy, but there is a plausible line of reasoning for how they got on the de l'Isle map. Since about the mid-1600s, hazy notions about land north of Japan had been drifting back to Europe from Spanish and Dutch sailors employed in the search for the elusive arctic sea route between Europe and Japan. They had apparently sailed near or through the Kuril Islands, where even an outstanding seventeenth-century mariner could have made serious plotting errors; as Martin Spangberg had discovered on his voyage for Bering, the Kurils are a region with a nasty combination of thick fog, strong tidal currents, and fierce storms. Other mapmakers had plotted nonexistent lands in the North Pacific based on the questionable Spanish and Dutch data, and Guillaume and Joseph-Nicolas de l'Isle had apparently followed suit, turning the Kurils into the misplaced and overgrown "lands" on their map.

To the council at Avacha Bay, the fictional De Gama Land looked enticing: it might lead to, or even be part of, America. But Bering and his officers had another route to America to consider. According to the accounts of Russian fur traders as early as 1711, the Chukchi—the Native people of the Chukchi Peninsula in northeastern Siberia—claimed that there was a *bolshaya zemlya,* a "Great Land," not an island, to the northeast of Kamchatka.

It was a land, they said, of big rivers, tall forests, great throngs of

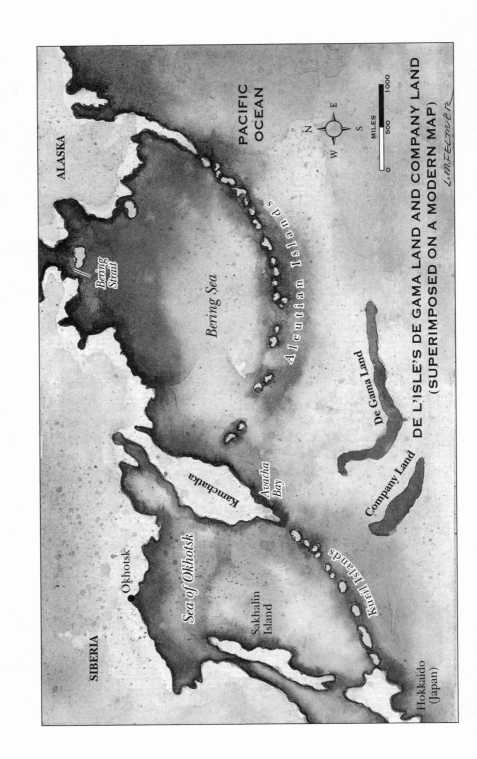

DE L'ISLE'S DE GAMA LAND AND COMPANY LAND
(SUPERIMPOSED ON A MODERN MAP)

PACIFIC
OCEAN

ALASKA

Bering
Strait

Bering Sea

Aleutian Islands

De Gama Land

Company Land

Avacha Bay

Kamchatka

Sea of Okhotsk

Okhotsk

SIBERIA

Sakhalin Island

Kuril Islands

Hokkaido (Japan)

MILES

0   500   1000

L.M.FELTNER

fur-bearing animals, and people who wore walrus ivory in their lips. And the Great Land was not that far away; the Chukchi told the Russians they had paddled there from Asia in their large, dorylike skin boats. They were right; what we now call Cape Prince of Wales, mainland Alaska's westernmost point of land, is only about 60 miles from Asia.

More evidence of how close America was had come from Mikhail Gvozdef's 1732 voyage into the strait Bering had discovered on his 1728 voyage. While Bering was back in St. Petersburg organizing his second expedition, Gvozdef sailed into the strait in Bering's ship the *St. Gavriel*. In his journal Gvozdef reports spotting four islands on his cruise; however, one member of his crew maintained afterward that the third sighting was no island, but "a large land with a coast of yellow sand," with "yurt dwellings," "many people walking about," and "many reindeer," all of which point to a sighting of the Seward Peninsula, on Alaska's mainland. Several of Gvozdef's sailors were with Bering's crew, so there's no doubt that Bering and Chirikov knew they could find the American coast by sailing northeast.

The question, then, for the council of naval officers: sail northeast toward the Great Land or southeast toward De Gama Land? Chirikov put a motion to the council to take the northeast course. But no one had sailed very far north so early in the year; on their 1728 voyage, Bering and Chirikov had sailed through the northern strait in August. The council decided that the sea to the north would probably be iced in and impassable until at least midsummer.

The council also had to consider the orders the Admiralty had given Bering, which directed him to find and chart any islands between Kamchatka and America. The Admiralty's orders seemed to put a priority on finding De Gama Land, and Bering and his officers may have thought that following orders from St. Petersburg would be wise; the Admiralty's commanders had already shown, in the case of Spangberg's repeat voyage to Japan, that they were capable of sending the expedition back to America if they were less than satisfied with the outcome.

The sea council agreed to point the *St. Peter* and the *St. Paul* toward the mythical De Gama Land. They would sail east-southeast from Avacha Bay, at latitude 53° north, as far south as 46°, and if they failed to sight land by then, would turn northeast until they met the American coast. From there they would sail north and west, following the coastline until they reached the point opposite Cape Chukchi, and then would turn south and west, back to Kamchatka. No matter what happened, however, they would aim for getting back to Avacha Bay by the end of September, the beginning of the stormy season. The plan was set, and it was time to rig the ships and go.

Years later, in reflecting on how such a good, logical plan could have gone so wrong, Waxell laid the blame squarely on de la Croyère and the de l'Isle map. "We were all led astray," Waxell remembered, "by the unreliable map . . . and my blood still boils whenever I think of the scandalous deception of which we were the victims." The time lost looking for De Gama Land, added to other delays, would cost the expedition dearly, but it would put Georg Steller on course to make scientific history.

———————

The *St. Peter*'s logbook begins with an entry for April 23, 1741, when the crews began rigging and loading the two ships. They were "packet boats," small ships like those used in Baltic Europe to ferry passengers and packets of mail between ports. Identical in size and design, they measured 80 feet long with a 22-foot beam and a draft of 9 feet, and each sported two square-rigged masts. All told, Bering was going to squeeze seventy-eight people onto the *St. Peter*, and Chirikov planned to pack seventy-six onto the *St. Paul*. The density of humanity on board is hard to imagine today in the United States, where two people routinely live in a house larger than either one of Bering's ships.

While wind squalls and snowstorms blew through the Petropavlovsk harbor, the crews built out bunks, hung doors on the cabins, calibrated compasses, caulked the seams, and set up the masts and rigging. In Bering's cabin on the *St. Peter*, a carpenter nailed in a bunk for Steller, the late arrival who needed a place to toss his blanket. Bering's usual physician was too sick to sail, so at the last minute the job of ship's doctor fell to Steller, and with it, a place in the captain's cabin.

Under the snow-covered volcanoes that border the bay, the crew ferried out spare rigging, anchors, cables, sails, eighteen tons of ballast and spare iron, eighteen tons of fuel wood, and a good bit of firepower: fourteen cannon, ten barrels of gunpowder, seven hundred cannon balls, and miscellaneous guns, ammunition, and grapeshot.

To handle all the weaponry the *St. Peter* was packing, Bering had signed on twenty-seven soldiers and gunners. The crew was setting up the *St. Peter* as a hybrid ship—part explorers' vessel, part warship. A common fear among sailors of the time was being caught in the open ocean unprepared for a naval attack, and they had no idea what kind of reception they might get from the "Americans," as they called the indigenous people they expected to meet on the expedition.

Even the ship's medical supplies had a heavy tilt toward battle. As Steller the doctor notes in his journal, the *St. Peter* was well stocked with plasters and splints for war wounds. However, there was not a single remedy in the ship's stores for scurvy, the real killer on long sea voyages, or for asthma, a common health problem in the close, fetid atmosphere of the common sailors' quarters.

No one expected much variety at mealtime. The provisions the crew heaved aboard the *St. Peter* included a hundred barrels of water; hundreds of pounds of wheat flour and ground grain (the log doesn't say what kind of grain); 15 kegs of dried beef, 11 of butter, and 6 each of pork and salt; and 382 sacks of sea biscuits (all that was left after Khitrovo's shipwreck). The two ships' stores could feed the expedition for about four months, possibly longer if rationed tightly. There was also a sizeable store of vodka—proof that this was a Russian expedition.

A Russian expedition, yes, but with an international crew: although Chirikov and most of the *St. Paul*'s crew except de la Croyère were Russian, the *St. Peter* was thick with crewmembers from other European countries, especially among the officers. On the *St. Peter* with Bering, a Dane, were Waxell, the Swedish first lieutenant and Bering's second in command on the ship, and Waxell's eleven-year-old son Laurentz; first mate and navigator Andreas Hesselberg, a German or Dane seventy years old who had spent fifty years at sea; the Germans Friedrich Plenisner, the surveyor and draftsman Steller had met in Okhotsk, and Johan Sind, a young midshipman; Matthias Betge, the assistant surgeon (a physician's assistant of the day), probably a Dane; and Boris Roselius, the constable or ship's policeman, most likely a Swede.

Most of the sailors and soldiers on the *St. Peter* were Russian, as was the third in command, the accident-prone second lieutenant Khitrovo. Other Russians included second mate and assistant navigator Kharlam Yushin and Dmitry Ovtsyn, a former lieutenant who had led one of Bering's arctic forays. The Admiralty had demoted Ovtsyn to the rank of common sailor after he was caught being friendly to a deposed prince who had fallen out of favor with Empress Anna; Bering, however, was bringing him aboard as his adjutant, or special assistant.

Steller brought aboard Stepan Krashenninikov's former assistant Thomas Lepekhin, a congenial Russian who was handy in the field and a good shot—just the type of companion a collection-minded biologist needed along. Bering also coaxed two Siberian Natives, a Chukchi and a Koryak, on board as interpreters in case they should meet any Americans on the voyage.

Finally, after more than a month of rigging and loading, the ships were ready to go. Each vessel had two wooden shore boats—one a larger longboat, the other a smaller yawl—mainly intended for rowing, but rigged for sailing when the conditions were right. The ships' logs don't go into the details, but the typical longboat of the time was about 25 feet long and held eight to ten oarsmen, and a yawl was roughly 15 feet long, built for four to six oars. (The term *yawl* now means something entirely different—a small, two-masted sailing vessel.)

On May 28 the crews of the *St. Peter* and the *St. Paul* put their shore boats to good use, rowing back to the village a few at a time, by watches, for a last bath. The next day oarsmen in the longboats towed the ships out of the harbor and into the broad bay, where they waited for the right wind to get the American Expedition under way.

And waited, and waited. They needed a breeze to get out of Avacha Bay, but for five days the wind would not cooperate. Finally, with a light northwest wind, they sailed toward the mouth of the bay, but the tide was running against them. They deployed the longboats again. Sailors rowed the anchors out ahead of the ships and set them, and then the crews on board hauled the ships to the anchors. Another round of hauling put the ships next to the point at the entrance to the bay; at last they caught a favorable wind and sailed into the North Pacific on June 4, 1741. Asia gradually receded, and soon the *St. Peter* and the *St. Paul* were sailing out of sight of land in a broad, uncharted ocean.

Bering retreated to his cabin, leaving Waxell in charge. Waxell needed time at the helm to work on his qualifications for a promotion to captain in Russia's navy, and Bering obliged. Bering also needed a break. He was nearly sixty years old and in the ninth year of his second expedition to the Russian Far East. All told, running expeditions to eastern Asia and the North Pacific had taken up nearly a third of Bering's life; he had outlasted four Russian rulers in his career as an explorer for the empire. The absurdly ambitious expedition had already exhausted him. The logistics burden had been stunning, and he had racked up huge cost overruns, running three thousand percent over his laughably inadequate budget. The Admiralty had cut his pay in half for two years as punishment for not accomplishing the impossible.

And the expedition's achievements had been less than stunning so far. First, the Admiralty had ordered Martin Spangberg to repeat his voyage to Japan. Second, the exploration of the Arctic Coast was not going well. Seven separate parties had filled in portions of the map, but they had failed to find an arctic sea passage. Scurvy and ship-crushing ice had derailed several of them, and one, a group that had traveled down the Lena River, had met complete disaster. The Lena expedition had started out with a crew of forty-six, but only nine returned alive after scurvy struck the party's winter camp on the frozen coast. Boris Roselius, Bering's constable on the *St. Peter*, was one of the survivors.

The American Expedition was having its problems, too. Bering's original idea was to take enough food along to winter in America if weather or other delays prevented them from returning to Kamchatka that fall. But Khitrovo's disastrous grounding of the *Nadezhda* in Okhotsk had left Bering well short of the supply of sea biscuits they would need for wintering in America. Then Khitrovo's failure to sail the rest of the supplies to Avacha the previous autumn had delayed the start of the voyage a month, from May to June. After all that had happened, Bering was apparently happy to leave the daily routine of running of the ship to Waxell.

Nothing was more important in the daily routine than computing the ship's position at sea. A noon sun sighting with a quadrant gave navigator Hesselberg and his assistant Yushin the latitude, or the north-south position, but longitude, the ship's east-west position, was much trickier to figure. The American Expedition sailed before there were reliable methods of fixing longitude at sea. The eventual answer to the longitude problem—the chronometer that English clockmaker John Harrison perfected, revolutionizing navigation—was still twenty years away.

The navigators calculated the *St. Peter*'s longitudinal position relative to Vaua, the point on the coast at the entrance to Avacha Bay. De la Croyère had calculated Vaua's position astronomically, which required several observations over time from a fixed point, something that could be done on land but was impossible at sea. From Vaua, the navigators computed the distance the ship traveled and logged every twist and turn of its course to keep up with where they were. To do that, he and his helpers used a compass, a log line, and a calibrated sandglass, the three tools of the trade in 1741.

Regular compass readings gave them the direction the ship was moving, and once an hour they figured their speed and therefore distance traveled with the log line and sandglass. They tossed the log line overboard, at the same time flipping the sandglass over to start its "timer." The log line, knotted at intervals in the same proportion to a nautical mile as the sandglass's running time was to an hour, paid out from a reel as the ship moved ahead. (The knot interval was 47¼ feet, and the sandglass running time 28 seconds.) When the sandglass ran out, they stopped the unreeling of the line and counted the number of knots that had paid out, giving them the speed of the ship in nautical miles per hour, or *knots*. A nautical mile is about 1.15 land, or statute, miles, the distance of a minute of longitude at the equator.

They computed the position of the ship each day by adding that day's direction and speed onto the previous day's position, a "deduced reckoning" method that sailors abbreviated to the term "dead reckoning." Khitrovo and Yushin each kept a log, carefully noting the figures for the speed and direction of travel and the deduced position of the ship at the end of the day.

Dead reckoning was notoriously inaccurate. Ocean and tidal currents caused drift that a navigator's measurements failed to pick up, and any small error in reading the compass or estimating speed could compound itself over weeks at sea into a major miscalculation. Like most seafarers of the time, the crew of the *St. Peter* would reach the limits of dead reckoning before the voyage was over.

Navigation was difficult enough, but the two ships had to stay together as well. In a written manifesto, Bering had laid out a set of protocols covering signals they would use in daylight, while under sail, in foggy weather, at night under sail, at night at anchor, and in many other situations; the signals were a complicated mix of shots fired, pennants and flags raised, and lanterns hung. Bering and Chirikov also had megaphones for ship-to-ship conversation when the *St. Peter* and the *St. Paul* were close enough for the captains to hear each other.

The ships sailed uneventfully together toward a rendezvous with De Gama Land until June 12, when the expedition reached latitude 46°. If De Gama Land had been where the de l'Isle map showed it was, they would have been sailing right through it. Using the megaphones, Bering and Chirikov agreed to give up the search and turn east-northeast. They had been sailing in the wrong direction for more than a week. If de la Croyère had anything to say at this point, no one wrote it down.

Steller, however, had something to say. He challenged the decision to change course, reasoning that there had to be land ahead in that direction because of the floating seaweed and the gulls and terns he saw from the deck. They were likely passing over a chain of seamounts at the time, possibly accounting for the seabirds Steller saw, but he was definitely wrong about land ahead; on their current course, there was only open ocean ahead of them for thousands of miles.

At this point Steller's journal reveals the first signs of tension between him and the naval officers:

> . . . if we continued our initial course farther, we would soon reach land. But [this is when] the unreasonable behavior of our officers began. They mocked, ridiculed, and cast to the winds whatever was said by anyone who was not a seaman, as if, with the rules of navigation, they had also acquired all other science and logic.

The heated tone of Steller's journal—the only account that mentions this disagreement—seems to appear out of nowhere. Steller undoubtedly thought that by giving his opinion, he was carrying out one of his duties; as Bering had told him in Avacha, he was to advise the officers on the direction and distance to land while they were at sea. Yet here he had done as he had been asked, and he was mocked for it. In little more than a week of sailing, patience was already fraying.

On June 20, near latitude 49°, a storm broke over the two ships, and in fog and gale-force winds they lost sight of each other. Bering's manifesto included a protocol for the situation: they would sail back to the place where they had separated and cruise the area for three days looking for each other. If they didn't find each other by then, they would each continue alone on the east-northeast course they had agreed upon back in Avacha.

In the storm, Chirikov and Bering both had a difficult time getting back to their point of separation. On the twentieth and twenty-first they searched for each other within the same tight circle only a few miles in radius, but the weather was too thick to see any distance. On the twenty-second Bering continued searching in the same area, but Chirikov decided to search to the south. Near the end of the day, Chirikov broke off the search, and the *St. Paul* turned east and went on its lonely way.

The officers of the *St. Peter* met and decided to turn southeast, to make one last try at finding De Gama Land and follow up on the slim possibility that Chirikov had sailed in that direction. They sailed southeast for four more days but saw no sign of either land or their sister ship. On the twenty-fifth Bering gave up and ordered an east-northeast course.

The two ships would never see each other again.

The parting of the *St. Peter* and the *St. Paul* led to one of the great coincidences—and one of the great mysteries—in the history of northern exploration. First, the coincidence: the crews of the two ships sighted the American coast on the same day—July 15, 1741—five hundred miles apart and twenty-five days after they went their separate ways.

Chirikov, who had given up the search first, took the lead, sailing east. For three weeks the crew of the *St. Paul* saw nothing to indicate that they were anywhere near land. Then, on July 13, they saw two tree trunks float by, and they made out a "shore duck" on the water. The next day it was more driftwood and more ducks; land had to be close.

Early on the morning of the fifteenth, someone on the ship spotted a range of mountains in the distance, and an hour later, a coastline with a thick topping of forest came into view. It was America, one of the islands of Southeast Alaska's Alexander Archipelago, and the crew's first sight of land after more than two thousand miles at sea. The nearest point of land to the ship was today's Cape Addington, the long, prominent cape of Noyes Island, off the coast of giant Prince of Wales Island and not far from present-day Ketchikan, Alaska.

On the *St. Peter*, Waxell had set a course a few degrees farther north than the *St. Paul* had sailed after the ships separated. Waxell crossed Chirikov's track on July 8, a week behind the *St. Paul*, in the wild, blue Pacific three hundred miles south of Kodiak. As they continued, Steller decided there had to be land not far to the north because he was seeing floating kelp, gulls, and harbor seals, none of which inhabit the open ocean. (Steller was only partially right; there was land to the north, but it was still a voyage of four or five days away.)

If they turned north, he argued, they would sight land in short order. But the officers "curtly and sarcastically refused all suggestions and proposals," Steller wrote in his journal, and quoted one unnamed officer as telling him, "You do not understand. You are, after all, no seaman." Bering, Steller wrote, agreed with him about a course change, but he was powerless to order one because the other officers didn't agree; the earlier decision of the sea council still held.

Finally, several days later, still with nothing but saltwater on the horizon, Bering mustered his arguments for changing course and called another sea council. Their water supply and the waning of the summer were on his mind. They were seven weeks into the voyage and still had seen no sign of America. Half the ship's fresh water was gone; the rest, if none of the barrels had leaked, might last until the first of September. Autumn storms could come at any time after that. Bering prevailed; the council decided to aim directly north in hopes of finding America. They changed course on the fourteenth, but it didn't matter: from their position at that point, America was about equally distant either to the north or to the east.

Late in the day on the fifteenth, Steller was out pacing the deck. The calm, sunny afternoon had yielded to a breezy, cloudy evening; to the north, clouds scudded along the horizon. One stood higher than the rest, and then for a few seconds Steller had a clear view. It was no cloud; it was a great, white peak that seemed to rise straight out of the ocean. With a shout he called on anybody in earshot to come to the rail and see. But the mountain faded into the clouds again, and the naval officers discounted the sighting. As Steller wrote in his journal, "it was, as usual, dismissed as one of my peculiarities."

The next day, the sixteenth, the clouds lifted, and a snow-covered mountain range materialized on the horizon, rising practically straight up from a narrow coastal plain; Steller wrote in his journal that he had not seen a higher range anywhere in Siberia. One mountain stood above the rest, the 18,000-foot peak we now call Mount St. Elias. It was the ice-cream mountain Steller had spotted the night before, on the evening of the day the *St. Paul*'s crew had sighted the islands and coastline of southern Southeast Alaska. With hundreds of twists and turns of the coastline between them, the American Expedition's two parties had spotted land the same day.

On the *St. Paul*, Chirikov sent a longboat party into one of the bays near their position to see whether there was a safe anchorage there. Four hours later, the party returned with their report: they had seen huge trees, an army of sea lions on the rocks, no evidence of people, and no sign of any protected cove for anchoring the ship. Going ashore was clearly out of the question, so Chirikov moved on, pointing the *St. Paul* northwest along the outside of an archipelago of green islands.

He followed the shoreline as closely as possible, navigating through a thick coastal fog that alternately lifted and fell. As the coastal mountains disappeared into the mist one minute and reappeared the next, he and his officers took compass readings to chart the coastline. They searched the islands for an anchorage, seeing great flights of seabirds and pods of whales and sea lions. After two days of cautious sailing, they finally made out an opening in the coastline, most likely off today's Yakobi Island, north of present-day Sitka.

Chirikov worked the ship into position near the opening and organized a scouting party. He put boatswain Avraam Dementiev in charge, and soon Dementiev and ten men were rowing away in the longboat toward what they thought must be a protected bay inside the opening. Chirikov had given them a long set of written instructions: they were to take compass bearings on the opening in the coastline, take soundings in the bay inside the opening, and sketch a map of the bay; if possible, they were to land and explore the shore. The crew was armed, but under orders not to start anything if they met Americans; they carried copper and iron pots, beads, needles, and cloth with them as gifts. If they met with any hostility, they were to return immediately to the ship. Dementiev took a week's worth of food along in case of an emergency, but agreed to return that day or the next at the latest.

The longboat left the ship on the afternoon of July 17. There was no anchorage where the *St. Paul* lay, so while Chirikov waited for his shore party to return, he beat up and down the coast, trying to stay as close as possible to shore while the wind and tide tried to carry the ship away. The eighteenth and then the nineteenth passed, and no longboat appeared. On July 20 a storm blew the *St. Paul* well offshore. On the twenty-first and the twenty-second the crew fought the wind and tide to bring the ship back into position near the entrance to the bay, but they still saw no sign of their shore party.

On the afternoon of the twenty-second they fired two cannon shots to signal the men on shore, and later they saw smoke rising from the trees. In the evening the sky cleared and the wind calmed, and they spotted a fire on shore. They fired seven more shots, but still no boat appeared.

Chirikov called a sea council, and the officers unanimously agreed to send the yawl to shore with a carpenter, a caulker, and tools, thinking that the longboat must have been damaged and Dementiev stranded. Chirikov ordered the boatswain in charge, Sidor Savelev, to find the shore party, build a fire to signal the ship that they had landed safely, leave the caulker and carpenter to work on the longboat if they needed to, and bring Dementiev back to the ship immediately.

The ship's crew watched the repair detachment row the second boat into the bay; it disappeared around a point before reaching shore. The men on the ship waited, looking in vain for the signal fire Chirikov had told Savelev to build. The afternoon and evening passed, and still they saw no sign of either boat. As daylight began to fade, they maneuvered closer to shore and fired the ship's guns again. Soon afterward they spotted a fire, but there was no way to tell if it was their shipmates' campfire.

The next day, July 24, they saw two boats moving out of the bay toward the ship. Any elation the crew might have felt at seeing the two boats died away quickly. They were not the ship's boats; they had sharp bows like canoes, not the rounded bows of the longboat and the yawl, and the people inside were paddling, not rowing. In the lead boat, one of the canoers stood at the stern and three sat or kneeled. Two Native dugout canoes—Tlingit, as we know now—were approaching the ship.

The canoes slowed and stopped well before reaching the ship. The canoers stood up in their craft, waved, and yelled a few syllables to the ship. Then they turned their canoes and paddled back toward land.

The men on the ship frantically waved white kerchiefs, yelling for the canoers to come back, but they disappeared around the point. It was too dangerous for the *St. Paul* to follow, and Chirikov had no more shore boats to send after the canoes.

Chirikov knew now that the men he had sent to shore were in serious trouble, if any of them were still alive at all. He held the *St. Paul* close to shore the rest of the day, and the crew hung a lantern in the rigging that night like a porch light for their missing mates. The next morning, July 25, they gave up the vigil at the entrance to the bay and slowly made their way up the coast to the northwest, hoping to catch sight of some of the sailors, if by chance they were stranded and not drowned or murdered.

By the twenty-sixth they concluded it was a futile search. They had lost fifteen men. There were really only two possibilities: either both parties had swamped and drowned in surf inside the bay or, as Chirikov thought, the Tlingits had captured or killed them. (But why, if it was the latter, did the two Tlingit canoes approach the ship?) The fate of the *St Paul*'s missing shore-boat crews is still a mystery.

For the crew on the ship, the voyage had devolved into a survival situation. They had no boats left to row to shore for fresh water, and the supply they had brought from Asia was going fast. Chirikov and his officers met to decide what to do. They had no choice; they voted to steer the ship back to Kamchatka. Chirikov ordered water to be rationed and spare sails set up to catch rainwater. The *St. Paul* turned west toward Asia.

On board the *St. Peter*, there was joy and more than a little bragging on July 16. The expedition was a success: they had found America. They were now 186° of longitude east of St. Petersburg, having traveled more than halfway around the northern part of the globe to get there. But Bering, when he came on deck to look at the coastline, in what should have been his supreme moment, just shrugged his shoulders and went back to his cabin.

Later, alone with Steller and Plenisner, he called the braggarts "pregnant windbags" and told the two Germans that he was worried about the expedition's prospects for a safe return to Avacha Bay. They were far away, ignorant of the country and the sea around them, short of supplies, and vulnerable to a seasonal wind-shift. If the prevailing fall winds blew out of the west, as Bering suspected, the crew's return to Asia could be in jeopardy.

Waxell maneuvered the ship to the northwest to work around a tall, forest-covered island and, he hoped, to find a secure anchorage. North winds forced the crew to tack back and forth to make headway. Steller took in the scene with anticipation: fine forests, great tidal flats, and sandy beaches lay at the foot of colossal coastal mountains. On July 19 they passed a great white-rock cape at the end of the island. The noon log calls it Cape St. Elias; the island was Kayak Island. Steller quibbled with the decision to call the point a cape, arguing that a cape meant a prominent feature on a mainland coast, and this was the outer point of an island. But Cape St. Elias it has stayed to this day.

Waxell steered toward a point west of the island and just south of another mass of land; the crew thought at this point it was the mainland, but it was actually the southern reaches of Wingham Island. With the wind more or less constantly from the north, an anchorage in the lee of the land to the north was their best opportunity for shelter.

Steller noticed a sea current running toward the ship out of the gap north of Kayak Island. He could see driftwood floating out on the current, and the seawater tasted low in salinity—a good indication that a major river emptied into the sea from the mainland somewhere out of sight behind the island. He argued for sailing around the island and anchoring in what he thought must be a protected bay at the mouth of the river. The officers, however, declined; in his journal, Steller called the discussion of his idea "a petty quarrel."

Steller was right; there is a major river to the north, the river we call the Bering River today. However, he was wrong about the anchorage. The ocean current running through Kayak Entrance and the silty shallows of Controller Bay, which is the dumping ground for the Bering River's great loads of glacial sediment, would have made any attempt at anchoring north of the island difficult and dangerous.

Early on the morning of July 20, Waxell anchored a mile off today's

Cape St. Peter and its rocky reef. The crew got both shore boats ready to launch; it was going to be a busy day. A crew in the yawl would take several round trips to Kayak Island to fill the water barrels, and Khitrovo would take the longboat to the north to explore the coast and locate any other possible anchorages.

Steller asked Bering for permission to go with Khitrovo, and Khitrovo seconded the request. Inexplicably to Steller, Bering refused, and Steller protested strongly in front of the crew. He obviously remembered Bering's reassurances back in Petropavlovsk that captain and crew would support the scientific work of the expedition. Now, at the most important moment for that work, the captain-commander was going back on his word. As he describes it in his journal, Steller threatened to report Bering to the Russian Senate:

> *To get ashore was, after all, my chief work, profession, and duty. Up to now I had served Her Majesty faithfully, and I was determined to continue to serve to the best of my ability in the future. And I said that if for reasons contrary to the purpose of the voyage I was not to go, I would report such conduct in the terms it deserved.*

Bering, for his part, had a larger concern. Their anchorage west of the island was not protected from a storm out of the west or south; if one materialized from either of those directions, they would have to move the ship into open water quickly to avoid being driven onto land. If Steller were to wander too far, Bering could be put in the position of having to abandon him to save the ship.

But Bering relented, telling Steller he could go with the watering party to Kayak Island instead. He would have no help, though, other than his assistant Thomas Lepekhin. At 10 AM, two hours after Khitrovo's longboat party had rowed away from the ship, the watering party was ready to leave for the island. As Steller climbed into the yawl, Bering had his trumpeters play a few flourishes, apparently as a bit of sarcastic humor aimed at Steller. Steller wrote in his journal later that he took the musical jab "in the spirit in which it was ordered."

About twenty minutes later the watering party landed on the beach. Steller, aware of how precious the next few hours would be, immediately hiked off with Lepekhin up the coast to the north. They had traveled only about a half-mile from the landing when they came upon a fading campfire on the beach—with live coals still glowing. Ten minutes in America, and they had found the first sign of Americans. And hot coals meant that people had been here not many minutes before; had they seen the yawl approaching from the *St. Peter* and run and hidden in the forest?

The fire was under a tree, next to a section of log that had been hewn out with an ax to form a shallow trough, and there was water in the trough. Scattered on the ground near the log and the fire pit were a wooden drill for kindling a fire, a small clump of dried seaweed, a few ax-felled trees, several stones, some large animal bones (a few with meat still on them), scraps of dried sockeye salmon, several mussel and scallop shells, and scrapings of "sweet grass"—cow-parsnip, the same big, leafy plant Steller had seen in vast stands in coastal Siberia.

He took a moment to think things through. The Americans had apparently started the campfire with the drill, using the sun-dried algae as tinder. They had heated the stones in the campfire and tossed them into the water-filled log trough to cook pieces of meat. Some of the bones appeared to have been roasted directly on the fire. The bones, he thought, looked like those of reindeer; he was familiar with the animals from his time among the reindeer-herding peoples of Siberia. The Americans seemed to have eaten the mussels and scallops raw, as Steller knew was the practice in Kamchatka. They had apparently poured water through the sweet grass, caught the sweet liquid in the shells, and drunk it, again as the Kamchatkans did.

At this one campsite, then, Steller had seen many obvious similarities between the Native people of Kamchatka and the Americans. Probably, he wrote, they were the same or related people, and the Americans were likely a people who had emigrated from Asia. With this entry in his journal, Steller became the first scientist to hypothesize an Asian origin for Native Americans.

Leaving the campsite, he and Lepekhin pushed on along the coast for another two miles, where they found a dark trail leading into thick forest. They stopped for a moment to consider their situation: they were clearly near an American camp, and they were lightly armed—Lepekhin with a musket, an ax, and a knife, Steller with only a long-handled knife he used for digging up plants. They needed to approach any Americans they met as friendly visitors, so Steller warned Lepekhin not to use his weapons unless Steller ordered him to fight.

With that, they plunged into the forest. In a few feet they found some branches lying haphazardly across the path, in what was apparently a hurried attempt to hide the trail. Just as at the campsite on the beach, Steller concluded, someone seemed to have rushed away only a few minutes before. He and Lepekhin continued through a forest of giant spruces, many of which the Americans had stripped of their bark. The trail splintered into several fainter paths, and they followed a few of them out, one at a time, until one led them into a small open area, about 20 feet by 12 feet, covered with cut cow-parsnip.

Steller and Lepekhin moved the blanket of vegetation aside and found a layer of rocks lying on a section of tree bark. They removed the rocks and bark and then the poles the bark rested on, and looked into what appeared to be a storage cellar about 12 feet deep. Steller clambered down into it and found a large cache of food and goods. There were bark boxes 4 feet square full of dried sockeye salmon fillets; Steller tasted a sample and wrote in his notes that it was delicious. Cow-parsnip and scraped nettle stems lay in heaps; Steller guessed that the Americans used the cow-parsnip for making liquor, as the Kamchatkans did, and the nettles for making fish nets. There were rolls of spruce bark, probably from some of the stripped trees he and Lepekhin had noticed earlier, bales of line made from kelp, and some finely made black arrows.

Steller says in his journal that while he was in the cellar, he was constantly in fear of being attacked; had the Americans returned and found him down in the pit, he would certainly have been trapped. Hurriedly, in the name of science, he pilfered two bundles of fish, the arrows, a fire drill, and samples of the kelp line, grass, and bark, sending Lepekhin back to the watering creek with his collection. Lepekhin hiked back to the stream and sent the samples from the cache back to the ship with the yawl, passing on Steller's request to Bering for more help. Lepekhin warned the watering party to be on their guard, with the Americans so close.

As for Steller, he pulled the cover back over the cache and continued roaming. He hiked back to the beach and turned north, collecting plants as he went. Harbor seals poked their gray heads out of the water to watch him as he walked along the beach, and he saw several whales offshore. There were sea otters in the water as well, but what impressed Steller was how much otter scat he passed on the beach:

Concerning the animals that are present here . . . there are seals, sharks, whales, and plenty of sea otters, whose excrement I found everywhere along the shore, which shows that the [human] inhabitants, with enough other food to be found, must not be much concerned with them, because otherwise they [the otters] would come ashore as infrequently as they do now in Kamchatka, where there are so many people interested in their pelts.

After another two-plus miles of hiking, Steller met a wall of rock jutting so far into the sea that he couldn't get around it. He climbed the slope south of the wall and made his way around it, but found that the slope back down to the beach on the far side was extremely steep, with no obvious safe route of descent. He retreated to the top of a forested hill to the south with the idea of crossing the island and checking out his theory of a big mainland river and harbor on the other side, but the forest was a tangle of shrubs so thick he could barely work his way through it. He realized he would never be able to make it to the other side of the island and back by the end of the day.

From the top of the hill, he looked out over the island, discouraged by how little he was going to be able to see in only one day ashore. He turned to the north, glancing out toward Wingham Island and the mainland, and a trail of smoke caught his eye. Below him, a half-mile to the north, smoke from a campfire curled into the sky. There were Americans almost within shouting distance.

Steller decided he needed reinforcements to approach them, so he crashed downhill through the brush to the beach and hurried the five miles back to the landing site with an armload of plants he had collected. He arrived at about four in the afternoon, just as the yawl crew was leaving for the ship with another load of water. Steller told them to ask Bering for the yawl and some help for a few hours so that he could approach the Americans at their camp.

Steller was exhausted from his near-sprint back to the creek; the seven weeks cooped up on the *St. Peter* had cost him some of his stamina.

He got a fire going for tea, dipping into the creek for the water. The tea revived him, and he started work on his plant collection, writing descriptions first of the ones he was afraid would wilt quickly. It was the beginning of his Kayak Island plant catalog, the first scientific account of the life of northwestern North America.

His prize find was the salmonberry, growing then, as it does today, in shrub thickets all over the island:

> *Of fruit-bearing bushes and plants, I met with only one new and else-where unknown species of raspberry, growing in great abundance but not yet fully ripe. Because of its exceptional size and its unique and exquisite taste, this fruit . . . deserved that a few bushes of it be taken along in a box with soil to be sent to St. Petersburg to be propagated.*

Salmonberry *(Rubus spectabilis)*

Steller dug up some specimens with his long-handled knife to take back aboard the ship.

At about 5 PM the yawl returned with Bering's answer to Steller's request for help: get back to the ship post-haste or Bering would leave him there. So, with only a few hours till sunset, Steller hurried off to the south to see what else he could see, first sending Lepekhin into the forest to shoot and collect an unfamiliar bird he had spotted. Meanwhile the men from the yawl hiked over to the underground cache and carried off some of the dried salmon, leaving a few European gifts in exchange: some cloth, two knives, an iron kettle, twenty strings of beads, some tobacco, and a pipe. Steller thought the tobacco was a bad idea; if the Americans were to try eating it, the next explorers to call at the island might get a hostile reception.

A little before 8 PM, Steller and Lepekhin boarded the yawl with Steller's biological treasures, and the boat left the island for the *St. Peter*. An hour after they were back on board, Khitrovo and his party in the longboat returned. They reported that what they had thought was the mainland was an island (today's Wingham Island). They had taken soundings in the passage between Wingham and Kayak and north of Wingham; the ship, they told Bering, could squeeze through the passage and anchor north of Wingham if necessary.

Khitrovo had found an American plank house on the north shore of the island. He had looked inside and come away with a bark basket full of seashells, a canoe or kayak paddle, and a whetstone with copper stains on it, proving that the Americans had copper (which, we know now, came in trade from the upper reaches of the Copper River).

Everyone was safe, and the crew celebrated what they thought was the first European landing on the northwest coast of America. It *was* the first day of science in the Northwest, but—something they could not have known at this point—the prize for the first landing probably had to go, in all likelihood posthumously, to Dementiev and his party from the *St. Paul*.

As the sun set, Bering served hot chocolate. It was a major luxury; chocolate was a plant of tropical America, expensive to import and still a drink only for the wealthy in mid-eighteenth-century Europe. This chocolate had come across the Atlantic from America to Europe, had been carried overland all the way across Asia, and had sailed the

Pacific to America, closing the circle back to its native continent. It was a totally fitting drink for the occasion.

Steller must have been happy with what he had accomplished on Kayak Island, yet he complained in his journal that no one had even set foot on the mainland, and that the time the expedition had taken to get there—nearly ten years—dwarfed the grand total of ten hours he had been able to spend ashore. Steller had traveled halfway around the world and had spent only part of one day on land in America. In his brief time ashore, though, he had made the first European scientific discoveries in western North America. And he had found the indigenous people's camp and cache, just missing out on meeting the Americans of Kayak Island.

But to Steller, his greatest find came in his last minutes on the island. "Luck, thanks to my hunter," as he describes it, "placed in my hands a single specimen"—of a raucous blue bird with a dark crest—"which I remembered having seen painted in vivid colors and written about in the newest description of Carolina plants and birds." The sight of the bird, the bird we now call Steller's jay, had dredged up a memory in Steller's mind: the image of a crested blue bird from English naturalist and artist Mark Catesby's 1731 book about the Carolinas, a book that Steller had read in Europe. In his acknowledgments Catesby mentions Steller's botanical garden supervisor and Academy sponsor, Johann Amman of St. Petersburg, so Steller probably came to the book through Amman.

What Steller remembered was Catesby's hand-colored plate of an eastern blue jay (now called *Cyanocitta cristata*). It was a different species from the jay he saw on Kayak Island (now *Cyanocitta stelleri*), but both are blue, crested jays found only in the Americas. Steller wrote in his journal that the Kayak Island jay proved, beyond any doubt, that they had landed in America.

Like the chocolate he drank to celebrate his day of pioneering science, the image of a blue, crested jay had closed a circle, from the Carolinas of Mark Catesby, to Europe, where Steller had seen Catesby's book, across Europe and Asia with Steller, and back to America. When Steller climbed back onto the *St. Peter* after his day on Kayak Island, the world was smaller than when he had left it.

Aleut kayaker

AUTUMN IN THE ISLANDS

*We were as well accustomed to storms as we were to
daily deaths.*

—Steller, *Journal*

Early on the morning of July 21, Bering came on deck and, with no council, no deliberation whatsoever, ordered the crew to weigh anchor and sail away toward Asia. Waxell protested the quick departure—the crew still had twenty empty water barrels to fill, 20 percent of the ship's fresh water capacity—but his plea fell on deaf ears. Bering was in no mood to wait; he was afraid that the winds might soon make a seasonal shift from east to west as the summer waned. If the wind did swing around to the west, the *St. Peter* would be hard pressed to make it back to Kamchatka before winter. Bering was right about the winds; as he and his men would find out, sailing west in the North Pacific in autumn is like swimming upstream against a waterfall.

He told the crew that they should be happy with their discovery of America for this year; summer was going fast, and they didn't have enough food for wintering on the east side of the Pacific. They should put as many miles behind them as quickly as they could on their return voyage. None of them had any idea what the coast ahead was like. It might run consistently west and north, allowing them to sail on a direct line back to Avacha Bay, but it could, he argued, just as well swing to the southwest, taking them well off a direct course. In fact, his fear about Alaska's coastline was just as valid as his concern with an autumn wind-shift: the Alaska Peninsula and the Aleutian Island chain do sweep southwest, forming an 1,800-mile arc of land they would have to skirt before sailing directly to Kamchatka.

Bering, the same cautious mariner who had turned back after passing East Cape on his first expedition, was once again far from home in unfamiliar territory, and he opted again to play it safe. Steller agreed with him, giving Bering credit in his journal for being the only officer who was thinking ahead about their situation.

As far from Asia as they were, they were unlikely to make it back to Kamchatka in good time if they followed the ins and outs of the coastline, charting it as they went—the plan that had been agreed upon at the sea council in Avacha Bay before they sailed. But Waxell, at the helm again, stuck closely to the coast as they sailed west, and nothing in any of the accounts suggests that the officers even discussed changing their earlier plan. So they had left Kayak Island in a hurry, with twenty empty water barrels, but now they were going to take their time and chart the coast on their way west.

After a day under sail, a storm front settled over the *St. Peter.* With clouds scraping the deck of the ship, Waxell held cautiously to a southwest course to keep from running aground, assuming that the coastline trended east-west. The storm persisted, and Steller continued to see floating kelp, a good clue that they were still close to land. By July 30 the storm cleared, the wind turned more favorably to the southeast, and the *St. Peter* finally began making decent progress.

In the darkness after midnight on August 2, however, a sailor tossed the sounding lead into the sea and hit bottom at four fathoms. With a draft of nine feet, the ship had only fifteen feet of water under her—not much room for error in a hard-to-maneuver sailing ship. Waxell inched ahead, looking for deeper water. After the crew passed a few nervous hours, a cast of the sounding lead found bottom at a comfortable eighteen fathoms. They lowered the anchor to wait out the night.

When dawn came, they saw an island ahead, less than two miles away; they had nearly stumbled over the shoals of an orphan island in the open sea. It was today's Chirikof Island, eighty miles southwest of Kodiak, named by British captain George Vancouver for the *St. Paul*'s captain fifty years after the American Expedition.

The weather improved, so Waxell turned the ship northwest, toward the coast. On August 3 the crew spotted the high, snow-covered volcanoes of the Alaska Peninsula. They were coming up on the peninsula at an oblique angle, and now it blocked their way to the north, west, and southwest. Waxell turned south, but the following day they found they were heading straight for a large group of islands, today's Semidi Islands.

They were hemmed in by land. Waxell steered southeast, turning back on their course as he tried to clear the coast and the coastal islands, bucking an east wind that could have pushed the ship well on its way toward Kamchatka if they had been in the open sea. By August 6 they were barely any farther west than they had been on July 30. Their preoccupation with the coastline had cost them another week.

While they were near the Semidis, Steller spent his time watching harbor seals, fur seals, sea lions, and sea otters. The crowds of North Pacific marine mammals he observed were definitely something new for European science. In the pinniped realm—the marine mammals with finlike limbs—Europe could claim only the North Atlantic subspecies of the walrus and a few species of true, or earless, seals like the harbor seal, the seal of the ice-free northern coasts. There were no counterparts in the seas off Europe to the eared seals—the fur seals and sea lions—and nothing at all there like the sea otter, the only seagoing member of the mustelid family, most closely related to the river otter and the mink and unrelated to any other marine mammal.

The South Pacific has several species similar to the marine mammals of the North Pacific. Sailors had run across them in the southern and mid-latitudes as far back as the fifteenth century, but except for one pirate with a scientific turn of mind, William Dampier, no one had studied or written about the Pacific's mammals in anything like the detail they deserved. They were still essentially *animalia incognita* to science when the *St. Peter* set sail.

On August 10, back in open water, one of the *incognita* approached the ship. Steller watched it for two hours at close range, close enough that he could have touched it with a pole. To Steller it was a "a very unusual and new animal." He christened it *simia marina,* "sea ape," from his recollection of an account he had read of an animal called Gesner's sea ape, which was reputed to live in the seas off Denmark.

It was five feet long, with a head like a dog, big eyes, erect ears, long whiskers, hair-covered skin, and a long, round body. Steller thought he saw a two-part, fin-shaped, sharklike tail, and he could not see any mammal-like front flippers when it drew itself up partly out of the water and held there, watching the ship, for a few minutes.

There was mutual curiosity at play. At one point the animal shot under the ship, had a look from that side, and then swam back to the original side and resurfaced. It liked this game so much it repeated the round-trip thirty times. Then it grabbed a long piece of kelp in its mouth and juggled it—comically, Steller thought—and now and then bit off a piece and swallowed it.

Scientific duty as he saw it finally got the better of Steller, and he had Thomas Lepekhin shoot at the creature with his musket, hoping to bring it aboard so he could write an accurate description. Lepekhin missed twice, and the animal vanished into the sea; the pale creatures on the floating island were not so friendly after all. It was Steller's last close look.

Eight generations of biologists later, no one has claimed another sighting of a so-called sea ape. The consensus is that what Steller saw was a young northern fur seal. Fur seals do have whiskers and external ear flaps (that's why they are called "eared" seals), and the sharklike tail Steller thought he saw could have been a fur seal's extra-long hind flippers. The front flippers are far enough back on the fur seal's body that Steller might not have caught a glimpse of them; also, fur seals are curious animals, and most young male fur seals are solitary at sea, as this creature was.

But Steller had observed fur seals in the Semidis for the past few days (he knew them already from Kamchatka), so why would he have failed to recognize this one? He probably had never seen a young fur seal at close range, and this was only a partial view of an animal in the water, late in the day, most likely in poor light. Then again, he studied fur seals in detail later on the voyage and left no indication in his writing that he ever changed his mind about the sea ape; in fact, he mentions the strange creature again in *The Beasts of the Sea*. Steller leaves us with both a drop of doubt and a realization that even a smart, well-educated biologist can conjure up a strange observation in ambiguous circumstances.

⌒‿⌒

When he was not at the rail looking for sea creatures, Steller spent most of his time in the tiny cabin he shared with Bering, catching up on his journal or working on one of his papers. A typical multilingual scientist of the day, he wrote his journal in German; he spoke both Russian and German on the ship, the former with the sailors and officers and the latter with his German friends. He wrote his scientific papers—for example, the catalog of Kayak Island plants—in Latin, the language of science.

Steller's plant catalog is an inventory of 140 different plants that he identified on the island. (Finding 140 species in the six hours he spent botanizing there calculates as a barely believable 2½ minutes per plant. Most, however, have been identified as present on the island in recent times, so modern biology has more or less verified Steller's feat.) His longest entry in the catalog is the description of the salmonberry. He identifies it as an American relative of the raspberry and blackberry, an upright shrub without thorns, bearing large scarlet flowers with thin petals and oval red fruit. He follows up this basic description with twelve lines of detail, including the size of the shrub and the shape and structure of its leaves.

Finally, he writes, "the berry is without doubt very delicious, even though these were not quite ripe yet." It was late July, and the berries probably *were* ripe; salmonberries are not the tastiest berry in the forest, but after several months without fresh food, Steller must have thought any palatable berry straight off the bush was a gift from the gods.

The naming format Steller used in the catalog, the biological convention of the time, was a single-word Latin genus name (*Rubus*, in the case of the salmonberry) followed by a few words to describe the characteristics that differentiate the plant from others of its genus. *Rubus* is Latin for "bramble," the Romans' grouping of bristly shrubs that included blackberries and raspberries; Steller chose the other dozen words in the introductory part of his description to differentiate this new bramble from others of its kind that he knew from Europe.

The convention of genus name followed by a string of descriptors—the "polynomial" that Steller used—was soon to be eclipsed by the "binomial," or two-word naming scheme, introduced by Carolus Linnaeus (the Latinized name of Swedish biologist Carl von Linné). Linnaeus's naming convention—a unique combination of genus name followed by species name—is a universal shorthand for referring to living things, and it is the system we still use today, more than 250 years after Linnaeus devised it. The binomial brought the level of recognition "down" from the genus to the species, in effect creating a more detailed understanding of life.

Linnaeus's scheme was comprehensive: he also extended the classification ladder "up" from the genus to more inclusive categories (order, class, and kingdom), and he laid out numerous methods and rules for applying the logic of his system. He applied one of those rules, for creating Latin-form words to refer to newly discovered plants and animals ("Generic names formed to preserve the memory of a botanist who has deserved well of the science, I retain as a religious duty"), when he christened a genus of Asian plants *Stellera* to honor Steller, whom he called "a born collector of plants."

Linnaeus had been working on his ideas for several years before the American Expedition, but his first true encyclopedia of life, *Species Plantarum* (*"The Species of Plants"*) came out in 1753, a decade after the expedition. In *Species Plantarum* he named and classified the six thousand plants then known to European science, using his full classification system. Neither it nor any of his later works, which ran to thousands of pages, included Steller's salmonberry. The salmonberry had to wait until 1814 for its binomial, *Rubus spectabilis;* it was named by botanist Frederick Pursh from a sample Meriwether Lewis brought back East from the banks of the Columbia River.

The "Linnaean hierarchy," as we call the system today, brought order and understanding to the surge in European knowledge of the natural world in the seventeenth and eighteenth centuries, the era known as the Enlightenment. Steller was one naturalist in a virtual army of scientists and philosophers of the time, whose quest to discover the order of the natural world and the character of the human mind modern biologist Edward O. Wilson calls "the West's greatest contribution to civilization."

To understand Steller, it helps to understand his time, and E. O. Wilson provides more insight on the subject: he describes the spirit of the Enlightenment in terms of "confidence, optimism, eyes to the horizon," "the thrill of discovery," and trust in "the power of science to reveal an orderly, understandable universe." All three describe Steller personally as well as the scientific thought of his time—and in our era, all are expressions of humanity at its best.

Steller and other Enlightenment scientists did not simply catalog and count; they were pioneers in a hopeful new world, filling in the family tree of life and unveiling the natural order of the universe.

In addition to the entertainment the "sea ape" provided, August 10 was a day to remember on the *St. Peter* for a second and more serious reason: the sea council Bering called. Since August 7, the wind had been steadily out of the west, in the explorers' faces; it looked as though Bering's prediction of a seasonal wind shift was coming true. And scurvy had appeared on board. Assistant surgeon Betge reported to the officers that five men were so sick they were unable to work, and sixteen more were sick but still able to stand their watches. (It is interesting that either Bering or Waxell apparently bypassed Steller, the physician, and asked for a report from Betge, the assistant.)

The first stages of scurvy—swollen and bleeding gums, loosened teeth, and stiff, sore joints—had progressed in the five on the disabled list to complete loss of the use of their arms and legs. If the *St. Peter* stayed at sea much longer, the crew could expect to see the sickness spread, bringing on life-threatening anemia and hemorrhage.

At the council the officers considered the scurvy outbreak, the wind shift, and the fact that autumn was coming on. They officially abandoned the plan to follow and chart the coastline and decided to sail due west along the 53rd parallel, the line of latitude they were now crossing, as directly as possible to Avacha Bay. There was still a lot of sea to cover; they calculated that Kamchatka was more than 1,700 nautical miles away.

A steady west wind blew for the next nine days, forcing Waxell to tack back and forth to the north and south, gaining precious little ocean to the west. After midnight on the nineteenth, the breeze shifted to the east for a few hours, but then it promptly died and the west wind came up again. The nights were getting longer now, and, for fear of running aground in the strong winds, the crew had to take in the sails after dark. Then a storm from the west blew in on August 24 and stayed with them until the twenty-sixth. The twenty-seventh dawned cold, clear, and bright, with the wind still strong from the west.

Since the sea council seventeen days earlier, the *St. Peter* had advanced only 300 miles closer to Avacha Bay. At that rate, it would take nearly three more months to reach Kamchatka, and Bering knew the weather was only going to grow worse as the fall progressed. The ship's supply of fresh water was down to twenty-six barrels; they were certain now to run out of water before making landfall in Asia again. Bering called another sea council, and the officers decided to steer for the American coast and find fresh water to refill their empty barrels—including the twenty they could have filled at Kayak Island.

They turned north, blown ahead by strong winds through storm clouds and heavy rain. On the morning of August 29 they spotted land about 25 miles to the north. The storm let up, and they sailed into a circle of islands, still a good 40 miles from the mainland. As night fell, they anchored between a small, barren, rocky island to the east and a long, narrow island to the west. They were in a partially protected bay, but they were exposed to the open sea to the south; the sailors on watch would have to stay alert in case another storm rolled in from that direction. In the night, one of the officers scanning the bay with a telescope spotted a campfire on an island several miles to the northeast. There were Americans in the islands.

Very early on the morning of the thirtieth Hesselberg organized a shore party. He and several sailors prepared the longboat for the three-mile trip to the long, narrow island (today's Nagai Island) to find fresh water. Khitrovo asked Steller whether he wanted to go ashore with Hesselberg. Meanwhile Khitrovo was organizing a crew to take the yawl to the island (today's Turner Island) where they had seen the fire the night before. Steller thought he saw through Khitrovo's invitation to join Hesselberg; Khitrovo, he was sure, intended to make first contact with Americans and claim the credit in Steller's absence. But Steller was not up to protesting and being denied yet again, so he climbed into the longboat without saying anything, taking Lepekhin and Plenisner with him to explore Nagai Island.

Waxell challenged Khitrovo's plan, questioning the idea of sending a party on a nonessential mission so far from the ship. The island was eight or ten miles away, and if a storm came up from the south, the crew would have to take the ship into open water to ride out the storm in safety, leaving the men in the yawl trapped indefinitely on the island. But Khitrovo insisted he be allowed to go.

Waxell left the decision up to Bering, who was lying sick in his cabin with scurvy. The captain told Waxell that if Khitrovo felt strongly about it, he should let him go. Khitrovo left for Turner Island in the yawl about 11 AM, taking with him four sailors and soldiers, one of the Siberian interpreters, and some cloth, mirrors, knives, and needles as gifts in case they met Americans on the island.

About 6 AM Steller landed on Nagai Island with the water carriers, and he immediately set off hiking ahead of the group to find a good water source. Fifty yards inland, he passed a big pool of water, cut off from the sea behind a beach berm. Knowing it was probably salty, he continued inland until he found the spring that fed the pool. Steller tasted the spring water; it was fresh and good. He hiked back to the beach, ready to lead the watering crew to the spring, but they were already filling the barrels from the pool.

Steller tried to convince them the pool water was salty; he pointed out that the level of the pool was rising with the tide, fed by seawater that was seeping through the berm. He tasted the pool water; it was obviously salty. He sent a sample of the spring water back to the ship with the ten barrels the crew had filled with the pool water, along with a brief report to Waxell: in Steller's medical opinion, the water from the pool would dehydrate the crew and make the scurvy patients worse.

On board the ship, Waxell tasted a sample of the pool water. He did taste the salt in it, but thought it was fine. He sent another sixteen empty barrels and a message back to the crew on the island: "The water is good; fill up with it!" At that, Steller checked farther along the beach and found a freshwater lake nearer to the beach than the salt pool was. Steller returned to the pool and told Hesselberg about it, but Hesselberg refused to move the watering crew to the lake. So, realizing he had

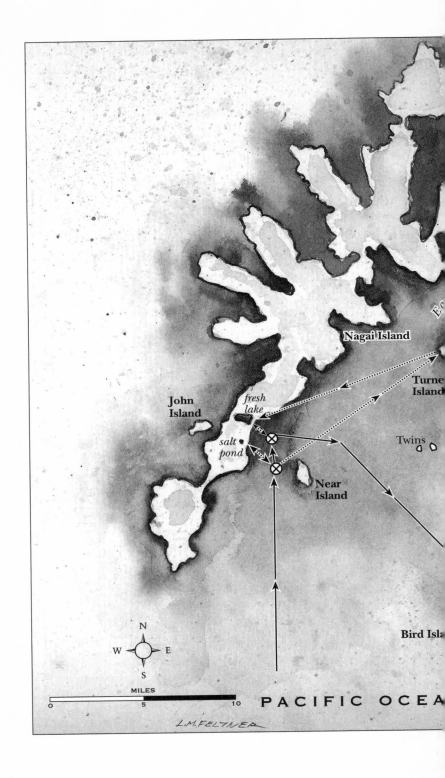

Nagai Island

John
Island

*fresh
lake*

Turne
Island

*salt
pond*

Near
Island

Twins

Bird Isla

N
W   E
S

MILES
0   5   10

PACIFIC OCEA

L.M.FELTNER

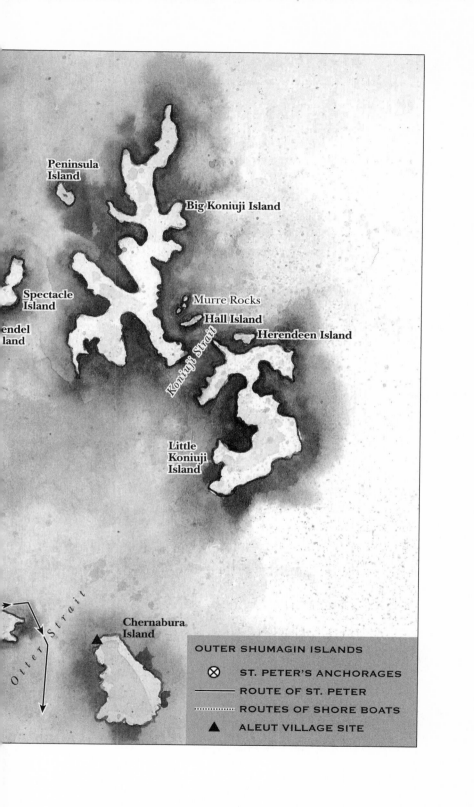

Peninsula
Island

Big Koniuji Island

Spectacle
Island

endel
land

Murre Rocks

Hall Island

Herendeen Island

Koniuji Strait

Little
Koniuji
Island

Outer Strait

Chernabura
Island

OUTER SHUMAGIN ISLANDS

⊗   ST. PETER'S ANCHORAGES

———   ROUTE OF ST. PETER

·········   ROUTES OF SHORE BOATS

▲   ALEUT VILLAGE SITE

done all he could do, Steller left Hesselberg to his work and set off to explore the island.

Nagai is not so much a single island as it is a confederation of peninsulas, a dozen narrow fingers and thumbs sewn together by a few delicate stitches of land. Steller and his friends hiked across one of the thumbs, a bulge of land three miles wide near the south end of the island. The land was treeless but green, and springs popped out of the rocky ground all around them. The plant cover grew no more than four feet high, and the vegetation was so wind-battered and gnarled, Steller wrote in his journal, that it was impossible to find a straight stick two feet long anywhere.

The first creature they encountered was a fox; it barked at them like a dog and showed no fear whatsoever. As they walked, Steller recognized many of the birds they saw: ptarmigan, ravens, flycatchers, and snow buntings over land, and swans, ducks, and loons on ponds and lakes. The seabird life was even more abundant: Steller recorded sightings of cormorants, murres, pigeon guillemots, and horned and tufted puffins near shore.

Steller, Plenisner, and Lepekhin built a small shelter for camping out that night on the island. Now, however, seeing the great variety of green plants growing in Nagai's lowlands—plants such as scurvy grass, gentian, and crowberry—Steller decided he had to go back to the ship and try to convince Waxell that fresh, green food and fresh water were vital for the scurvy patients. He tramped back to the beach, where the longboat had just landed with another load of empty water barrels and some of the scurvy patients.

Waxell had sent the sickest sailors ashore on the theory that the fresh air would help them, but for one of the sailors, it was the end of the line. As soon as his mates moved him ashore, Nikita Shumagin died. They buried him, the first of the *St. Peter*'s scurvy victims, on a grassy slope by the salt pond. They erected a small wooden cross to mark the grave, consecrating his body and his name to the small archipelago we now call the Shumagin Islands.

Steller went back to the ship to ask Waxell to fill the barrels with fresh water and to assign some men to help him gather greens for the scurvy patients. He got nowhere with either request. The water from the pond was fine, Waxell told him, and it was all right to bring a few plants on board, but there was no sense in sending a group of sailors ashore to pick them. Waxell told Steller to collect the plants himself, without any help from the crew.

From then on, Steller vowed in his journal, he would stop giving advice and would look out only for himself. The naval officers ignored him, even when it came to the health and safety of the crew. But, despite the sharp words in his journal, Steller (probably with the help of Plenisner and Lepekhin) harvested a supply of plants from the island, and over the next few days he fed them to anyone who would eat them. Eight days later Bering, who had been unable to stand, was up and about on deck again, and most of the sick sailors had improved. Steller's Nagai Island greens staved off the shipboard epidemic for the moment.

With his prescription of green plants for treating scurvy, Steller became one of the first ship's physicians to successfully treat the disease at sea. Sailors and overland expedition crews of the time still thought of it as an occupational hazard they could do very little about. We know now, of course, that scurvy is an easily preventable Vitamin C–deficiency disease. Ignorance of its precise cause, however, persisted into the twentieth century.

In his time with the Itelmen and other Siberian people, Steller had learned how to prevent or treat the disease. With his quick mind, he could not have missed the sharp differences between the indigenous diet and propensity for the disease and that of the members of Bering's expedition. The Native people he had studied ate a diet of mostly fresh food, tilted strongly at times toward pure meat and fat, and they never contracted scurvy; the Europeans ate mostly flour, grain, and dried meat, and during their explorations of the Russian Arctic during the Second Kamchatka Expedition, they died of the disease like mosquitoes in a hard freeze. Steller's discovery came well in advance of "official" medicine; it was still a dozen years before Scottish naval doctor James Lind would write the first medical paper about it, and fifty years before lime juice became standard preventive medicine on British ships.

Early on the morning of August 31, Waxell began the longboat relay again, shuttling more empty barrels to Nagai Island for water. Steller returned to Nagai on the first trip and continued exploring. In the early afternoon the wind picked up from the east, blowing mare's-tail clouds high over the *St. Peter,* and the crew on the ship tightened up the rigging in anticipation of a storm. By late afternoon the watering crew had shuttled a total of fifty-two full barrels back to the ship, and at 6 PM Waxell sent the longboat to shore to pick up the last of the barrels, the sick sailors, and Steller, Plenisner, and Lepekhin.

The storm was gathering intensity as the longboat landed. A Russian sailor hiked off to find Steller's party and found them on the other side of the island, unaware of the change in the weather. They trotted back to the landing beach. A strong surf was running, and the crew was hurriedly loading the sick sailors into the longboat. Steller, Plenisner, and Lepekhin waded waist-deep through breaking waves to the boat, which the sailors on board were holding with difficulty off the beach.

In the confusion of pushing off from shore, they left the last few water barrels behind. These were the only barrels the water carriers had filled with fresh water from the spring above the salt pool; Steller found out from the sailors in the longboat that Waxell had ordered a few barrels filled with spring water for the officers. Now everyone would have to drink the briny water from the pool.

The longboat crew was barely back on board the *St. Peter* when one of the sailors spotted a campfire on Nagai Island, near the position of the freshwater lake Steller had found. It was Khitrovo and his party, stranded three or four miles from the ship, in an impossible situation in the breaking storm. There was no way for them to return to the ship safely, and no way for a crew in the longboat to get to them for a rescue.

Khitrovo had landed on Turner Island the day before and had found warm embers from the campfire, but no Americans. He and his crew had spent the night on the island, and then, trying to beat the approaching storm back to the ship, they had nearly overturned the yawl in the waves the east wind had kicked up in the bay. Their direct course to the ship had put the waves on the beam of the boat, an extremely dangerous situation; knowing that it was impossible to reach the ship, they had made a run for the east side of Nagai. A wave had hurled them onto the beach, and the hard landing had damaged the yawl. Now they were safe but soaked. On the verge of hypothermia, they scavenged wood for a fire and huddled around it. Beyond being wet and cold, they had another major problem: the yawl was not sea-worthy enough now to row back to the ship even if the ocean calmed.

Mounting a rescue from the ship was impossible for the next day and a half; nobody was going anywhere in the storm. At 1:00 in the morning of September 1, Yushin wrote a single word in the log of the *St. Peter:* "Gale." At 9 AM, it was "Gale blowing." At 10:00, the crew took in every last square inch of sail, and "made ready for whatever might come." The barrage of the storm continued all day; by 5 PM four inches of seawater had seeped into the ship's hold.

The storm finally began to wane that night; the wind turned gusty and swung around to the southeast. The ship was exposed in that di-rection, so at daybreak on September 2 Waxell moved her farther into the bay for more protection. They anchored again at a point about two miles from where Khitrovo and his party were holed up. At noon, with the seas calm again, Waxell sent the longboat for them. For sev-eral hours, the crew of the *St. Peter* saw no sign of either the yawl or the longboat. By 6 PM the wind had come up and the seas were build-ing yet again. They spotted two campfires near Khitrovo's bivouac; it looked as though both rescuers and rescuees would be spending the night ashore.

The next morning the wind quartered around to the southwest and the seas began to die down. Both parties on Nagai piled into the longboat and rowed out to the ship. No one was lost, but they had left the broken yawl on the island.

Now Waxell had the crew pull up the anchor and turned the ship for the open sea. But the southwest wind was pushing squarely against them; there was no escape in the direction they needed to go. Instead, Waxell tucked the ship into a protected bay in the north-ern lee of one of the outer islands, today known as Bird Island. They waited there all day for a favorable breeze, but they couldn't clear the island in the southerly winds.

After his rescue Khitrovo quickly got back to the business of the ship, taking charge of the sounding lead as the crew navigated the waters off Bird Island. On his first cast he parted the line and left the lead at the bottom of the sea. Khitrovo had done it again; after delaying the expedition for four days—time they definitely did not have to spare—he had committed one of the most ominous sins of life at sea. To eighteenth-century mariners, losing a sounding lead was a terrible omen. The Russian sailors muttered to themselves that it had been exactly a year before that Khitrovo had run aground in the *Nadezhda* and drowned their provisions.

The next day, September 4, Waxell stuck the *St. Peter*'s nose around the western corner of Bird Island, but the southerly winds were still howling; there was no escape yet. The crew turned the ship about and limped back into the same anchorage north of Bird Island where they had spent the previous night.

Standing at the rail again, Steller thought he could hear the roaring of sea lions from beneath a cliff in the inner bay. He scanned the shoreline, but did not see any animals. Then he thought he could make out two small boats against the cliff. The objects slowly drew closer, and after several more minutes of anticipation, Steller realized that two Americans, each paddling a small, decked boat, were approaching the ship.

The boats were kayaks, and Steller's sighting was a preliminary to the first contact between Europeans and the Unangan people of the Aleutian Islands, more commonly known to us today as Aleuts. What Steller had thought was a sea lion's roar was a chant the Aleut kayakers were shouting as they paddled toward the alien ship. Behind them, several other islanders called in unison from shore.

The Aleuts cruised closer, and their high-pitched shouting crystallized into words and phrases, but in a language neither of the Siberian interpreters understood. Steller guessed that it was either a greeting or a prayer for courage and protection. The kayakers stopped a hundred feet from the ship. Steller and his shipmates waved to them, trying to convince them that it was safe to come closer. The Aleuts waved back. They pointed to their mouths, scooped up seawater with their hands and pointed to shore, apparently inviting the Europeans to Bird Island for food and water.

After smearing his cheeks with ochre-colored earth and filling his nostrils with grass, one of the Aleuts bravely paddled up to the ship. From beneath the rigging on the deck of his kayak, he pulled out a length of red-stained spruce and lashed two falcon wings to it with baleen cord.

Then he tossed the spruce stick to the Koryak interpreter on the ship. One of the men on the ship then tied two smoking pipes and some glass beads onto a piece of board and floated it toward the kayak.

The Aleut picked the board out of the water and paddled back to his companion; they looked the gift over and stuck it under the rigging of the second kayaker's boat. Then the first Aleut paddled back to the ship and offered up another spruce stick, this time with an entire falcon lashed to it. The *St. Peter*'s crew launched another gift from the ship in return: a mirror and some Chinese silk. The kayakers scooped them up and started paddling back to shore, motioning to the ship for the Europeans to follow.

There was a lively discussion on the *St. Peter* as the two Aleuts paddled away. The plan that emerged was to send Waxell, Steller, the Koryak interpreter, and nine sailors and soldiers to the island in the longboat. It was a big risk. The longboat was now their only shore boat; if Waxell and his party wrecked it, they would be stranded.

They lowered the boat over the side and packed it with gifts for the Aleuts. In the bottom of the boat, hidden under sailcloth, they stowed several guns and swords in case of trouble. They launched and rowed away from the ship. As they neared shore, they could see that waves were crashing heavily on the rocky beach. They couldn't risk landing in the surf, so Waxell had an anchor dropped when they were still well offshore. The longboat drifted in among the rocks, stern first, to a point barely twenty feet off the beach. Nine kayaks lay here and there along the beach; the Aleuts obviously had no trouble landing in surf.

A group of nine Aleuts, both men and women, came down to the water, waving for the strangers to come ashore. They apparently could not understand why their visitors had not landed on the beach. Waxell saw that the Americans were having some doubts about their visitors, so he decided to send two sailors and the interpreter ashore. The three took off their clothes and hopped out of the boat, up to their armpits in the sea. They waded to the beach, carrying the longboat's stern line, which they tied off to one of the rocks on shore.

The Aleuts took each of the three by the arm and led them to their outdoor kitchen, where the Americans offered their guests whale meat. Attempts at conversation produced a jumble of unintelligible syllables, and the Europeans and Americans resorted to arm waving and signing. Pointing over the island, one of the Americans seemed to be saying that they lived in a village somewhere to the east.

A few of the Aleuts still stood along the beach, gesturing for the rest of the Europeans to come ashore. The eldest of the Americans decided to paddle out to the longboat. He picked up his kayak with one hand and his paddle with the other, carried them to the water, and launched into the surf. When he reached the longboat, Waxell offered him a cup of vodka. Then, as Waxell described it, "he put [it] to his lips, but spat the vodka out again at once and, turning to his fellows, screeched most horribly," not very impressed with the Russians' favorite drink. Next, one of the sailors offered him a lighted pipe; Steller, who had advised against giving the Americans tobacco or liquor, says that the sailor "tried to make up for one annoyance with a new one." The Aleut took a puff, handed back the pipe in disgust, turned his kayak, and paddled back to shore.

Night was coming on, and the surf was getting rougher. The longboat crew still had the return journey to the ship ahead of them, so Waxell shouted to his three men on shore to get back to the boat. They made their farewells and began to walk toward the beach, but the Americans had taken a liking to the Koryak and held onto him as though they wanted him to stay. Meanwhile, one of the Aleuts picked up the longboat's stern line and began to tug on it, dragging the boat through the waves toward shore. The *St. Peter*'s last shore boat was about to end up on the rocks. Desperate to save the longboat, Waxell ordered two muskets fired over the heads of the people on shore.

The sharp crack of the muskets echoed off the cliff face behind the beach; the Aleuts dropped everything and dove to the ground. The shore party sprinted through the water to the longboat and climbed in. But as the crew tried to row away, the anchor stuck firmly to the bottom. Waxell yelled for someone to cut the line. One of the sailors sliced it, and they rowed into deeper water.

The Aleuts got to their feet and began shouting, apparently scolding the Europeans for repaying their hospitality with rude behavior. A few of them picked up stones from the beach as if to throw them at the strangers, but they held off as the longboat retreated. Waxell left them with a smile and a few gestures intended as an invitation to come out to the ship later. The whole incident had lasted only fifteen minutes.

That night the wind and waves that had threatened the longboat turned into a blow, and the Americans' fire burned all night on the beach in a heavy rain. The next day, the fifth of September, rain continued to come down in torrents. About 3 PM the wind shifted to the southwest, exposing the ship to the storm, so Waxell had the crew pull the anchor for a move to a more protected spot. As the anchor was coming up, Steller spotted two of the Aleuts paddling their kayaks from sea to shore.

Waxell moved the *St. Peter* to the east, and at about 5 PM they anchored again to wait out the storm. Half an hour later seven Aleuts came paddling toward the ship. They were shouting again, the same roar-chant the two paddlers had called out the day before. Two of the kayakers split off from the group and approached the ship.

Waxell put the idea to Bering to lure the Americans on board and take them as prisoners. Bering refused, ordering Waxell not to use any kind of force against them. Steller, meanwhile, had his eye on the visors they were wearing. They were thin, wooden, open-crowned hats, stained red and green, and some of them had small, sewn-on bone or ivory carvings. Bering offered to trade for one of them, and the Aleuts responded by handing up two of the visors. Bering gave them a rusty iron pot and some needles and thread in exchange. Then, with the sea beginning to build again, the Aleuts paddled back to the island.

The next day the sea had calmed, and Waxell took the ship around the east side of Bird Island. The Americans shouted again from shore to the *St. Peter* as she sailed away. The ship turned toward the open sea through a channel, now called Otter Strait, between Bird Island and today's Chernabura Island, the island to the southeast. As they sailed past, Steller could see people and houses on Chernabura—most likely the village of the Aleuts they had met.

The *St. Peter* cleared the islands, caught a west-southwest wind in her sails, and raced south. By 2:00 that afternoon the expedition had put the islands over the horizon to the north. The first meeting of Europeans and the people of the Aleutians was over.

To Steller, the people the expedition met at Bird Island were simply "Americans." After the expedition, the Russians who came to the Aleutian chain referred to the island people as "Aleut," a term that apparently came from a Kamchatka coastal people known as the Aliutor, who had a similar sea hunting and fishing culture. The Russians did not differentiate among the peoples they met later as they moved east along the American islands and coastline; all were "Aleuts," from the far western Aleutians to the Alaska Peninsula and all the way to Kodiak Island.

Of course the case was, and still is, much more complex than that. The people of the Aleutian Islands and the western Alaska Peninsula consider themselves to comprise eight different groups. The terms for these people as a whole, in their languages, derive from the root *unanga,* which translates as "seasider." The term "Aleut" lives on, now in a much more limited sense than the Russians used it, for the people who share an indigenous language, the language also referred to as "Aleut."

The Russians called all the forms of the kayak on the Alaska coast "baidarkas," or "little boats." We do essentially the same thing with the word *kayak*—which comes from *qajaq,* the Inuit word for the craft—corralling within the term at least a dozen different styles of decked, canoelike small boats.

For the coastal people, kayaks were silent sea-hunting craft built for stalking marine mammals. They were indispensable in the Aleutians. Most of the other peoples who used kayaks had at least some large land mammals available to them, but that was not the case in the islands; the Aleuts' food had to come from the sea, and sea mammals were the crucial resource. Aleutian villagers also ate fish and shellfish, which gave them plenty of protein, but there was no major source of carbohydrates in their environment. The source of the critical calories in the Aleut diet was fat—the fat of sea mammals. Aleut culture would have been very different—if it had survived at all—without marine mammals and the kayak.

A traditional story from the eastern Aleutians tells of six brothers who set out in kayaks from their village one morning, following a multicolored bird. Soon they were well out of sight of land. The bird disappeared ahead of them, and when they reached the point where it had disappeared, they came upon an island. They landed, and from the beach they heard the roaring and growling of strange animals. The animals were sea lions.

The six brothers built a hut and stayed the winter, living on sea lion meat. When spring came, they put on sea lion skins, swam into the sea, and began to live as sea lions. Then the sea lion brothers swam back to their human village to see their parents and wives, carrying several sea lion skins with them.

They convinced their parents and wives to join them, and the parents and wives put on the sea lion skins, waded into the ocean, and swam away as sea lions. From there they traveled to the bird island and then to an outlying reef, where they hauled out. They decided to live on the reef, the story concludes, and all the children born to the brothers and their wives were sea lions.

It was when they paddled their *iqyan*—the Aleut name for the kayaks Steller observed in the islands—that the people of the Aleutians swam like sea lions. The *iqyan* were as good an approximation of the animals as humans could devise. They were about the length of a large Steller sea lion bull, and sea lion skins were used as the outer membrane of the kayak. The frame inside the skin cover was almost literally a skeleton, and the connective tissue that held the skeleton together was sinew from sea lions and other marine mammals. The spine of the frame was its three-piece keel; it flexed like a very limber backbone, which is one of the prime adaptations of sea lions and seals to life in the ocean. Small pieces of bone and ivory in the keel joints, and in more than fifty other joints in the frame, gave the joints flex and prevented wear, like cartilage in an animal's joints.

The *iqyan* were sleek and supple in the water, like sea lions. The flex of the elastic frame and the skin cover allowed the kayak to absorb and transmit the force of Aleutian storm waves through the entire length of the boat, protecting it from breaking up in seas that would destroy a rigid boat. The *iqyan* were as seaworthy as marine mammals, and they had to be; the Aleut way of life depended on them.

The first European description of an Aleutian kayak is Steller's. In his brief encounters with Aleut kayaks and kayakers off Bird Island, he absorbed enough to write this detailed verbal sketch:

> *The American boats are about two fathoms [twelve feet] long, two feet high and two feet long on the deck, in front pointed toward the nose, but in the stern truncated and smooth. To judge by appearance, the frame is of poles fitted to each other at both ends and spread apart on the inside by crosspieces. On the outside, this frame is covered with skins, perhaps of seals, and colored black-brown. . . .*

About five feet from the rear is a round opening, around which a piece of whale gut is sewn. Its outer edge has a hollow hem made fast by a string pulled through it, by means of which it can be pulled tight or loosened like a purse. As soon as the American has seated himself in the opening with his feet stretched forward under the deck, he pulls this hem together around his body and fastens it by a slipknot to keep any water from getting in. Behind the paddler on the deck lie ten or more round red sticks pointed at one end and bound together, all formed in the same way as the one we got from them—for what purpose I cannot guess, unless perhaps they serve to repair the boat in case the frame should break.

The American sticks his right hand into the opening of the boat, holding the paddle in the other, and because it is so light carries it from the land to the water, and sits down and fastens himself in it. For paddling, he makes use of a long, thick stick, on both ends equipped with a blade the width of a hand. With this paddle, he strikes the water alternately to the right and to the left and in this way propels his boat with great agility even among the highest waves. On the whole, this boat is very little different, if at all, from those of the Samoyeds and the Americans in New Denmark.

Steller was right about the Aleutian kayak's connection with the watercraft of "New Denmark" (Greenland) and Siberia (home of "the Samoyeds," not a people of the kayak, although the Koryak and Chukchi of Siberia were). Almost all across the arctic and subarctic landscape, from eastern Siberia to Greenland, indigenous peoples built and paddled hunting kayaks. Kayak historians lean toward the Aleutian Islands as the craft's birthplace, or if not the birthplace, at least the place where it evolved into a sophisticated technology. Kayaks were most likely in use in the Aleutians at least seven thousand years ago, and perhaps even further back in time. In any case, the craft spread southeast as far as Prince William Sound and hopped across the North American Arctic, eventually reaching Greenland, speciating as it went into a dozen or so different major forms.

In the hands of a skilled paddler, the kayak of the Aleutians was an unmatched small watercraft. Early European visitors left a string of superlatives behind in their accounts of Aleutian kayaks and kayakers. Ioann Veniaminov, the first Russian Orthodox priest in the Aleutians, wrote in a memoir that an Aleut kayaker could outdistance a bird; apparently he had watched kayakers zip past marbled murrelets as the seabirds ran and flapped to get airborne off the surface of the sea. Martin Sauer, secretary of the Joseph Billings–Gavriil Sarychev expedition, a voyage half a century after Bering's, watched a group of kayakers paddling their *iqyan* into violently breaking seas along the rocky coastline, submerging their boats and "sporting about more like amphibious animals than human beings."

The kayakers Steller met off Bird Island, like all Aleutian hunters, were skilled at stalking sea otters, and a channel we call Otter Strait today was surely a good place to hunt them in 1741. The painted, pointed wooden sticks the Aleuts kept on the rear decks of their kayaks—the sticks Steller thought might be spare parts for repairing the frame—were "dart harpoons" for hunting otters. A hunter hurled a dart at his prey with the help of a throwing board, which acted as an extension of the hunter's arm. It was no simple feat to balance the kayak with a paddle in one hand and throw a dart harpoon with the other, but a good shot could hit an otter at 100 feet.

Aleuts hunted the furry, low-fat sea otters primarily to make warm coats. For most of their sea mammal food, they hunted seals, sea lions, and whales. Of all the mammals, a hunter's greatest prize was a whale. One of the great whales, a humpback or a gray, gave the people meat and fat to eat, oil for heat and light, ribs for framing their earth-covered, semi-subterranean homes, bone for tools and harpoon heads, gut for waterproof parkas and kayak spray skirts, tendons and ligaments for cord and line, and vertebrae and shoulder blades for furniture.

The whale hunt was also the most spectacular of the kayak hunts. Imagine an Aleut hunter in his kayak, perched on a wave crest, the bow of the kayak hanging in the air just above the great, blue-black back of a humpback whale as it breaks the surface of the sea in a boiling of waves. The whale, at four or five times the length of the kayak and several *hundred* times the mass, dwarfs the tiny kayak. The hunter has only a split second to aim and thrust his harpoon into the huge animal. He cannot kill the whale outright; his harpoon head is tipped with monkshood poison, and it will take some time to take effect. So, even if his strike is true, he will have to put the kayak in reverse in a very big hurry to avoid the thrashing of the whale. One wrong move, and he is finished. In the instant before he strikes, the whale hunter is on the verge of either great success or total annihilation.

The whale hunt is a good metaphor for traditional Aleut existence: a precarious life in one of the richest seascapes on the planet. The seas of the Aleutians were an abundant source of food, but the constant wind and never-ending cycle of storms made hunting in small watercraft a risky way to make a living. One storm follows another for most of the year, as though this corner of the earth had to create enough weather for the entire planet. Add in a jagged coastline, tricky tidal currents, and fog as thick as fish chowder, and successful hunting at sea was anything but a sure bet.

The strategy was to become masters of the sea. It was undoubtedly a hard life, and famine was probably very often a danger, but the strategy worked. Something on the order of 15,000 people lived in the Aleutians when the *St. Peter* came calling, nearly double the population of the chain today. Dozens of small villages peppered the eastern Aleutians near the passes between the Pacific and the Bering Sea, where sea currents concentrate plankton, fish, and marine mammals. There were about twenty-five villages in the vicinity of Unalaska Island alone.

At the meeting on Bird Island, the contrast between the Aleuts and Bering's crew could not have been starker. The Europeans were sick and beginning to run out of food. They were unable to land their longboat on the island, and they were having serious trouble positioning the *St. Peter* to keep her out of the winds that were roaring into the bay. Meanwhile, the Americans were freely handing out whale meat, beaching their kayaks in the surf, and paddling the heavy seas with the ease and grace of sea lions swimming.

Aleksei Chirikov and the crew of the *St. Paul* were not in a good position. They had lost both of their shore boats and fifteen men in their attempt to land in America. Food was short, but the lack of water was the crisis; with the longboat and the yawl gone, they had no way to get to shore for more. Their situation must have seemed absurd—sailing offshore of a coast that was teeming with creeks and rivers, yet knowing that they were going to have to make do with the water they had brought from Asia. Chirikov ordered strict water rationing, and they hurriedly sailed away in the direction of Kamchatka.

They left the coast near the great snowy wall of Mount Fairweather, the signature peak in today's Glacier Bay National Park. They passed south of Kayak Island on July 29 and crossed Bering's track on the thirtieth. By August 4 they were off Kodiak at about the same position where Bering had been ten days earlier. While Waxell was working to get free of land off the Alaska Peninsula the first week of August, Chirikov closed the gap. He passed the point where Steller had seen the sea ape just two days behind Bering's ship, on the twelfth. Neither captain had any idea the two ships were so near each other.

Steady west winds held up both ships for the next two weeks, and Chirikov ordered a new water inventory. Not liking what he learned, he had the crew begin distilling seawater to augment the rainwater they were catching in buckets and wringing out of the sails. There was scurvy on board now, and the sailors who were coming down with it noticed something about the water coming off the sails: it tasted horribly bitter, but it made them feel better. The source of the bitter flavor was the pine tar they had used to seal the rigging and sails from the corrosive seawater. They had boiled down the tar from fresh pine pitch, so it probably was a passable scurvy remedy.

The wind shifted to the east on August 31, and Chirikov sped by the Shumagins, leaving Bering and the *St. Peter* behind. The wind continued to carry Chirikov's ship west while Bering's crew sat at anchor, waiting to rescue Khitrovo. By the time the *St. Peter* sailed back out of the islands into the open sea, Chirikov had covered half the distance between the Shumagins and Kamchatka, opening an 800-knot lead on Bering.

Chirikov was sailing west along the 53rd parallel, the latitude of Avacha Bay. If America's geography and the weather cooperated, and if their calculations were right, he and his crew could be home in a week. But islands kept appearing in their path; the edge of the continent was swinging out in a southwestern arc, cutting off their westerly course.

On September 8, with land in front of them, the wind died and a heavy fog set in. Darkness fell, and they felt their way ahead with the sounding lead as if by braille. Rolling swells carried the ship into progressively shallower water, and then they heard the worst sound a sailor can hear in a fog: surf crashing on rocks. They dropped anchor in a panic. Luckily, it held, and they began a long wait for daylight.

The next day, in the middle of the morning, the fog lifted enough for them to see, less than a quarter-mile to the west, the rocky coast where the surf was breaking. They were anchored off today's Adak Island, and they were trapped there until the wind came up again.

Glassing the coastline, one of the officers spotted two Americans walking along the shore. They quickly disappeared from sight as the fog swept in again, but an hour later, seven small boats materialized out of the mist, one paddler in each, moving toward the ship. Five days after Bering and Steller had met the people of the Aleutians, Chirikov and his crew were about to have their own Aleut experience.

At 300 feet from the ship, the Americans stopped paddling and began to shout in unison, a roaring chant like the one the Shumagin islanders had directed at Bering's ship. After seven or eight minutes they stopped their chanting, and Chirikov and his officers waved for them to come closer. Eventually they did, and Chirikov got the message across that his men were low on water.

Chirikov offered the Aleuts a cup, boxes, bells, and needles as gifts, but they showed no interest whatsoever until he produced a knife. As if on cue, three of the kayakers paddled back to the island and filled sealskins with fresh water. Back at the ship, each one demanded and received a knife for his skin of water.

Later in the day another fourteen kayakers paddled out to see the Europeans. They spent three or four hours signing and bartering at the ship, but then the wind began to pick up from the west, the direction that would push the ship out of the bay. Chirikov abruptly called a halt to the visiting and ordered his crew to sail. They had the anchor only part way up when a great gust of wind ripped down from the mountains, whipping the ship from side to side. With not a second to waste, they cut the anchor line, crowded on all the sails, and harnessed the wild wind for a run for the open sea.

They skirted the rocks and made it, but all they got for their sailing heroics was more headwinds and little progress toward Asia. On September 15 they lowered the body of their first scurvy casualty into the sea—the ship's sailmaker, who had been one of the strongest members of the crew. Disease and short water rations were pushing the crew to the edge; most of the sailors were so weak now that they had a tough time just climbing out of their bunks.

Chirikov, the log says, was very sick too; by the twentieth he was unable to get out of his bunk. His lieutenants were also down, so the task of running the ship fell entirely to Chirikov's navigator, Ivan Yelagin, who was also sick with scurvy but still able to drag himself to the helm. Chirikov helped as much as he could with the steering of the ship from his bed, "for, thanks to God," he wrote in his account, "my mind did not leave me."

On September 25 the ship's constable died of scurvy; everyone on board now was showing signs of the disease. On September 26, 27, and 30 storms drove the *St. Paul* back on her course; they were losing miles, not gaining them. As each storm broke over them, the sickly crew somehow managed to lower the sails and avoid losing the ship and all their lives to the wind and waves. The storms were cold now, dumping first hail and then heavy snow on the ship. They were down to six small barrels of water. To top off their predicament, their reckoning of longitude had fallen apart. Their calculations showed they should have been off the Kamchatka coast, but they were in the middle of the ocean with no land in sight.

Yelagin, on deck nearly twenty-four hours a day now, kept them as close to the latitude of Avacha Bay as he could in the storms. Then, the first week of October, the weather broke their way. The snow subsided, and with decent sailing winds, they cruised west unimpeded for several days in a row. Their faulty reckoning by now showed the ship 350 knots *west* of Avacha Bay. Over two days, October 6 and 7, four more men died, and cascading death seemed only a matter of days away.

But at dawn on October 8, one of the crew spotted snow-covered mountains to the west, hanging above a fog-marbled coast. Everyone who could crawl out of his bunk must have been on deck, trying to see Asia in the distant land. It took several agonizing hours for them to see enough of the coastline to fix their position.

It was Kamchatka. They were looking at the coastline north of Vaua, the point with the lighthouse that led into Avacha Bay. They cut southwest in the direction of home, and the next day they sailed past the lighthouse into Avacha Bay. Cruising up to the little garrison of Petropavlovsk, they fired five cannon shots to signal the village. Ye-lagin had brought them back to Russia, and they had made it just in time. All their fresh water was gone, including the skins of water the Aleuts had traded them. The only water left on board was two small barrels of distilled seawater.

Boats came out from the village to ferry the sick to shore, and Chirikov learned that Bering had not made it back. The captain went ashore in poor but stable condition. De la Croyère heaved himself out of bed and dressed up for the occasion; it would be his first time ashore in four months. But as he waited for his turn in the boat, he collapsed and died—the seventh and last of the *St. Paul*'s crew to fall to scurvy. The only scientist on the American Expedition besides Steller had died without ever setting foot in America.

It was already the sixth of September when the *St. Peter* sailed out of the Shumagin Islands into the open sea. Steller, standing at his self-appointed post along the rail, had a good look at the seabird rookeries on the south side of Bird Island as the ship passed by. He spotted great flocks of familiar birds on the rocky coast: murres, cormorants, kittiwakes, puffins, and pigeon guillemots. Steller wrote the list into his journal, using the contemporary European names for the puffins ("sea parrots") and guillemots ("Greenland sea pigeons"). It was here that he recorded the first European sighting of the black oystercatcher, the common shorebird that inhabits rocky shorelines and islets from the Aleutians to Baja California: "an entirely black snipe with red bill and feet, which continuously nodded its head." Steller's journal also mentions "a very beautiful black-and-white pied diver never seen before," probably either a marbled or a Kittlitz's murrelet, from a sighting of a juvenile or an adult already in winter plumage. Once the ship reached the open sea, a group of whales swam by, and one rose vertically out of the ocean for a closer look at the *St. Peter* and its crew.

The idyllic wildlife watching ended shortly. The wind and sea began to build the next afternoon, and that night a furious storm struck them from the southwest. Two weeks of favorable winds were all they needed to get home to Kamchatka, but the next two weeks were dismal. Fighting the prevailing westerly winds, they could make only about a knot an hour, just half the speed of a leisurely walking pace. On September 22 their reckoning showed that they were still a daunting 900 knots from Kamchatka, and the talk among the crew turned to wintering in America. If there was any hope left that they would make Avacha Bay before winter, it was going fast.

They reached latitude 51°, and Waxell, apparently thinking they had finally cleared the American coast, changed course that night to northwest. The next afternoon, at 5 PM, Yushin wrote another scurvy death into the log: "By the will of God died of scurvy the grenadier Andrei Tretyakov." The disease was back, and their only cure, the supply of Nagai Island greens Steller had picked, was all but gone.

A group of islands suddenly shot out of the fog on the evening of September 24, and in danger of running aground, they tacked hard to the east; the *St. Peter* had come up against the Andreanof Islands. One of the islands they could see to the west was Adak, the island where Chirikov had met the Aleuts two weeks before. Now Waxell had to turn southeast—in the wrong direction—to get away from the land.

On September 25 they had to take in the sails and let the ship drift in a howling storm. The wind drove them thirty knots east, back on their course, and the spars and masts heaved and groaned as if they were going to break apart any minute. The next day the west wind slacked off, but the sea, still rolling wildly to the east, pushed the ship back another forty knots. On the twenty-seventh an even more violent storm roared in, and Steller thought their time was up:

> . . . we heard the wind charge periodically as if out of a channel with such terrible whistling, rage, and frenzy that we were every moment in danger of losing the mast or the rudder. . . . The waves struck like shot out of a cannon, and we expected the final blow and death every instant.

Navigator Hesselberg, in his fifty years at sea, had never seen anything like the storm of September 27. Then, on the thirtieth, an even more powerful storm struck. Steller again:

> On September 30, at five o'clock in the morning, we got a storm out of the southwest that was double the violence of any storm we met with on

the voyage. . . . Every moment we expected the shattering of our ship, and no one could sit, lie down, or stand. No one could remain at his station, but we were drifting under God's terrible power wherever the enraged heavens wanted to take us.

The ship survived it, but the storms were not played out yet. One gale after another hit the *St. Peter* over the next two weeks. The ship bobbed helplessly in the Pacific, on a constant roller coaster of giant wave crests and deep troughs, and blasts of seawater washed completely over the deck time after time.

On October 6 the vodka ran out. The storms now carried hail and snow. The exhausted, scurvy-riddled crew could barely keep up with the changing of the sails and the repairing of damaged rigging. On the tenth Waxell tried to convince Bering to let them land and winter in America, but Bering refused. By the eleventh the cycle of storms that had begun on September 25 had driven them back 260 knots to the east, away from Avacha Bay.

Over the next two weeks, three more sailors died, and the ship made slow progress west against intermittent storms. Waxell came up with a passable plan on the twenty-fourth: they would sail northwest to latitude 52° and then try to hold that latitude to Kamchatka. The winds were coming predominantly out of the southwest, so sailing at 52° would give them the leeway to get to Avacha, at 53°, if the winds forced them north off their course. If the wind shifted to the north, they could sail for the Kuril Islands.

On the morning of October 29, they spotted two islands, the Semichis, near the end of the Aleutian chain. They were sailing at latitude 52°, right where they wanted to be, but now dead reckoning failed them; with few chances for a noon sun sighting the entire autumn, their calculations had broken down. The accounts are confused and contradictory at this point, but Steller, at least, thought they were at latitude 50° and that the islands they were looking at were the northernmost Kurils, south of Kamchatka. Apparently not trusting their computation of longitude, which showed them still well east of Asia, Waxell turned the ship north.

The wind twisted around to the southeast on November 1. The *St. Peter* began to drift west—a ghost ship, for all practical purposes unmanned, a toy boat at the mercy of the ocean. Yushin's hands and feet hurt so much now that he was barely able to drag himself on deck. The death toll was at six, and nearly everyone was seriously ill with scurvy. Water was down to six barrels, all of it brackish, and the sea biscuits were gone. The sails were so worn they could fall apart at any minute. Waxell heard several of the crew praying for a speedy death. Meanwhile, Steller and his small circle of friends—Plenisner, Betge, and Lepekhin—remained healthy, thanks to earlier large doses of Steller's greens. They were inexperienced as seamen, but they did what they could to help manage the ship.

At sunset on the third, the crew lowered the body of the latest scurvy victim, the army drummer, into the sea. They shortened sail to keep from running aground that night; by Yushin and Khitrovo's reckoning, they were close enough to the Kamchatka coast for that to be a worry. And, in fact, at 8 AM on the fourth, they sighted land to the northwest, topped by snow-covered mountains.

The near-dead clawed up to the deck to see. Comparing the land ahead to a sketch map of the Kamchatka coast they brought out, Waxell and Khitrovo thought they could make out the mouth of Avacha Bay. Hidden stores of vodka appeared, and the crew shouted toasts to the navigators.

But by noon the clouds cleared, and Yushin took a sun sighting that sobered them all. It gave him a latitude of 54° 30'; there was no way this could be Avacha. As they sailed closer, what had looked like a single coastline split into two land masses, an island to the south and a second coastline farther ahead to the west. The snowy mountain mass resolved into a single, rugged ridge crest rising from the second coastline. There were no symmetrical volcanic cones on this skyline like the peaks around Avacha Bay.

They continued toward the second coastline. The snowy ridge was now to the southwest, and the ship was riding a northeast swell toward it. As night came on, the wind began to pick up. Waxell ordered the ship brought around; they would have to leave the battered sails unfurled on the masts, ready for maneuvering, to stay off the land in the dark. At midnight they let another dead crewman slide into the sea.

The wind accelerated, tearing through the rigging the rest of the night. In the morning they saw that it had ripped the rotten mainsails apart. The *St. Peter* was helpless now; they had no hope of surviving another storm at sea. The crew's death toll was up to twelve, and thirty-four more were in dire straits. Bering, so sick with scurvy that he had had himself tied into his bunk, called a sea council in his cabin. In addition to the other officers, he also invited two of the crew from outside the naval command: Steller and Dmitry Ovtsyn, the former lieutenant, demoted now to common sailor, who had led one of Bering's arctic expeditions seven years before.

Waxell and Khitrovo argued that it was impossible to go on, that they should land on the coast ahead. They insisted that it had to be Kamchatka; if not, Khitrovo said, they could chop off his head. Bering at first argued for continuing southwest toward Avacha. They had already suffered so much, and Avacha had to be close; they could probably get there using just the foremast sail. He asked Ovtsyn to give his opinion, and Ovtsyn agreed with Bering. But Waxell and Khitrovo shouted Ovtsyn down.

Then they turned to Steller, who for once declined to give his opinion. They had never consulted him before, he explained, and they had ignored his advice time after time; they would ignore him now if his opinion was not in line with theirs. Bering yielded too, and they decided to land in a bay they thought they could make out in the coastline ahead.

They steered straight for the bay. At sunset they were a mile from shore, and they began to use the sounding lead to pilot the *St. Peter* toward it. The moon came up. At a half-mile from shore, they dropped anchor in nine fathoms of water and relaxed.

But half an hour later, the sea began to build just as the outgoing tide exposed a hidden reef ahead of the ship. The swells from the open sea crashed against the reef, and a heavy surf deflected back, alternately throwing the *St. Peter* forward toward shore and backward toward the open sea. As the ship bounced violently in the waves, the men who still had the strength to move hobbled onto the deck.

It was complete chaos; in the shouting of the crew and the roaring of the waves, nobody could tell who was giving orders or whom they were meant for. The anchor line parted, and somebody threw a second anchor into the sea. It caught the bottom, held for an instant, and then that anchor line parted too. Some of the sailors were about to throw the last anchor into the sea in a desperate attempt to keep from plowing onto the reef, but Ovtsyn and the assistant boatswain, Aleksei Ivanov, shouted for the sailors to hang onto the anchor and let the ship float. Waxell and Khitrovo were nowhere to be seen, "as customary in all dangerous circumstances," wrote Steller.

Now some of the crew, in a panic over having unlucky corpses on board, threw the bodies of two soldiers, the latest scurvy casualties, into the foaming sea. As the waves hurled the ship around the bay, some of the crew screamed in terror and others laughed insanely. Steller overheard one sailor ask no one in particular whether the water was very salty—"as if," Steller wrote in his journal, "death were sweeter in fresh water."

And then a great wave rolled into the bay, a rogue, towering over the swells that were sloshing the ship between the reef and the open sea. The wave picked them up, lifted them over the reef, and set them down gently behind it. In a matter of seconds the *St. Peter* was lying quietly inside the reef in a peaceful lagoon. The crew set their last anchor by moonlight in clean sand 600 yards off the beach.

Sea otter *(Enhydra lutris)*

OTTERS, BEARS, LIONS, AND COWS

These sea animals live on the islands in large numbers
and in security . . . because since the beginning of
the world they have never seen a human being or
been disturbed.

—Steller, letter to Johann Gmelin

A well-known principle of backcountry safety holds that it usually takes more than a single mistake or turn of bad luck in the outdoors to create a survival situation. Usually several factors have to come into play (the technical term is "multiple point failure") to put survival on the line.

For example, an unseasonal blizzard will not push a hiker or climber into hypothermia if he is at least minimally prepared. But if he lost his only pair of gloves on the hike to camp, forgot to clean his camp stove before leaving home, failed to bring enough stakes to pitch his tent tightly, and packed a lightweight sleeping bag for the trip, the multiple negatives could add up to trouble. Say the hiker is in his tent, asleep, when the blizzard blows in. The snow and wind cause the loosely pitched tent to sag, and the tent wall presses against the thin sleeping bag. Moisture from the snow soaks through the tent fabric into the bag. The wet chill wakes the hiker, and he leaves the tent to fire up the stove and warm up with a hot drink, but the stove fails. He spends so much time trying to unclog the stove with his ungloved hands that they become too numb to function. He starts to shiver, and within minutes hypothermia sets in.

Multiple point failure is essentially what happened on the voyage of the *St. Peter*. Mistakes and problems accumulated over months, stacking one on top of another, until they finally reached critical mass in November in the uncharted North Pacific. Picking out ten or more things that went wrong is relatively easy to do:

- The month lost because Khitrovo failed to sail the expedition's supplies around the southern tip of Kamchatka to Avacha Bay.
- Khitrovo's drowning of the sea biscuits, which left the expedition without a margin of safety and forced Bering to try to squeeze an ambitious itinerary into one short northern summer.
- The lack of scurvy remedies in the medical supplies.
- The three weeks lost in the fruitless search for De Gama Land and in the attempt to find the *St. Paul* after the ships separated.
- The failure to fill up all the water barrels at Kayak Island.
- The week lost trying to get clear of land near the Semidi Islands.
- The ten days spent on the water stop in the Shumagin Islands, a stop they might have avoided entirely had they filled all the barrels at Kayak Island.
- Waxell's refusal to listen to Steller's advice about fresh water and scurvy remedies.
- Khitrovo's foray to Turner Island, which, combined with the storm of August 31, delayed their leaving the Shumagins and caused them to waste several days of favorable winds.
- The autumn storms that drove them back on their course.
- Their navigation errors over five months at sea, compounded by the stormy weather—errors that led them to turn north instead of continuing west toward Kamchatka at the end of October.

Winter was coming on, and the *St. Peter* was at anchor off an unknown coast, on the verge of complete collapse. Most of the crew thought the land ahead of them was Kamchatka; they knew they had to be close to Asia, and this was obviously not an island near the coast, or it would be on their charts. Their best guess was that they were off Cape Kronotski, a bulge in the south-central Kamchatka coastline about 150 miles north of Avacha Bay. Waxell spoke confidently of landing the crew and the provisions they had left, and then sending a party of the strongest on foot to the Russian post on the Kamchatka River, where they could organize a rescue by horseback.

Steller was skeptical. He was sure that this piece of coastline was longer than any cape on the coast of Kamchatka, and that the land was trending in the wrong direction; the coastline of Kamchatka runs northeast-southwest, but the coastline ahead ran northwest-southeast. Steller was right; it was not the Asian mainland. They were about to land on an island at the western end of the Aleutian chain, today's Bering Island, due east of Cape Kronotski. Waxell and the others who thought they were anchored off Kronotski were right, in a way, but they were more than 100 miles east of the cape, not 600 yards.

Their situation was grim. Most of the survivors were incapacitated to some degree with scurvy. They were essentially out of provisions: all they had left was six barrels of brackish drinking water, a small supply of ground grain, and a few hundred pounds of three-year-old flour. And the last was questionable: not only had saltwater seeped into the hold, soaking the bags, but the flour had also had picked up the unmistakable taste of gunpowder from a keg that had broken open and spilled onto it.

But they had had one great stroke of luck in their run of misfortune: Bering Island is almost completely ringed by reefs, and they had taken the ship into the only bay on the east side where they could have landed safely. In Steller's words:

> From the continual pounding of the waves on the rocks, the sea became so frothy that it looked like milk. During our stay we came to know only a single narrow passage on this side [of the island] that was clear of rocks, so that one could anchor there in calm seas, and this is precisely the place, only eighty fathoms [about 500 feet] wide, into which God wisely and lovingly led us as we blindly ran under full sail toward the land. . . .

And in Waxell's:

*We later realized there was no other place anywhere round the entire
island where a ship could have got in to shore, but only this one. On
the island's every side were large expanses of shelving rocks extending to upwards of half a German mile [about two miles] out into the
sea. The place where we had come was so narrow that had we been
but 20 fathoms [120 feet] farther to the north or south, we would
have become hung up on a shelf of rock and from there not one of us
would have escaped. In this one can see God's miraculous, merciful
assistance, for it was already quite dark when we anchored, so that we
were quite unable to choose our anchorage in that unknown spot, but
had to leave that to chance.*

On November 7, on the morning after the wave had delivered
them into the lagoon, heavy swells from the open sea began rolling
under the ship again. The tide had risen, covering the reef and exposing the ship to the sea. Their peaceful lagoon of the night before,
they could see now, was a low-tide phenomenon only. It took several
hours for the tide to drop, and when the swells finally died down, they
lowered the longboat and sent a party to shore. The scouting party consisted of Waxell, Steller, Lepekhin, Plenisner, Waxell's son Laurentz,
and a handful of sailors and soldiers; a few of the completely disabled
sailors also went ashore to escape the foul air of their quarters.

As they rowed toward shore, they saw several animals slide into the
water from the beach and swim out toward the boat. Some of the crew
thought they were bears, others that they were wolverines, but when
the animals came closer, Steller could see that they were sea otters, apparently curious as to who the intruders were. Obviously no one had
hunted these fearless otters before.

The longboat landed on the beach, a curving, sandy shoreline
backed by tall, grass-covered dunes. The crew climbed out, and the ambulatory helped the sick above the high-water mark and made them
comfortable. Then Steller and Plenisner hiked inland.

Topping the dunes, they saw a valley open up ahead of them.
The lower valley was a cove of more or less level terrain carved into
the mountainous island, and a mosaic of low sandhills spread across

MILES
0   5   10

Cape Waxell

Sarana Lake

Bering Island

Wood Creek

St. Peter's approach November 1741

fur seal and sea lion rookeries

1741–42 camp

Commander Bay

Mount Steller

Yushin's Valley

PACIFIC OCEAN

L.M. FELTNER

BERING ISLAND

Cape Manati

it. Nestled among the sandhills were many small, protected depressions. High bluffs flanked the valley on either side, the outliers of ridges that ran down to the coast from the snow-covered mountain crest they had seen from the ship. Steller and Plenisner had a panoramic view from the top of the dunes, and they could see no trees or tall shrubs in any direction.

A creek meandered through the valley, flowing down fresh and clear from the mountains. After they had drunk only stale, salty water for weeks, this pure, cold stream was the greatest gift the island could have given them. Steller later wrote in his account of the island that all the castaways drank the "excellent and wholesome water" "with great benefit and joy."

After they surveyed the area where they had landed, Plenisner hiked off with a shotgun to look for game, and Steller walked into the valley to explore. After a few hours Steller returned to the beach, carrying a bundle of green plants. Much of it was brooklime, a trailing, succulent plant that was growing on the margin of the stream, which Steller knew to be a good scurvy remedy.

At the beach he found Waxell flat on his back, very sick and weak. Plenisner joined them a few minutes later, carrying a half-dozen ptarmigan he had shot. Three of the other crewmembers returned with the pelts of two sea otters and two harbor seals. Steller berated them for wasting the meat, and one of them went back for it. The ambulatory sailors loaded Waxell into the longboat, and they pushed off for the trip back to the ship, carrying a few barrels of water and some of the ptarmigan meat and brooklime for Bering, who was still lying sick in his bunk. Steller, Plenisner, Lepekhin, and Laurentz Waxell stayed behind, planning to camp overnight on the island with the sick sailors they had brought to shore.

The only wood to be found was driftwood on the beach. There was precious little of it, and much of it was partially buried and frozen in the snow. The campers hacked some of it free for a fire. Steller cooked a big pot of ptarmigan soup for dinner; the sickest of the sailors, their gums grown black and spongy until they practically covered their teeth, could eat only liquids and very soft food. Plenisner pieced together a rough shelter out of driftwood and an old sail, and they all slept under it that night.

In the morning Steller and Lepekhin hiked away to explore more of the coast, and Plenisner went off in search of more ptarmigan. As Steller and Lepekhin trudged through the sand along the beach, scatterings of small animals barked at them from the dunes, and several ran down to the beach toward the hikers. The animals were arctic foxes, and they showed no fear whatsoever; they sniffed and snapped at Steller and Lepekhin. Startled by the aggressive animals, Lepekhin shot eight of them and finally succeeded in driving the rest away.

The hikers passed the bluff at the southern edge of the valley, and the beach narrowed and grew rocky. It was high tide, and the offshore reef was covered by the sea. In the water Steller saw the protruding, dark back of what was obviously a very large creature floating in the shallow water covering the reef. Every few minutes a great snout rose out of the water, took in a loud, snorting breath of air, and disappeared into the sea again.

Steller had never seen anything like it. He ran through the possibilities of the creatures he knew from the waters off Okhotsk and Kamchatka. Whales and sharks came to mind, but this animal was different. Lepekhin, who had traveled all over Kamchatka with the Academy student assistant Stepan Krashenninikov, had no idea what it was either.

It was Steller's first sighting of a sea cow, but his focus for the moment was less on science than on their desperate situation. The evidence was mounting that they were on an uninhabited island, not on the coast of Kamchatka. The animal in the water was nothing they knew from Asia. Neither the foxes nor the otters showed any sign that they had ever seen humans. Kamchatka was forested, and this island did not have a stick growing on it that was more than a few inches high. And Steller thought he could see on the clouds, beyond the top of the mountain ridge crest, the "water-sky" known to sailors and explorers in the North—the dark reflection of water against the bright reflection of a snowy landscape—that meant there was open sea across the mountains.

That night, around the campfire by their sailcloth shelter, as the campers were eating another ptarmigan dinner, a fox darted in and stole two uncooked birds they had set aside for breakfast. As if the theft of their next meal was not depressing enough, Steller then confided in his campmates that he was fairly sure they were stranded on a deserted island. The news disheartened Lepekhin so much that he confronted Steller, who had talked him into coming along on this unlucky voyage. Why, Lepekhin asked, had Steller not been content with exploring Kamchatka?

Steller responded that he was confident they would survive, even if they were on a remote island; they certainly would not die of hunger in a place so full of animals that had no fear of humans. Steller thanked him for his good work on the expedition and told him, "You have in me, with God's help, a lifelong friend." Then he reminded

Lepekhin that they had no idea what might have happened to them if they had stayed in Kamchatka.

Later, with Plenisner, Steller talked over a plan for building a shelter. They would need it if, as they suspected, they were going to be here for a while. The hollows in the sandhills offered the only natural protection from wind and weather, and Steller proposed that they build a shelter in one. Plenisner agreed.

They scouted the hills and found a good place to build their hut, but they had to rout the resident foxes first. Steller and Plenisner axed and stabbed sixty of the aggressive foxes before they felt they had a secure, fox-free area, but by that time so much of the day was gone that they had to retreat to their beach shelter of the night before.

The next day, their fourth on the island, they moved their belongings to the shelter site. In the early evening, over a campfire and cups of tea, they agreed on how to set up their new home. Digging in below ground level would protect them from the biting wind, so they excavated a pit in the sand, which, with the freezing nights, had set up

Arctic fox *(Alopex lagopus)*

solidly enough so that it didn't slough back into the pit. They erected a framework of driftwood over the depression and covered the frame with a blanket and extra clothes. Into the cracks in the frame they stuffed the bodies of the foxes they had killed the day before.

All seemed fine, and Steller, Plenisner, and Lepekhin crawled in and went to sleep. But at about midnight a storm tore across the island, and their shelter failed its first test; the squall blew the roof off the hut and covered them in fresh snow. They ran out into the storm, found a more protected hollow and dug it out, gathered more driftwood, and set up a new framework for their roof and walls. The new shelter held up in the storm, and they slept well the rest of the night.

The next day they shored up their new hut and settled in. They called it their "grave"; with a small fire ring inside, however, it was passably cozy for a winter camp in the subarctic. Up to now the rest of Bering's crew had spent the nights on board the ship, debating whether it would be better to stay on the *St. Peter* or move to shore. But when word spread on the ship about how comfortable the new pit house was, collective opinion shifted toward quarters on land. The longboat, shuttling between ship and shore, carried most of the crew to the beach over the next few days. Waxell and Khitrovo stayed on the ship with a small contingent of the crew to keep the *St. Peter* secure in the lagoon; if a storm drove the ship on shore or, worse yet, sent it out to sea, they would be in even deeper trouble than they were already.

The crew on shore went to work building pit houses like Steller's, and a small village began to take shape in the sandhills. Two groups organized themselves as households and got shelters under way; other hut builders put up an infirmary for the scurvy patients. A fifth pit house was built for the crew remaining on the ship, who would eventually be coming ashore. The construction boom quickly exhausted the supply of nearby driftwood, so to find enough framing for all the huts, the builders had to hike as far as three miles up the coast.

Betge, Roselius, and Johan Sind, a junior officer who was very sick with scurvy, moved in with Steller, Plenisner, and Lepekhin; two other Russian assistants joined them, bringing their household up to eight. The crew settled Bering into a sailcloth-roofed hollow near Steller's hut.

While the work on the huts was being finished, Steller and Plenisner went otter hunting. They found a group of otters sleeping on shore, sneaked up on them, and clubbed and bagged four of them. They cooked the liver, heart, kidneys, and meat and served up an otter smorgasbord the evening of their hunt. Steller thought all of it fine and delicious, but not everyone shared his opinion; reviews of the otter feast ranged from moderately tasty to extremely rank. Wondering aloud about Steller's taste, Bering turned down his naturalist's offer of the meat of an otter pup.

Bering was gravely ill, but he amazed Steller with his composure and contentment. Steller explained to Bering his theory that they were on an island, but one not far off the coast of Asia: not too far, because Steller had found, buried in the sand, a window shutter of Russian workmanship. Bering agreed that they were probably on an island, and, he confided, the ship might be doomed where they had anchored her. "May God spare us our longboat," he told Steller.

The hut builders had left the sick on the beach while they worked on the shelters, and several more died of scurvy in a short time after landing. Then, Steller says in his journal, the foxes returned:

> Even before they could be buried, the dead were mutilated by foxes that sniffed at and even dared to attack the sick—still alive and helpless—who were lying on the beach everywhere without cover under the open sky.

In revulsion, the crew killed foxes by the dozen, but the slaughter didn't deter them. Steller again:

> The foxes . . . dragged apart all the baggage, ate the leather sacks, scattered the provisions, stole and dragged away from one his boots, from another his socks and pants. . . . It even seemed that the more of them we killed . . . the more malicious and determined the others became, breaking into our dwellings and dragging away everything they could get to, even iron and all kinds of gear.

It was constant warfare, the crew against the foxes:

> Every morning we dragged the prisoners we had captured alive out by their tails for execution in front of the barracks. . . . Nevertheless, they would not be warned and keep away from our huts. . . .

Waxell, meanwhile, was still on the ship with twelve sick crewmen and five corpses. When they had drawn down the ship's water supply to only four buckets, Waxell tried to signal the men on shore to come pick them up by firing several shots, but an east wind was gusting so hard that no one could hear his signals. In any case, the wind was driving heavy surf onto the beach, making it impossible to launch the longboat. Luckily, it began to snow; Waxell and the sailors melted the snow that accumulated on the deck for drinking water. Finally the storm subsided and the longboat came out to the ship. On November 20 Waxell and the rest of the crew left for shore, leaving the ship lying at anchor with no one on board.

Waxell barely made it to the beach alive, and Steller ministered to him in near-desperation. Bering was not likely to survive the winter; if they lost Waxell, the command would fall to Khitrovo, and almost no one trusted him now. With Khitrovo in command, a major conflict could break out, possibly even mutiny, and there was a good chance none of them would survive that upheaval.

On November 21 the navigator Hesselberg died of scurvy, ending his fifty years of service at sea. Steller, in his journal, laments the loss of such an experienced hand, who almost alone among the senior officers under Bering had impressed him with his knowledge and ability.

Hesselberg's death brought the toll to twenty, and the dying was surely not over; many of the crew were still very sick. By this time the entire company was depressed at their slim prospects for surviving the winter. Steller wrote that "want, lack of clothing, cold, dampness, exhaustion, illness, impatience, and despair were our daily guests." And it didn't help when a scouting party Bering had sent out several days earlier returned with discouraging news: there was no sign of humanity anywhere near their camp, no forests for shelter and fuel, and no evidence that they were on the Kamchatka coast.

On the twenty-second Bering called the officers to his tent for a council on how to save the *St. Peter*. The ship was almost certainly their only way home, and she could not survive a storm where she was anchored. The officers decided they had to beach the ship to save her.

Bering ordered Khitrovo to organize a crew to run the ship onto the beach on a high tide, but for several days howling winds kept him from carrying out Bering's order. Then, at the end of the month, a winter gale blew in. The sea snapped the *St. Peter*'s anchor cables and sent her crashing ashore high up on the beach below the sandhill village. The morning after the storm, the crew found her, lying on her port side, her bottom torn open and her rudder gone. The tide flowed through the ship, piling up sand inside. The crew was helpless to do anything. Two days later the beached ship had sunk to her gunwales, nine feet into the sand.

The men were stuck. They were going to have to survive the winter in semi-underground shelters, subsisting on marine mammals, just as the indigenous people of the coast did. They did have one thing in their favor: they had a naturalist along who knew something about sea animals and Native ways.

On December 8, 1741, the single entry in the expedition log reads:

5 AM Captain Commander Bering died, and Lieutenant Waxell succeeded to the command.

The crew had to dig Bering out of his hollow to give him a formal burial. He had lain under a sailcloth tarp in a narrow trench in the sand for the previous four weeks; sand trickling down the sides had gradually filled in the trench, covering the lower half of the captain's body. He had preferred that the crew not dig him out, as it was warmer under the blanket of sand. Now that he was gone, they pulled him out of the trench and moved him to the growing cemetery next to their village. Bering's death was the twenty-seventh among the officers and crew of the *St. Peter.*

What exactly Bering succumbed to is still not entirely clear. His scurvy had apparently stopped progressing, so it could not have been the only factor. One theory is that the disease had weakened his immune system and that he died of an infection contracted months earlier. Other theories suggest kidney or liver disease or heart failure. Steller, though, says Bering "died more from hunger, cold, thirst, vermin, and grief than from a disease" and that he would have survived if they had made it to Avacha Bay that fall.

Steller, who doctored Bering to the end, left a written eulogy for the captain in his journal. What successes the Second Kamchatka Expedition had achieved, Steller tells us, were due to Bering's patience, caution, and wisdom. He faults the captain in only one respect: for trusting and delegating too much to his officers—a pointed reference to Khitrovo and Waxell. In Bering's last days, Steller says, he had focused his concern completely on the survival of his crew, knowing at that point that he would never leave the island. "He might well not have found a better place to prepare himself for eternity," Steller ends his eulogy, "than this deathbed under the open sky."

The survivors settled into their five shelters to wait out the shortest days of the northern winter. The cold of an Aleutian winter is not the deep cold of the mainland interior; temperatures usually fall only into the twenties and thirties Fahrenheit, but fog, mist, snow, and high winds—not to mention the foxes—made the situation difficult enough for the crew of the *St. Peter.* To keep the foxes out of their food, each of the five households set up several barrels for meat storage and slapped together wooden racks for hanging clothes and other gear out of their reach.

Steller's household divided the daily chores into three work details: cooking and housekeeping, gathering wood, and hunting. The other four households, again following suit, organized themselves the same way. Steller took on the duties of lead cook in his hut and doctor to all the households.

The castaways shot and devoured ptarmigan by the dozens. The few times they were able to take harbor seals, the meat was a welcome addition to the larder, but they rarely found seals on shore, and they were much more difficult to stalk than the sea otters were. When they had seal, the cooks made a dish that was a company favorite: small cakes of the gunpowder-flavored wheat flour fried in seal oil.

They also found one completely new and very convenient source of food: a new species of cormorant. Cormorants are a genus of swimming, fish-eating, goose-size birds that snorkel along on the surface, heads submerged, looking for fish below and diving to capture them when they spot a choice morsel. Unlike any other cormorant known at that time, these birds were flightless and therefore easy pickings for the camp's hunters. The company's cooks prepared them according to an old Kamchatka method for cooking sea birds, one that called for

Spectacled cormorant *(Phalacrocorax perspicillatus)*

slathering clay all over the bird, stuffing the wad of clay and bird into a fire pit, and slow-roasting it.

Food here was apparently so plentiful and the predators so scarce that the wings of this cormorant, today called the spectacled cormorant, had withered over the eons to the point that the bird was no longer capable of full flight. Steller says the coast of the island was thick with them. They were so easy to hunt, however, that they were destined to disappear from Bering Island, their only home on earth, by the mid-1800s. Steller was the only European naturalist ever to see a spectacled cormorant alive. Today a single species of flightless cormorant survives on the Galapagos Islands, a species that also evolved in a predator-free environment.

Sea otter hunting, however, was the main pastime of the crew. The island's fearless otters were relatively easy targets at first, completely unwary of danger from the land—in stark contrast to the cautious otters of Kamchatka and the Kuril Islands, animals that almost never went ashore because of their fear of human hunters. The Bering Island otters spent a lot of time on shore, Steller wrote in his journal: they slept, ate, rested, mated, and played on land, mainly near the water but sometimes the better part of a mile inland.

A typical Bering Island otter hunt began after nightfall. Carrying stout birch poles, a small group of hunters set out along the shoreline, hiking against the wind as much as possible to limit scent and sound. When they found an otter lying down or sleeping, one hunter approached it quietly while the others cut off its escape route to the sea. If it woke and took off before the first hunter clubbed it, the others would force it away from the water, run it down, and kill it. Sometimes the hunters came across a group of otters and managed to bag several at once; that rare luck meant that they could fill their storage barrels in just one outing.

Gradually, in spite of the snow, the damp cold, and the clamminess of their burrows, the fresh food they were eating began to take the edge off the scurvy epidemic. Waxell, to the relief of nearly everyone, was making a solid recovery. Christmas came, and the company gathered for a celebration of fried wheat cakes and tea.

The holiday spirit they managed to muster for Christmas, though, was deflated the next day. A few days before he died, Bering had sent out a second search party, hoping to find any evidence that would pinpoint their location, and on December 26 the party returned. The three men, led by the strongest of the sailors left alive, had spent twenty-five days afoot along the coast, carrying little food and no shelter with them, huddling out of the weather as best they could each night. They had crossed the high ridge of mountains to the west, and had seen only open ocean to the west and north. The search party returned convinced that they were marooned on an island.

However, the searchers had found more evidence—a boat rudder and the remains of some fish barrels—that they were close to Kamchatka. Some of the crew still could not be convinced that they were on an island, but all agreed that they were in remote country, far from any Russian outpost, with no hope of rescue anytime soon.

A week into the new year, 1742, the scurvy epidemic carried off its last victim. Five more men had died after Bering, bringing the total number of deaths to thirty-two. The forty-six survivors were out of immediate danger from the disease, but it would be months before they were all back to full strength.

As the crew of the *St. Peter* waited out the winter on Bering Island, the bored sailors and soldiers began spending their spare time gambling at cards. The stakes, the only things of value they could lay their hands on, were otter furs. The gamblers wiped out the animals within any reasonable distance of camp; worse yet, they carried off only the furs, leaving the meat for the foxes. As a result, the camp's meat hunters had to hike farther and farther to find otters when they needed food.

To Steller, the gambling was a stupid outbreak of greed that could jeopardize the crew's chances of surviving the winter. He complained to Waxell, but Waxell refused to intervene. Waxell's tenuous hold on power may have influenced his thinking; his authority had eroded considerably since the November landfall, and the sandhill village was functioning now more like a federation of independent huts than a single group with a hierarchical command. Steller had a slightly different theory about why Waxell let the gambling go on, when it had the obvious downside of threatening their survival: "[T]he officers themselves were addicts."

In November and December, the hunting details found enough otters within two or three miles of camp to feed the company. By January, it was three to five miles, and by February, they had to hike twelve to fifteen miles one way. By March and April, all the otters on the east side of the island had been killed or driven off or had turned too wild for the hunters to approach. Hunting parties had to cross to the west side of the island, as much as twenty-five miles away, to find otters they could hunt.

On his hunts and rambles, Steller watched and recorded otter behavior in detail. He began to piece together his Bering Island observations with what he had learned about the animals in Kamchatka, on Kayak Island, and in the Shumagin Islands, and, working in what passed for an office in his sand-hut, started to write up his observations and theories. His notes on the otters were the beginnings of *The Beasts of the Sea*, the first written account of the North Pacific's marine mammals.

The opening words in Steller's description of the sea otter describe its luxurious fur:

> *These animals are very beautiful, and because of their beauty they are very valuable, as one may well believe of a skin the hairs of which, an inch or an inch and a half in length, are very soft, very thickly set, jet black and glossy.*

He correctly notes that the otter sheds its coat continually, a few hairs at a time, so that it always has a fine shell of thick, heavy fur to protect it from the cold sea. Otter furs, Steller says, are actually *too* heavy for full-length women's coats, and the skins of the marten, the mainstay of the Russian fur trade in Asia, "never shine with so deep a natural blackness as the otter's."

Steller's sketch of the fur and its value takes up more than half the description. His long account is appropriate, though, given the sea otter's total dependence on its fur; the animal would not survive half an hour in the northern seas without it. Unlike most other marine mammals, otters have little fat for insulation, so their fur is their main physical defense against the cold. They have the thickest fur of any animal on earth, as thick as a million hairs *per square inch*, compared to the 100,000 hairs *in total* on an average human head. The otter's double-layered fur (a layer of guard hairs over a dense underfur) also traps air, allowing the animal to float effortlessly on the surface of the sea; it is both fur coat and personal flotation device.

Steller also noted the second piece of the sea otter's survival strategy: a ravenous appetite paired with a metabolism that is always running at full tilt. He notes that otters cannot survive long without food, and that they have cosmopolitan tastes, eating just about anything in their near-shore marine world, from crabs and octopus, to clams, mussels, and snails, to fin-fish of many kinds. He also recorded seeing one otter eating the remains of another otter after the camp gamblers had killed and skinned it and left the meat behind.

Steller's observations were the first step in sorting out the omnivorous appetites of sea otters. We have records today of one hundred or so species of marine creatures that otters eat. A sea otter devours up to 30 percent of its body weight in meat every day, the equivalent of a human male downing fifty pounds of steak daily. (A fat-cloaked walrus, by comparison, eats only about 6 percent of its weight per day.)

What Steller could not see in the underwater world of the otters was how much they rely on their handlike front paws to procure all that food. Sea otters are the only marine mammals with anything like true hands; their paws, because there is no fur on the inner surface, work well for grasping and manipulating. As it forages beneath the surface, an otter captures prey with its paws, sometimes carrying a rock to use as a tool to pry loose a sea urchin from a crevice or crack open a shellfish clinging to a rock. Steller never mentions seeing what we think of today as the classic sea otter pose—an otter floating on its back, cracking open a clam or mussel by whacking it against a rock resting on its chest.

Steller's account has numerous passages about sea otter behavior, some of which probably cross the line into anthropomorphism:

> As they come out of the sea, like dogs they shake off all the water before they lie down to sleep; then with their paws they wash their faces, just as cats do, smooth out their bodies, straighten out their fur, turn their heads from one side to the other as they look themselves over, and seem to be greatly pleased with their personal appearance.

and

> . . . they fall down at the first blow and pretend they are dead, and then as soon as they see that we turn our attention to others they suddenly take to flight. . . . If they escape the club, they gesticulate in a very ridiculous manner, as if making fun of the hunter.

Steller saw otters as very social animals, congregating in huge droves, even stationing sentries to warn the rest of the otters of approaching hunters once they became aware of their new human predators. The females he observed were loving mothers:

> When they sleep at sea they fold their young in their arms just as mothers do their babes. They throw the young ones into the water to

teach them to swim, and when tired out they bring them to shore again and kiss them just like human beings. . . . with them they engage in all the delightful and gentle games that a fond mother can play with her children. . . . They embrace their young with an affection that is scarcely credible.

And once, when he and Plenisner approached a group of unwary otters, one female noticed them and reacted:

When she caught sight of us, the mother ran to her offspring, woke him up, and warned him to flee; but, as he preferred to go on sleeping rather than to run away, she picked him up in her paws in spite of himself and rolled him like a stone down into the sea.

Steller notes that in contrast to sea lions and fur seals, otters "are not naturally of a roving disposition," staying for the most part within relatively small coastal territories. He cites three factors in this otter-as-homebody theory: they are not strong swimmers, they are not able to "hold out against hunger" for long, and they cannot stay underwater long enough to feed in the deep waters they would have to cross if they were truly migratory.

And, in fact, modern science has confirmed most of what Steller concluded on this score. Sea otters are the smallest, the least stream-lined in body shape, and the most closely tied to coastal habitat of the marine mammals. They are also the youngest species of sea mammals—a relatively recent offshoot of the land dwellers of the mustelid family (otters, weasels, badgers, minks)—and so are the least adapted to the sea. They are not well equipped for long-distance swimming, for migrating from place to place, or for living in deep water.

Steller's generally accurate description of the otter's habitat and range veered off course on one point: he claimed the sea otter is "a genuine American sea animal, existing in Asia more as a guest" than as a full-time resident. Otters probably got to Asia intermittently, he thought, by island-hopping and riding ice floes. In reality, sea otters occupied a range around the rim of the North Pacific from Baja California to Japan before Europeans arrived on the scene.

He also wrote that otters "always give birth to their young on land," and he mentions seeing groups of otters well inland from the sea. These observations have turned out to be specific to the undisturbed Bering Island otters, which, until the *St. Peter* arrived, had never been threatened by any predator. Sea otters never actually *need* to come ashore, as they are able to mate and bear their young without ever leaving the water—in contrast to harbor seals, fur seals, and sea lions, all of which have to retreat to land for mating and birthing. The trapped air inside the otter's thick fur helps it stay afloat, and therefore the fur is truly the animal's primary adaptation for full-time ocean living.

Steller recorded his observations of the otter's reproductive strategy, correctly noting that otters have no rigidly timed cycle, that females bear no more than one, very well developed pup at a time, and that they care for their pups in many cases for more than a year before the young go their own ways. Biologists today identify those traits with species that build future generations by banking on high survival rates of a small number of young, like all marine mammals and like *Homo sapiens*. This low reproduction–high survival strategy works best in stable, rich environments like the northern seas the otters inhabit.

From the point of view of the crew of the *St. Peter,* the Bering Island otters were packaging the wealth of the northern seas in their meat, and those nutrients were keeping the castaways alive. There was disagreement over how appetizing otter at every meal was, but Steller waxes eloquent about it: adult otter meat, he says, is "tender and savory," young otters taste like lamb, and otter gravy is "most delicious." Maybe it helped that there was not much else to eat.

Near the end of his sea otter account, Steller gives the animals the credit for the expedition's survival through the winter of 1741–42. Sea otters, he says, were both their prime food and medicine, and they deserved "the greatest reverence" for saving the party from both starvation and scurvy.

Things continued to look up in the sandhill camp as the winter progressed. On January 28, 1742, the company held a birthday party for Empress Anna, not knowing that she had died in 1740. The next day a hunting detail from Steller's hut managed to kill a young sea lion, which everyone agreed was the best-tasting delicacy they had eaten so far; Steller, once again, goes on in superlatives about it, comparing the meat to the finest veal. The sea-mammal food was working its magic; Waxell says in his account that by the end of the month every man in the party was able to get on his feet and do at least some work.

In late February another in the series of scouting parties left camp, this time led by second mate Kharlam Yushin. Yushin's expedition, according to Steller, devolved into an otter hunt, and the group came back to camp on March 8 with no new insight into their situation.

The crew gathered to talk over what to do next and decided to send out yet another scouting party. To lead this fourth exploring party, they elected Aleksei Ivanov, the boatswain who had helped save the ship when they first anchored off the island and who had taken the lead in building one of the huts. As their trials on the island unfolded, Ivanov became one of the most trusted officers; he had risen into the officer ranks when he inherited the job of head boatswain after the original boatswain, Nils Jansen, had died of scurvy in November.

Ivanov's party left camp on March 15 and headed across the mountains to the west side of the island. Hiking was a lot easier now. Spring was coming on, and with the temperatures warming above freezing during the day but still freezing at night, the snow had settled and crusted over to form a good walking surface. Once they reached the west side, though, Ivanov's route north along the coast was cut off by cliffs reaching into the sea, and he and his party gave up and hiked back to camp on March 19.

They had nothing new to report about the geography of the country where they were shipwrecked, but they did bring back two interesting bits of news. First, they had found wood chips on the western beach—chips that one of the soldiers in the party was sure he had hewn out in the building of the longboat at Avacha Bay the year before. Second, they had seen a big, unfamiliar animal on shore on the far side of the mountains. From their description, Steller decided it must have been a fur seal.

On March 22 Ivanov set out on another attempt to cross to the west coast and hike north, and Steller and three of his hut mates went with him. This time they crossed the island summit by a different route, hiking up the valley of the stream they called Wood Creek three miles north of camp, where they had found most of the wood used in building their huts. It turned out to be an easier traverse, and once they were on the west side it put them north of the impassable cliffs that had blocked Ivanov's passage on his first try. Ivanov continued north while Steller and his mates "caused a severe defeat among the sea otters," a new herd of the animals they had not hunted yet. After bagging ten, they stopped, since that was all the meat they could carry back to camp; Steller says they could have killed a hundred.

The discovery of a better route to the sea otter grounds on the west side of the island was important news back at camp, and a procession of hunting parties followed the Wood Creek route over the mountains to the opposite coast. It was still rugged country and a dangerous time of year, however, and three of the parties wound up in survival situations.

First, a zero-visibility blizzard on April 1 caught a party from Steller's household—Betge, Sind, Roselius, and one of the unnamed Russian assistants—out on a hunt far from camp. In the storm Sind was separated from the group and, in dire straits, the other three dug into a snowdrift for shelter. Six feet of snow fell that night. At dawn the next day, the storm finally began to peter out.

The snowstorm had buried the entrance to Steller's pit house, and he and his remaining three housemates had to dig through wind-packed snow for several hours to get out of the hut. As they finally cleared the entrance, the hunting party staggered back into camp without Sind. Betge was snow-blind, and the others were stiff and nearly senseless from the cold. Their mates undressed the three hypothermic hunters, wrapped them in blankets, and fed them hot tea. Then their concern shifted to Sind, and a party set out to look for him.

They found him an hour later, on his feet, on the beach. He had fallen into a creek, and his clothes were frozen to his skin. The searchers brought him back to camp and warmed him in time, and he revived. Betge was slower to recover; it took him eight days to regain his sight.

A day or two before Betge and Sind's party left camp, another party of five hunters led by Yushin had crossed the island to hunt on the west coast. The same storm that caught Betge and Sind sent Yushin's group scrambling for shelter, and they crawled into a crevice in the sea cliffs. The crevice was exposed only because the tide was very low when the storm struck, so when the storm passed they found themselves trapped by the sea in the narrow cave. They had to wait a week, with no food, for the next tide low enough to allow them to escape. They finally made it back to camp, nine days after they had left; nearly everyone had given them up for dead.

One of the hunters with Yushin was a journeyman carpenter named Sava Starodubtsov, the only person left alive on the expedition who knew anything about shipbuilding and ship repair; the expedition's three more experienced shipwrights and carpenters were dead from scurvy. Steller wrote in his journal that it was "joyful news" to the company when Starodubtsov, "on which all hope of our deliverance rested," returned alive to camp.

Then Steller's household ran out of food, and he, Plenisner, Lepekhin, and one other Russian assistant left camp in fine weather for a hunt on the far side of the island, "believing that we were forecasting the weather better" than the previous parties, according to Steller. As soon as they reached the beach on the west coast, they stumbled onto a pod of otters lounging on shore and in short order took as many as they could carry. Evening was coming on, so they bivouacked around a campfire on the beach and waited for daylight the next morning to hike back to camp.

At midnight another storm blew in, blasting them with wind and thick clouds of snow. The fire died, and it was impossible to get it going again. Lepekhin burrowed into the fresh snow while Steller sat hunched over on the sand, smoking a pipe for the bit of heat it afforded. The other two hunters ran back and forth along the beach to keep up their body heat. The snow piled up all night, and at dawn the storm showed no sign of letting up. Plenisner forced Steller to his feet to help him look for shelter. Finding nothing, they returned to their bivouac, cold and discouraged. Lepekhin was still buried in the snow; they had to dig him out and revive him. The four men split into two pairs and went off on another search for shelter from the storm.

Lepekhin found a refuge, a roomy cave that was home to a company of foxes. The humans moved in, and the foxes retreated into a crevice. The hunters built a fire in the cave with a bit of dry driftwood they found inside; the smoke ran up and out through the crevice, causing a fit of sneezing and spitting among the foxes. Steller and his party warmed and dried by the fire while the storm raged outside.

When the blizzard abated, they left the cave and returned to their bivouac site to pick up the otter meat, but foxes had eaten some and dragged away the rest. So Steller and his mates stayed on the west side of the island for another three days, hunting from their base camp in the cave and carefully guarding the fresh meat from the foxes.

When they finally made it back to the pit-house village on April 8, they learned that Ivanov had returned from another reconnaissance trip two days earlier, having rounded a cape about 25 miles to the north, where he had seen only sea ahead. The crew knew from their earlier forays that there was ocean to the east, south, and west, and this piece of news proved to everyone, beyond any doubt, that they were stranded on an island, not on the coast of Asia. Some of the crew may have thought of it, but no one seems to have reminded Khitrovo about his offer to let them chop off his head if this was not Kamchatka.

On the ninth Waxell called a council to debate what they should do. The expedition log lists as a participant "Doctor Georg Steller" immediately following the names of Waxell and Khitrovo, and before mentioning the junior officers. Steller, whose stock had risen with his role in the company's recovery on the island, was apparently now on equal footing with the naval command.

The company discussed its options. They could send a crew in the longboat to find help, try to dig out and refloat the *St. Peter* as she was, or tear apart the ship and rebuild her as a smaller vessel. They rejected the longboat option; from their experience on the voyage, this sea was no place for a small boat. The second option, refloating the ship, would be virtually impossible because the hull was badly damaged, the hold was full of sand, and the prospect of being able to move the ship back into the water was dim. They were left with the third option—to break up the ship and rebuild it.

After the council, journeyman carpenter Starodubtsov came to Waxell and asked him to work out the dimensions of the new vessel; from there, Starodubtsov said, he could lead the crew in building it. Waxell agreed.

Starodubtsov's confidence was infectious. Steller sketched out a strategy for organizing the crew for the job, and once the details were agreed on, they went to work immediately. The twelve best builders and ax-handlers were assigned as a permanent construction detail. Everyone else except Waxell, Khitrovo, and Steller would shift among assignments of shipbuilding, hunting, and doing the cooking and household chores. All the meat the hunters brought home would now go to a central commissary, where a junior officer would divide it equally among the households; they had to be sure none of the full-time shipbuilders went hungry.

The work crews spent the next eleven days getting prepared to rebuild the ship. They cleaned and sharpened tools, set up a forge, and fabricated hammers, crowbars, and other tools from the spare iron they had brought with them on the voyage. Meanwhile, the northern spring was breaking around them. The thaw shrank the snowpack, and the driftwood that had been covered all winter began to show itself, making the crew's forays for wood much easier.

Steller, though still cook and doctor, was free to be a rambling scientist much of the time. He could not be sure that anything he observed and recorded would ever reach the outside world—the party's escape from the island and safe return to Asia was still very much in doubt—but rather than worry about it, he set out to explore the island and observe the coming of spring. Seabirds began to arrive at their sea-cliff rookeries, and the flocks of sea ducks that had floated offshore all winter grew into great rafts. One of the species of duck was definitely new—a bright, black-and-white bird that Steller identified and described in his notes. Years later, another German scientist named it *Polysticta stelleri*—"Steller's eider."

On April 20 one of the hunting details found a dead whale, fifty feet long, washed up on a beach three miles north of camp—probably a northern right whale. It was already slightly rancid, but whatever its condition, it would be a welcome change in camp cuisine. The hunters carved out chunks of the blubber and carried it back, a load at a time, to the village kitchens, where the cooks boiled out the oil and put it up in barrels. Steller hiked to the site to measure the beached whale and describe it in detail.

On April 21 the crew began tearing apart the *St. Peter.* It was going to be a long, hard job to build a new vessel, and they would need much more food now that they were all active again. The whale's meat and blubber were crucial because the otters on the west side of the island were already becoming too wary to hunt. But they were about to receive another gift from the sea: the arrival of the fur seals.

The story of the pinnipeds—the fur seals, sea lions, true seals, and the walrus—began about twenty-five million years ago, when these animals' earliest ancestors entered the eastern North Pacific Ocean from the part of the North American continent that is now Oregon. They went to the sea like an evolutionary version of pioneers in search of a better life, attracted by the cold, nutrient-rich coastal waters and their wealth of fish and other marine life.

Their exodus is one of four known mammal migrations from land to sea. The earliest migrants were ancestors of the cetaceans and the sirenians, both beginning about fifty million years ago, as mammals spread across the globe following the mass extinction of the dinosaurs. The cetaceans—whales, dolphins, and porpoises—swelled into more than eighty species and dispersed throughout the oceans. The sea cows, or sirenians, named for the mythological mermaids of classical Greece, were never as widespread; these days this group, the only vegetarian marine mammals, consists of just four species with a limited distribution in the tropics and subtropics. The last immigration of mammals into the ocean was that of the sea otter, beginning about twelve million years ago.

The pinnipeds have not dispersed as widely as the cetaceans; they are still mainly creatures of the Pacific. Biologists recognize thirty-three species, grouped into three clusters: the sea lions and fur seals, together called the *eared seals* for their small but visible earflaps; the *earless* or "true" seals, such as the harbor seal; and the walrus, a subgroup made up of only a single living species.

All the pinnipeds still retain four limbs from their days on land (in contrast to the whales and sea cows, in which the rear limbs have disappeared and the front ones have been reduced to small, paddle-like "arms"). Pinniped limbs are flattened "flippers," but they look a bit like "hands" and "feet " with webbed "fingers." And the pinnipeds are the only group of marine mammals that have kept a solid tie with the land; they all mate and bear their young on land or ice.

That last biological fact kept the survivors of Bering's expedition alive from mid-April through June. They had their first taste of fur seal the third week of April, when the first males arrived on the island's breeding grounds. Hunters took two big males on the west side of the island, on successive days—April 18, which was Easter Sunday, and April 19. The two seals, weighing about 700 pounds apiece, gave the crew a mountain of meat. It looked to be enough, Steller says, to feed the whole company for a week.

Unfortunately, the holiday fur seal feast was not as grand as they thought it would be. The fatty meat threw off a horrible stench, and after they had forced down as much of it as they could, nearly every member of the crew fell victim to fits of vomiting and diarrhea. As another fur seal scientist put it a century and a half later, the yellow fat of the older males "is sickening to the smell, and will, nine times out of ten, cause any civilized stomach to throw it up as quickly as it was swallowed."

The older fur seal males, however, were only the vanguard of the masses that were swimming toward the island, and there was better eating to come. As May progressed, adult females and juveniles at first dribbled and then poured onto the beaches. Steller, as always relentlessly cheery about food, described the young and female seals as his favorite island food so far.

Kharlam Yushin found a quicker and easier route over the mountains to the fur seals' side of the island, a discovery that made an efficient new system possible. A permanent, rotating team of two hunters camped near the seals, hunting them and piling up seal meat in a cache for daily pickup by crewmembers who hiked over from the sandhill village. Yushin's route ran up the right fork of their village stream and then led over a pass to the west side of the island into a protected, southwest-facing valley, which the company began calling "Yushin's Valley."

At the end of April male sea lions began arriving to claim mating territories on the beach just as the fur seals had done. The lions were much bigger than the fur seals, and they were so ferocious that none of the hunters dared to approach one close enough to try to kill it. But when a freshly dead sea lion washed up on one of the western beaches, the company fed happily on it. They found a Kamchatka Native harpoon head buried in the animal—the apparent cause of death and another indication that Asia lay not far to the west.

As April turned into May, the shipbuilding crew finished fashioning the keel, the stem piece, and the sternpost for the new ship. On May 5 they joined the pieces together, and it was time to celebrate. Waxell invited the entire company to his hut for saturnan, a thick, hot drink that was the Siberian equivalent of hot chocolate. Waxell made a big batch of it in the ship's largest pot by frying some of their musty flour in seal oil, pouring boiling-hot cranberry-leaf tea into the flour, and stirring it all together. He was improvising; the usual ingredients were flour, butter, and black tea, but Waxell's version tasted so good to palates used to an all-meat diet that no one seemed to care.

The shipbuilders were re-creating the *St. Peter* as a "hooker," a small, no-frills sailing vessel with a single mast, about half the size of the original packet boat. She would be open-decked except for one very small cabin. At this point the hooker measured 42 feet from stem to stern and 36 feet along the keel. When built out, she would have a 12-foot beam and a depth of 5 feet from the deck to the bottom of the hull.

The work was going well, and now spring came on with a rush. A series of downpours in mid-May drove the men out of their pit houses; the combination of melting snow and several inches of cold rain flooded the entire area where their village lay, and they had to move to higher ground. The moisture and the lengthening daylight coaxed green shoots out of the bare soil, and soon the island was alive with plants, some of them shooting up toward the sun at a rate of a few inches a day. Steller took up botany again, wandering for miles, recording the island's vegetable bounty and picking plants for salads and stews.

Steller gathered batches of the thicket-forming cow-parsnip for its edible roots and sweet inner stalk; it was the same species of plant he had found in both the cache and the camp on Kayak Island. He also harvested supplies of the cow-parsnip's carrot-family cousins the hemlock-parsley, or wild carrot, and one of the species of the genus *Angelica,* or wild celery.

Steller collected many other food plants as well. There was *Fritillaria camschatcensis,* variously known as chocolate, Kamchatka, or sarana lily today, and also called northern rice-root and Indian rice for the clump-of-sticky-rice look of its bulb, which was eaten by every Native group on the American coast from Vancouver Island to the Aleutians. He picked fireweed, a common plant with a hot-pink flower, an edible root and inner stalk, and leaves high in Vitamin C. For tea, there were the leaves of wintergreen and the dwarf, evergreen cranberry that Waxell used in his saturnan concoction. Later in the season, if they were still stranded, the cranberry would give them edible fruit. From low-lying areas along streams, Steller gathered alpine bistort, with its edible and tasty rhizome, and brooklime and scurvy grass, two of the scurvy remedies he had found on Nagai Island.

The energy level of the crew increased noticeably as they ate the freshly sprouted, nutrient-filled plants. Even Waxell, who had so dismissively rejected Steller's advice about green plants in the Shumagins, finally acknowledged that Steller was right:

> *Adjunct Steller . . . collected and showed us many green herbs, some for drinking, some for eating, and by taking them we found our health noticeably improved. From my own experience I can assert that none of us became well or recovered his strength completely before we began eating something green. . . .*

On his spring jaunts Steller managed to work in some zoology, too. The hated foxes were shedding their fur quickly, and soon their hair was so thin they "looked as if they were going about in shirts." They retreated to caves in the mountains to bear their young, in litters of up to ten pups, and they barked at Steller from their birthing dens as he peered in to see what was going on. He watched as an eagle—the striking black-and-white Asian coastal eagle we call Steller's sea-eagle today—nabbed a fox, circled high into the air with the fox in its talons, dropped it onto the rocks to kill it, and then lazily descended to the ground and picked at the animal with its chunky beak.

On May 28 Steller returned to the fur seal beach and killed and dissected one of the big bulls. To his surprise, he found that its stomach and intestines were completely empty. Steller had discovered that these dominant animals, the males that American sealers would later name "beachmasters" for their command of the rookeries, stay nearly constantly on guard and never leave the beach to feed during the entire time they are defending their breeding territories. During their two-month fast, they lose as much as a quarter of their body mass. Steller confirmed this fasting process with several more dissections:

Although at different times I dissected the old males, I found nothing at all in their stomachs except froth and gastric juice, and no feces in the bowels. Also, I noted that as time passed the layers of fat wasted away more and more, their bodies shrank, and the skin became so loose that it hung like a sack and swayed with each motion of the body.

By mid-June the rookery was a city of fur seals. As new males arrived and tried to haul out onto the rookery, the bulls that had already claimed territories charged them in furious attempts to drive them off. Once the battles were over, the winners held sway over breeding homesteads each about the size of a living room, and the losers gathered outside the breeding area in a sort of bachelors' suburb. Immature animals hauled out and took up residence at a respectful distance from the rookery. Then the females arrived and blended into the breeding bulls'

Northern fur seals *(Callorhinus ursinus)*

territories, from a few to four dozen or so per bull. Each fur seal bull patrolled his territory ferociously, constantly on the lookout for defectors from his harem.

The females were so much smaller than the bulls, Steller wrote in his notes, that "a careless observer might almost take them for a different species." In fact, males weigh about three to five times as much as females. In the language of biology, that is extreme sexual dimorphism, a common trait of all the species of fur seals and sea lions. (If humans were as dimorphic as fur seals, the weight of the average man would have to balloon to five or six hundred pounds to correspond to that of the average-sized woman.)

Within a few days of arriving on the breeding grounds, the fur seal females, most of them pregnant from the previous year's mating season, bore the current year's band of pups. For the first few days afterwards, each female stayed ashore to nurse its single newborn. Then the females began leaving the rookeries for five to ten days at a time to feed in the open sea. The new mothers were eating for two now, and they needed to fatten up on fish to produce enough milk for their young.

While their mothers were gone, the pups fended for themselves, mobbing together like kindergarten children at recess. When the fur seal mothers returned, each one picked its pup out of the crowd by its scent and by its voice response to her call. Then the females nursed their young for two days or so before leaving on another feeding trip. Within about a week of giving birth, the females came into estrus and each bred with her harem bull.

The beach was alive with animals. They drowned out the breaking of the sea in a deafening disharmony of roars, grunts, growls, woofs, barks, and bleats. The denser the mass of animals grew, the more agitated and aggressive the fur seal beachmasters became. Steller found that he could no longer walk safely along the beach:

> There is no doubt that many of us would have been killed by [the male fur seals] if their legs were worth as much on land as they are in the water. . . . Steep places were always our refuge of safety, because they cannot climb up on them. They sometimes laid siege to me for more than six hours, and at length compelled me, at very great peril of my life, to climb a precipice to escape from the infuriated animals.

Steller fails to mention in this part of his account that he tested the aggressiveness of the beachmasters by throwing rocks at them; this was clearly not one of his brighter ideas. Adding insult to injury, he came upon a mating pair of seals and, for some reason needing to know how absorbed the male was in his passion, ran down and whacked it on the back. The male reared up and "attacked me so angrily that I got away only with difficulty."

Witnessing this breeding spectacle and remembering stories from Asia about the "sea cats," as the Russians called the fur seals, Steller began to piece together the story of the animals' great migrations. He knew that Kuril Islanders regularly spotted masses of fur seals swimming north past the islands in the spring, and a few weeks later the people of the southern half of Kamchatka's Pacific coast would see them cruising north near the shore. Hunters there took some of the animals and found that many of them were pregnant females, so heavy that they seemed to be ready to give birth any day.

From Kamchatka, the seals swam east and disappeared. No one on the coast of Asia saw anything of them again until fall, when they passed by Kamchatka once more, this time heading south with smaller, younger seals among them. Steller summed up the mystery of the fur seals in *The Beasts of the Sea*:

> *For many years these migratory animals have been a source of wonder and speculation. . . . Where did these animals come from in early spring? Where were these very fat, these pregnant beasts, going in countless droves? What are the reasons for this migration? Why do they return with their young in the fall . . . ? And where are they going?*

On Bering Island, Steller had stumbled onto one of the few great breeding grounds of northern fur seals on the planet. The full story of the species would not be known for another century and a half, but while he was shipwrecked on the island Steller produced a good sketch of how they live.

He concluded that these fur seals must winter in the south, in the vicinity of Japan, and swim north to remote rookeries near rich feeding areas to mate and bear their young. There were plenty of clues already that Steller and his shipmates were on an island not far east of Kamchatka; if the fur seals swam east from Kamchatka, this island would likely be right on their path. The fact that they gathered only on the beaches on the west side of the island was another piece of evidence; the west side was the coast that faced Kamchatka, the side the fur seals would reach first as they swam out from the Asian mainland. Then, he reasoned, with the pups born and weaned, and the next generation already growing inside the females, the fur seals swam west, back to the Kamchatka coast, and then south to their wintering grounds.

He was right about the Asian seals, but he could not know that there were also millions of fur seals on the American side of the Pacific, seals that bred primarily on the huge Pribilof Island rookeries in the Bering Sea. Biologists think that before the coming of Europeans, the rookeries of Bering Island and its neighbor, now called Copper Island (the two collectively called the Commander Islands, after Bering), were the summer homes of one to two million fur seals—roughly equivalent to the human population of the Portland, Oregon, urban area. About double that number—say, the equivalent of metropolitan San Diego—swarmed the Pribilofs during the breeding season. There were also breeding grounds on a few other North Pacific islands, but the Commanders and the Pribilofs were where most of the world's northern fur seals congregated in summer.

The male fur seals' size, the way they moved, and their roaring and growling reminded Steller of bears, and through this mental connection he recalled the "sea bear" of the Southern Hemisphere as described by William Dampier, the seventeenth-century British pirate and amateur naturalist. Steller realized that the seals he was studying on the island were related to Dampier's sea bears. The seas where Dampier had seen his sea bears, Steller hypothesized, was much too far away for the animals he was seeing on Bering Island to be part of the same population. Steller's educated guess was that the seals of Bering Island migrated to a latitude in the Northern Hemisphere that corresponded to the latitude in the Southern Hemisphere where Dampier had seen his seals.

It was a good guess. The Juan Fernández Islands (one of which was the home of the real-life Robinson Crusoe), the islands where Dampier observed seals, sea lions, and fur seals, lie off the South American coast at latitude 33° 50' south. Northern fur seals migrate as far south as 35° north in the western Pacific, to the Sea of Japan, and to 33° north in the eastern Pacific, the latitude of southern California. (The journey of the seals that migrate between the Pribilofs and southern California, more than 3,000 miles one way, is the longest migration of any pinniped on earth.)

As a rule fur seals touch land only when they come ashore on the breeding grounds. Most of the Asian breeders winter on the western, Asian side of the North Pacific, and most of the Pribilof breeders winter on the eastern, American side. A few fur seals, however, cross the Pacific each year to breed or winter on the side opposite their birthplace, so there is a constant mingling of the populations.

Steller agreed with Dampier's choice of name for the animal; he refers to it in *The Beasts of the Sea* as *ursus marinus,* "sea bear," and with the hindsight of more than 250 years, we can see that that was a decent call. First, the skulls of bears and eared seals are very similar—the reason the genus name for the southern fur seals is *Arctocephalus,* from the Greek words for "bear" and "head." Second, fossil evidence indicates that bears are very likely the closest living terrestrial relatives of the pinnipeds in general and the eared seals in particular.

The name "sea bear," however, failed to stick. Linnaeus changed the scientific name in 1758 to *Phoca ursina* ("bearlike seal"). The Latin name today, *Callorhinus ursinus,* still retains a thread of the bear connection. The genus name, *Callorhinus,* means "beautiful nose," a reference to the fur seal's slender snout, which, with the seal's smaller head, makes it possible to distinguish it in the water from a Steller sea lion, which has a broad forehead and a short, rounded nose.

As the breeding season wore on, Steller studied sea lions as they came to shore to breed in much the same way the fur seals did. They were even more aggressive than the seals:

> *[Sea lions] far surpass the sea bear in strength and size. . . . They also give to the eye and mind the impression of a lion. . . . If one of them is cornered and all chance for flight is shut off he turns against his enemy with a great roar, shakes his head in wrath, rages, cries out, and puts even the bravest man to flight. The first time I tried this experiment was almost the last of me.*

During the time of the summer solstice, Steller built a driftwood blind on a rise in the middle of the seal and sea lion rookery, and for the next six days camped there and observed the animals. He must have slept very little; at that latitude, during the longest days of the year, an obsessed biologist could stay on watch for all but three or four hours a night.

Steller's observations from his makeshift blind convinced him that fur seals and sea lions are very closely related. (So they are; the genetic differences among the seventeen species of eared seals are so small that some sea lions and fur seals have been observed to mate and produce hybrid pups. The eared seals are a close-knit family because they radiated into many species very quickly and recently in evolutionary time.) Steller reported that the two species swim, lie, stand, and walk nearly identically, and that they are both true amphibians. (In fact, both sea lions and fur seals swim by flapping their powerful front flippers and ruddering with their smaller hind flippers, similar to the way a stern paddler in a canoe steers, and both rotate their hind flippers, turning them into "feet" for running.) Steller tossed pups of both species into the water and noted that they simply flailed away with their little flippers and struggled straight back to land, correctly observing that the young are unable to swim for their first few weeks of life.

Steller recorded two major differences between the species. First, their travel habits: Sea lions do not migrate as far as fur seals. As a rule, they stay much closer to their favorite rocky haulouts along the coast, while the fur seals travel widely. Second, the skins of the two species are very different: Sea lions have a hide that is tough and more or less bald, covered only with a sparse layer of guard hairs and little or no underfur; their skins are good for shoe soles, Steller tells us, and as the Aleut people knew, for boat skins, but they were not likely to attract a fur trader. The fur seal, in contrast, has a thick coat of fur, double-layered like the sea otter's. It is only half as dense as the otter's, but luxurious enough to be very valuable in the fur trade of Steller's day.

Steller decided not to waste his time trying to count the fur seals on Bering Island. In the only passage in his notes approaching a census of the seals, he says:

> If I had to say how many I saw on Bering Island I would truthfully say that I could not guess. They were countless.

It would not always be that way.

———— ⁀ ————

As May wore on, the shipbuilding crew finished cutting the hull planks for the new *St. Peter* and began setting the planks on the hooker's keel. The work was going well, but fur seal meat, laboriously packed across the island's mountain spine, was still essentially their only source of food. The work of hauling the meat had been back-breaking, and the packers were exhausted.

Meanwhile, herds of sea cows cruised the offshore kelp beds, a potential food source only a few hundred yards from the castaways' huts, but they couldn't devise a plan to land one. The cows were huge, powerful animals, blimplike creatures, the largest 25 to 30 feet long; they were about the size of an orca and almost half the volume of the hooker the crew was building. It was easy enough to get near them; at high tide they sometimes swam so close to shore that Steller was able to reach out and stroke the rough, hard crust of hide on their backs. However, piercing the tough hide and wounding one of them seri-ously enough to haul it ashore was another matter entirely.

Over the winter, Steller studied the sea cows from the beach below the company's village. The animals always roamed in herds, he observed, with the adults surrounding the young. Their favorite habitats were sandy-bottomed bays where freshwater streams emp-tied, like the cove where the *St. Peter*'s survivors were camped. They never completely submerged; their backs and half of their sides were always out of the water. Gulls often perched on them, pecking at parasites living in the rough skin. The sea cows slept floating on their backs—usually after swimming a few hundred feet out from the beach, apparently to keep the sea from pushing them ashore while they slept.

The animals spent most of their waking hours eating. They kept their heads underwater as they fed, raising their noses out of the sea only once every four or five minutes to suck in a breath of air. They fed on kelp, the giant brown algae of the North Pacific, cropping off pieces of the rubbery leaves as the plants waved in the swells. Where the sea cows foraged, the tide washed in piles of kelp that the creatures had torn from their holdfasts on the bottom of the bay.

Steller's sea cow *(Hydrodamalis gigas)* and its palate plate (inset)

As they fed, the sea cows faced out to open water, holding themselves in place against the force of the incoming waves by swishing
their big, whalelike tails and bracing against submerged rocks with
their truncated "arms." Steller wrote in his notes that, using both
their tails and their forelimbs, they "half swim and half walk" in the
kelp-bed shallows.

He again remembered the travelogue of William Dampier, who had
seen animals like these in the Caribbean Sea and the tropical South Pacific. Steller thought that the animals he was observing on Bering Island

were the same creatures that Dampier had seen in the tropics—the animal known in Spanish as *manatí* (corrupted to "manatee"), and called "sea cow" by the English. In reality the tropical and northern sea cows were sirenian cousins, but not the same species.

Before the end of May, the *St. Peter*'s crew finally devised a plan to hunt the beefy animals. They forged heavy pieces of iron into what looked like giant fishhooks and tied long, stout ropes to them. Then a small group of hunters waded into the shallows to give their new sea cow tackle a try. On their first attempt they pierced the hide of one of the animals, but it pulled away, ripped out the hook, and escaped. The same technique failed several more times, and the crew gave up for the time being.

Near the end of June, they worked out another approach. The idea was Steller's, from his memory of an account of Native whaling in Greenland. The key elements were a boat and a harpoon. The crew repaired the longboat, which had been hurled onto the rocks and damaged during a surf landing back in November. Then they reforged one of the iron hooks to resemble a harpoon point, attached it to a makeshift harpoon shaft, and attached the shaft to a long, heavy rope four inches in diameter.

A crew of six launched the longboat, with a harpooner in the bow and the rope coiled neatly in the boat so it would pay out without fouling. All the other castaways—forty of them—waited on the beach, holding the free end of the rope. The longboat slowly and quietly made its way into the bay's herd of sea cows.

The harpooner struck an animal, the harpoon point stuck, and a battle between forty-six humans and one sea cow began. The longboat crew hauled at the oars while the forty men on shore tugged on the rope, all trying to tow the wounded sea cow toward shore. At first all they could do was prevent it from swimming out to sea, but eventually it tired, and they managed to pull it into the shallows, where they knifed and bayoneted the huge animal until it finally succumbed.

It was a full-grown adult, about four tons of sea cow altogether. They sliced it into big cakes of meat and fat and carried them up the dunes and home. The meat barrels overflowed with sea cow, and it was fine eating. Steller wrote that the steaks were as good as the best beef, but he saved his longest string of superlatives for the fat:

The boiled fat is sweeter and better tasting than the best beef fat, is like fresh olive oil in color and fluidity, resembles sweet almond oil in taste, and is exceptional in smell and nourishment. We drank it by the cupful. . . .

Drinking a cup of fat—olive or sea cow oil or melted butter or anything else—may sound revolting, but by this time the *St. Peter*'s crew had lived outdoors full-time for seven months, sheltered only by sailcloth tarps. Their reserves were slim, and the thick, heavy liquid tasted like manna from marine mammal heaven.

Now that they had a workable method of hunting the sea cows, the crew was usually able to land one when they needed food. The animals' herding and feeding habits made them relatively easy to hunt, although their apparent loyalty to each other sometimes made landing a cow difficult. Steller wrote:

. . . they have an uncommon love for one another, extending so far that, when one of them was hooked, all the others tried to save it. Some tried to prevent their wounded comrade from being pulled to the beach by forming a circle around it; some tried to capsize the boat; others laid themselves over the rope and tried to sever it, or attempted to dislodge the harpoon with a blow from their tails, and several times they succeeded.

A single sea cow lasted the hungry crew two weeks. Waxell says that they finally had all they wanted to eat: "each cooked as much and as often as he liked." Their food troubles, it seemed, were over. One hunt every two weeks was enough to keep their pantry full, they could give up the daily round-trips across the island for fur seal meat, and the sea cow meat and fat were delicious, in contrast to the survival food the otters and fur seals had provided. The savings in hunting time and effort freed more hands for the job of shipbuilding, and the pace of the work picked up considerably.

As the hooker took shape, Steller spent his time recording the biology of the sea cow. He killed a calf and painstakingly skinned it, preserved its skeleton, and stuffed the skin with dry grass to take back to Russia. He also chose a full-grown female, killed on July 12, for close examination and dissection. Lepekhin and Plenisner helped, but it was too big a job for the three of them. Steller resorted to bribery, with tobacco, to get assistance from a few of the other crewmembers.

It was not comfortable, sterile lab work. The weather had turned wet and cold, the tide carried away anything left too close to the waterline, the foxes tried to make off with Steller's notebook, and his tobacco-wage help had no real interest in what he was trying to do. But Steller persevered, and because he did we have one, and only one, comprehensive firsthand account of the animal we call Steller's sea cow.

The female sea cow was nearly 25 feet long and measured 6 feet in diameter at the abdomen; lying on its side, it overtopped most of the people who were examining it. It had seventeen massive ribs. Its tongue was a foot long, its tail 6½ feet wide, and its neck more than 2 feet thick. It had an extremely flexible backbone of twenty-five vertebrae, and thirty-five more vertebrae made up the framework of its tail.

The cow's inch-thick epidermis, the hairless outer hide, was as rough and hard as "the bark of an ancient oak." Steller at first could not find the animal's ear openings; they turned out to be pea-sized apertures almost completely hidden in the warty, irregular hide. He found dozens of the parasites the gulls pecked off the sea cows; they were half-inch-long, shrimplike crustaceans known as amphipods, which had burrowed into hollows in the sea cow's skin.

When Steller sliced through the sea cow's outer "bark," he found a thin layer of softer skin under it, followed by a layer of fat four finger widths deep—about three inches of solid blubber. (Other sea cows he examined later had seams of fat as much as nine inches thick.) The blubber and the impervious hide, Steller wrote in his notes, were a good double layer of insulation from the cold sea. The hide was also a tough armor that protected the animal from rocks and ice; it took Steller some effort to penetrate it even with an ax.

The sea cow's mouth was curious, and Steller spent considerable space in his notes describing it. Protruding from its double set of lips was a thicket of hard, white bristles, which Steller says the sea cow used to snip off the seaweed it ate. The bristles also sealed its lips when the animal had a mouthful of kelp to chew. But it was not really *chewing* the kelp; the animal had no teeth. The sea cow *mashed* its food between two flat plates, one attached to the palate above and one to the lower jaw below.

The plates had corresponding patterns of wavy valleys and ridges, which allowed them to fit snugly together when the animal closed its maw.

To Steller, one of the strangest things about the sea cow's anatomy was its forelimbs, which as in all the cetaceans and sirenians are its only true limbs. The structure of the animal's forelimb was very much like that of a human arm, but it had no finger bones; Steller describes the end of the limb as being like a blunt claw or a horse's hoof, with hairlike bristles on the inner surface. Besides "walking" and bracing itself in the shallow water among the coastal rocks, the sea cow used its forelimbs to dig out kelp from the rocks, like a horse pawing the ground, and to embrace its partner when mating. But the arms were far too weak to move the great animals on land; when one sea cow washed ashore as it slept, it was hopelessly beached, and the crew soon converted it to meat for their larder.

Steller found the sea cow's heart and each of its kidneys to be more or less the same size, each about the volume of a county-fair blue-ribbon watermelon. But for sheer size and bulk, he found nothing that could match the digestive organs:

> The stomach is of stupendous size, 6 feet long, 5 feet wide, and so stuffed with food and seaweed that four strong men with a rope attached to it could with great effort scarcely move it from its place and drag it out.

The intestines were six inches in diameter, and packed into the abdomen so tightly that when Steller made a tiny incision in the thick membrane around the gut, air gushed out with the sound of hissing steam. He made a long slice through the membrane, and the intestines began to pour out of the abdomen. As Steller and his helpers tugged them out of the animal to measure them, the assistants saw an opportunity for a great practical joke:

> If only a very slight aperture were made with the point of a knife, the liquid excrement (a ridiculous thing to behold) would squirt out violently like blood from a ruptured vein, and often the face of a spectator would be drenched by this springing fountain whenever someone opened a canal upon his neighbor opposite, for a joke.

Steller and the jokers laid out the entire digestive tract, from craw to rectum, and put a measuring tape to it. It came to 500 feet, nearly two city blocks long and twenty times the length of the animal. (The human digestive tract is about 30 feet long, or five to six times the height of an average person.) "The final product of this workshop," Steller wrote, "is so much like the excrement of horses" that, when washed up on the beach, "it would deceive the most expert stable boy." He admits in *The Beasts of the Sea* that it had fooled him in his first days on the island; Steller had briefly believed that it was the dung of American horses, and that it might be evidence that they were shipwrecked near the American mainland.

Steller had discovered that the sea cows of Bering Island were kelp-devouring machines, finely tuned for turning seaweed into fuel and insulation. The cows did live well in the summer, but the pickings were slimmer in winter. Algal growth at the latitude of Bering Island slows considerably in the low sun of the cold season, and the animals, apparently having a hard time finding enough to eat, grew progressively more emaciated over the winter, as Steller saw from the beach:

> *When the animals are fat, as they are in spring and summer, the back is slightly convex; but in winter, when they are thin, the back is flat and excavated at the spine with a hollow on either side, and then all the vertebrae . . . can be seen.*

The withering of the Bering Island sea cows in winter is one significant piece of evidence that they were a much-diminished population, living at the outer limits of survivable habitat. In the late nineteenth century scientists explored the island and found only fifteen bays where the animals could have lived. Altogether, they estimated, there had been probably only one to two thousand Steller's sea cows left alive at the time Steller studied them.

The animals Steller observed were the ragged remnants of a species that had been far more widespread in the past, and Steller's account, a few skeletal remains from Bering Island, and fifty-plus fossils of the sea cows' ancestors have provided enough information to tell their story. Twenty million years ago some pioneering tropical sea cows crossed from the western Atlantic to the eastern Pacific via the Central

American Seaway, the saltwater connection between the two oceans that existed before Central America rose out of the sea. When the sea-cow colonists arrived on the Pacific Coast of California and Baja California, it was a flat-lying shoreline of deeply indented, protected bays and estuaries that sheltered great underwater prairies of sea grasses, the bottom-feeding tropical sea cows' favorite food.

Over the next few million years, however, the climate cooled in fits and starts, on a trajectory toward the Pleistocene ice ages; eventually the subtropical coastal life that had been thriving as far north as Kodiak Island would retreat 30 to 35 degrees of latitude to the south. At the same time, the Coast Ranges rose along the margins of the eastern Pacific, draining the extensive bays that had dominated the earlier coastline, and the coast of California and Baja California took on the rugged, rocky shape of today. Sea-grass habitat shrank, and for the sea-grass eaters, it was time to adapt or die.

Some of the animals adapted to the new climate and physical habitat by feeding on the leaves of early kelplike plants that grew up from the sea floor. These sea cows grew larger—much larger—eventually bloating into Steller's sea cow, which was two to three times the size of its nearest living relative today, the dugong of the Indopacific tropics (a different species from the familiar manatee of Florida and the Caribbean). The North Pacific sea cows grew a thick double layer of hide and blubber, reduced the number of their teeth and finally lost them, shortened and lost the finlike shape and finger bones of their forelimbs, and developed a powerful, flexible neck and jaws. Paleontologists have traced these and other body changes, step by step, through three intermediate forms between the early eastern Pacific sea cows and the Steller's sea cow.

This was a radical set of changes for the sirenians, which as a group had changed little over the course of their evolution, but it was a package of changes that worked in the new environment. Ballooning in size gave the North Pacific sea cow a lower surface-to-volume ratio, and with the thick blubber and hide as insulation, the new version of the sea cow retained body heat much more efficiently. Teeth were not much use on the rubbery kelp fronds, so the sea cow replaced them with mashing plates. The clawlike forelimbs gave the animal traction on the slippery rocks where it fed. A flexible neck allowed the Steller's sea cow to reach widely from side to side and so feed over a large area of kelp from one position, avoiding the need to move and restabilize often in the turbulent seas where it fed.

At one time the cold-water sea cows' range stretched around the North Pacific from California to Japan, more or less the same distribution as that of the sea otter, northern fur seal, and Steller sea lion. Their empire began roughly eight to ten million years ago and lasted until a new predator—human beings—arrived in the Americas, only a few thousand years ago. It was a dramatic change in fortune; the sea cows were slow moving, unaggressive, herding, and tasty—overall, an easy and inviting target for human hunters.

Early American hunting pushed the sea cow to the outer limits of its habitat in the Commander Islands. The evidence is circumstantial, but it is compelling, and there is no other workable explanation for the species' retreat to just two northern islands—which happened to be the only islands with suitable habitat where humans had never lived.

Bering Island and neighboring Copper Island were the last strongholds of the sea cow in the northern oceans, the final outpost of a lineage of mammals that had lived along the North Pacific coast for twenty million years. Steller's account would be the only scientific record of the living animals before they disappeared from the earth.

The sea cows were feeding the *St. Peter*'s crew perfectly well, and then the salmon started running in July. With their first haul of a tattered, half-rotten fish net, the castaways caught enough salmon to last them eight days. They had survived the season of scarcity; now the season of abundance was providing all they needed and more.

They were growing more confident every day that the small vessel they were building from the wreck of the old ship would sail well enough to take them back to Kamchatka. Steller says that Waxell had a lot to do with that confidence, that he had risen to the occasion as a leader with his "constant efforts and encouragement [that] raised the spirit of the men."

The increasing evidence that they were close to the Asian mainland also helped morale. While hunting fur seals on the west side of the island, some of the crew had seen what they were certain was a row of very Kamchatka-like snowcapped volcanoes on the western horizon. They also found, washed up on one of the western beaches, pieces of sleds that they identified as the reindeer sleds of the Koryak people of Kamchatka.

By late July, most of the work of building the new *St. Peter* was done. They had built the vessel on a platform 175 feet back from the usual high-tide line, cautiously keeping their only hope of salvation out of the range of storm-driven waves. Now they began building a wooden slipway for the hooker; the plan was to slide the vessel off the construction platform, onto the slipway, and down the slipway to the sea.

The summer was waning. They had to sail soon if they were to avoid spending another winter on the island, but there was still much to do before they could leave. Besides building the slipway, they repaired the sails and rigging, dried and salted sea cow meat for the voyage, and mended their leaky water barrels. They used more salvaged lumber from the original ship to build a small dinghy as a shore boat and to put up a storage building for the equipment they would have to leave behind.

They also faced the problem of sealing the seams in the new vessel. The usual method was to trickle pine pitch into them, but for that they would have needed pine trees, and they were on a treeless island. They had a supply of extra rope that they had waterproofed earlier with Siberian pine pitch, so, once again, they improvised, heating the ropes in a cauldron, melting out the pitch, and dripping it into a wooden box.

On August 8 they were ready to slide the hooker into the water. Everyone gathered on the beach at high tide to pray for success, and they officially named the vessel as the reborn *St. Peter*. Then they began to winch her toward the sea, but the platform she was resting on buckled under the weight; the vessel stopped dead in her tracks. They had to winch the hooker up and shove some planks underneath to raise her high enough so that she would slide onto the slipway. By the time they finished, the tide had receded, and they had to delay the launch till the next day.

The afternoon of August 9, on the high tide, they slid her into the sea and anchored in eighteen feet of water. That night Waxell hosted another saturnan party. Their spirits were soaring with the anticipation of sailing away.

On the tenth and the eleventh the crew worked day and night getting ready to leave. They set the mast, rigged the sails and rudder, and ferried out the ten barrels of water, five kegs of sea cow meat, and eleven sacks of flour that would be their chief provisions for what they hoped would be a very short voyage. They loaded iron, three cannon, and several hundred cannon balls into the hold for ballast, secured their new dinghy on deck, and carried aboard the nine hundred sea otter furs they had accumulated over their nine months on the island.

Yet Waxell refused to allow Steller's plant and animal collections on board. His hundreds of dried and pressed plants, the stuffed sea cow calf's skin, and the calf's skeleton all had to be left on Bering Island. Steller protested, but it was no use. All he managed to squeeze on board from the first scientific foray to western North America were his manuscripts, a collection of dried seeds from the plants of Kayak and Bering Islands, and a sea cow's kelp-mashing palate plate. Steller doesn't dwell on his disappointment in his journal, but it must have nearly killed him to leave his collections behind—and they were never recovered.

On the afternoon of August 12, the company erected a wooden cross over Bering's grave. Khitrovo, in his log, says they named the island Bering Island for the captain-commander. The next morning the crew, as Steller describes it,

> . . . one and all, with much inner emotion, left their dwellings for the last time and went on board the vessel, which was going either to bring us back to our country or to decide our fate in some other way.

The island was free of people once more, and the arctic foxes moved back into their sandhill burrows as if the *St. Peter*'s crew had never been there.

The forty-six survivors crowded onto the hooker *St. Peter.* Steller again:

> We lay one on top of the other and crawled over one another. Lieutenant Waxell, Master Khitrovo, I, and the Lieutenant's son had the best space, in the narrow cabin. The other 42 men were lying in the hold, which was packed so full with water barrels, provisions, and baggage

that the crew could scarcely lie down between all that and the deck. Three men shared two places because the crew had been divided into three watches. But because the space was still too crowded, we began to throw into the sea the pillows, bedding, and clothing we had brought from shore.

At 6 AM on August 13, after another assembly to pray for success, they got under way. The nearly windless weather had been perfect while they launched, loaded, and rigged the vessel, but now the lack of a sailing breeze kept them from pulling out of the bay. They had to set the anchor and haul to it several times, just as they had done when they left Avacha Bay more than a year before.

By 11 AM they were clear of the bay, and they raised their sails and began to coast south with a light breeze from the north. The new *St. Peter* was sailing well; Starodubtsov's little ship was seaworthy and responsive. They rounded the southeast point of Bering Island, which they named Cape Manati for the island's sea cows, and Kharlam Yushin began reckoning their position from there. For the last time they all looked out on the valleys and mountains and coastline they knew so well. "The more we gazed at the island on our farewell," Steller says, "the clearer appeared to us, as in a mirror, God's wonderful and loving guidance."

They headed a little south of west, a course they guessed would take them toward Avacha Bay. The next afternoon, the fourteenth, the wind and waves came up. The longboat, which they were towing behind the hooker because there was no room for it on board, began to founder in the sea, and they decided to cut it adrift. It was goodbye to their sea cow–hunting craft, the ship's boat that had served them so well.

At 11 PM they discovered that seawater was pouring into the hold. The *St. Peter* had sprung a serious leak, and their pumps were not able to keep up with the rising water. The crew bailed furiously with buckets, heaved the cannon balls overboard to lighten the ship, and moved the gear around in the hold, looking for the leak. In the crowded hold it was chaos, and, as Steller describes it, "everyone was in everyone else's way." Forty miles out from Bering Island, they were at risk of sinking, and their tiny dinghy was the only avenue of escape if they could not stanch the flow of seawater.

Starodubtsov had an idea where to look for the leak—in the section of the hull where the collapse of the building platform had put the most strain. He was right, and he found it early that morning. By 3 AM on the fifteenth they had plugged the leak and were out of danger.

It had been foggy, drizzly, and squally since the weather change of the previous afternoon. For two more days clouds hung over the deck of the hooker while the wind carried them west. On the morning of August 17 the fog cleared, and the crew saw that they were only four or five miles off a coastline capped by a snowy volcano. They were looking at a large headland, and soon someone recognized it as Cape Kronotski, the prominent Kamchatka cape where most of the crew had thought they had landed in November.

They knew where they were: 150 miles northeast of Avacha Bay. They turned southwest for home, but the wind swung around in their faces, and a heavy swell from the south pushed hard against the *St. Peter*. For the next nine days, alternating south winds and calms slowed them to a crawl.

On August 23 they pulled out a set of eight oars they had made for the hooker and started rowing. It was hard work and none too speedy; they advanced all of three-quarters of a knot in their first three hours at the oars. For the next three days they rowed more than they sailed, and at 1 AM on the twenty-sixth they finally pulled into the entrance to Avacha Bay.

They anchored there to wait a few hours for the tide to turn and for a headwind to die. Then, at 5 AM on August 26, 1742, they pulled in the anchor and rowed into Avacha Bay, and, once again, they all stepped ashore in Asia.

Chirikov, they learned, had made it back the previous autumn, and then in late May had sailed east again to try to find Bering's crew. It had been a near impossibility in the vast ocean; Chirikov had sailed the *St. Paul* as far as the middle of the Aleutian chain before the poor shape of his ship and crew had convinced him to turn back. Now he and the crew were in Okhotsk.

The joy of the company's homecoming faded when the people of Petropavlovsk told them that everyone had given them up for dead, and that most of the belongings they had left in the village had been divided up and carried off. It was another blow for Steller: he had lost almost his entire collection of plants and animals from the expedition, and now he found out that the possessions he had left in Avacha Bay were gone too.

He and the crew, however, still had something of value: the nine hundred sea otter furs they had collected on Bering Island. The survivors of the expedition, knowing he had saved their lives, gave Steller the largest share of the furs in gratitude—eighty furs, a nice nest egg for a poor biologist.

The tidy village, the warm cabins, the warehouse full of food—it all seemed so unreal after the months of hardship. Steller writes that being back in civilization (a relative term for a tiny village at the far edge of eighteenth-century Siberia) was like living in a dream world:

> We were all by this time so used to misery and wretched living that, instead of looking ahead to better times, we thought that our previous circumstances would always continue and that we were dreaming the present ones.

They gathered one last time to give a prayer of thanks for their deliverance. Then Waxell and most of the crew reboarded the *St. Peter* to sail to Okhotsk for the winter. Steller and Lepekhin started hiking the 140 miles across Kamchatka to Bol'sheretsk, where Steller meant to winter with his friends in the village, turn his notes into professional papers, and make plans for more biological rambles in Kamchatka.

As he hiked away from Avacha Bay, Steller turned his back to America. He would never return to the New World, but his legacy was secure. With the publication of *The Beasts of the Sea*, European scientists would know the marine mammals of the distant North Pacific better than they did their own, more familiar sea creatures. From the sea otter furs Steller and the crew had brought back to Asia, Europeans would learn about the wealth of life of the northern seas. For better or worse, Steller and the other survivors of the American Expedition were about to introduce the creatures of the North Pacific to the outside world of humanity.

Steller sea lion *(Eumetopias jubatus)*

KAYAK ISLAND

I do not doubt that the American shores are to become better known to us.

—Steller, *The Beasts of the Sea*

On Kayak Island, the place where science began in western North America, Phil North and I are inside the Cape St. Elias lighthouse, climbing a set of stairs into the light tower. Passing around the navigation light, we reach a small doorway and squeeze through it, onto the narrow balcony encircling the tower. The view to the south is raw and magnificent. In the foreground is the pyramid of Pinnacle Rock, set against gray sky, surrounded by swirls of glaucous-winged gulls and enveloped in the bawling and roaring of sea lions. I pull out my binoculars and scan the more distant coastal rocks, catching a glimpse of sea lion silhouettes against the white foam of breaking waves. Out to sea, alone in the expanse of the blue Pacific, a cruise ship is plowing its way toward Prince William Sound.

The view is fine, but the sea is in full retreat, and tide-pool exploring will be at its best very soon. This afternoon's tide is a super-low minus three feet; much of the alien, subtidal world will emerge from the ocean today. We leave the lighthouse and hike down to the shoreline for the show.

Out on the island's tidal shelf we meander through a vast array of small shellfish—limpets, barnacles, and the sea snails known as periwinkles—clinging en masse to thousands of exposed rocks in the upper tidal zone. In pools left behind by the last high tide, I pick out scuttling hermit crabs, darting sculpins, and anemones waving their mop-head tentacles, blindly groping for their next meal. The walking is slimy, a process of hopping from one seaweed-draped stone to the next.

We descend the sloping shelf, following the tide line as it retreats, and the color of the seaweeds shifts from the greens of the upper tidal zone to the lower zone's browns and reds. The darker pigments in the algae that live at this depth, which mask the reflected green of chlorophyll, help the plants absorb the muted sunlight they receive when they're covered with several feet of seawater. Kelp lies over the lower rocks in thick bunches of flat, brown, yard-long fronds like lasagna noodles spilling over the sides of a pasta dish. Peeking underneath the dense canopy of kelp turns out to be great sport; we find several shellfish predators of the sea star persuasion, hiding out in the shade and damp underneath: fat, red and blue leather stars; spiny, yellowish, six-rayed stars; and one long-legged, bright-red blood star. Peeling back another layer of kelp I come across a feathery, delicate, lichen-like red alga, a sea plant that, as Phil remembers, survives only in the shelter of the kelp.

Kelp beds are a layered, living forest as wild and rich as any forest on land. They are the best shelter a sea creature can hope to find along this coast, here at the downwind end of an ocean with a fetch that reaches to Australia. The thick beds of vegetation, anchored to rocks on the bottom, soothe the ocean the way a stand of timber on land breaks the force of the wind.

With the tide out, this mosaic of life appears two-dimensional and almost dormant. But, an hour or so into our exploration, the tide begins its return, lifting the kelp off the rocks, floating the plants' fronds up to the sunlight, and reanimating the forest. The rising sea rolls in a fresh supply of water, dissolved oxygen, organic particles, and plankton, and the shallow sea grows cloudy with eggs, larvae, and detritus. We lose our window on the subtidal world as the sea closes in, but we know it's coming back to three-dimensional life.

When the tide is in, the kelp fronds are as busy as a subway station at rush hour. Creatures called kelp lace—like a crust of tiny doilies bonded to the surface of the fronds—wave food into their mouths with tiny tentacles. Gelatinous, bloblike sea slugs rasp the lace off the fronds. Tiny shellfish crawl along the waving leaves, out of reach of their sea-star predators. Pillbuglike isopods graze on the fronds, and small fish dart in and gulp them down. On the bottom, under the canopy of the kelp, small crabs scavenge carcasses and swallow fish and snail eggs. Clams siphon-feed on drift-food washing by in the tide. Carnivorous snails attack shellfish, drilling into their shells to reach the soft meat inside. Greenling, rockfish, and pricklebacks feed among the fronds, and bald eagles and harbor seals dip into the kelp beds and eat their fill of the fish. It's an ark-load of creatures under the flood of the tide; Charles Darwin, apparently the first scientist to recognize the teeming abundance of the Pacific kelp forest, called it the equal of terrestrial tropical forests in wealth of life.

And although we haven't seen any sea otters yet, the healthy kelp is a good sign that they are alive and well off Kayak Island. Otters prey on sea urchins, pincushion-like animals that are voracious kelp grazers. By keeping them under control, sea otters allow the kelp forests' intricate web of life to thrive. We didn't find any urchins in our tide ramble; there may be a few hanging on in inaccessible crevices, hidden away where the local otters can't find them, but there are apparently so few that they're not much of a factor here.

Where otters are missing from the undersea world, urchins proliferate, thin out the canopy-forming kelps, and totally change the character of the near-shore marine world. A seascape without otters can be rich with animals like urchins, clams, crabs, snails, and sea stars, but it's missing the kelp forest's physical texture and protected nooks and crannies, all of which attract so many other creatures. Areas with otters and kelp harbor fewer shellfish but many more species and a greater sheer mass of life than those without. In areas with otters, the total amount of plant life—the ultimate foundation of any food web—is triple that of similar areas without otters. In the language of biology, the top-predator sea otter is the "keystone" species—a reference to the stone in the center of an arch that holds the entire structure together—in the North Pacific kelp forest. Otters, say the biologists who study them, may be one of the most powerful keystone species on the planet.

They may not have always been the lone keystone creature along the North Pacific coastline, however. One animal is missing from the kelp forest today that was around for much of its existence in evolutionary time: the Steller's sea cow. The story of kelp, otters, and sea cows began with the cooling of the North Pacific, which gave rise to the blossoming of the species that now call this ocean home. The forest-forming kelps thrived and diversified into what are now recognized as three dozen genera of plants, at the same time fanning out widely from their North Pacific birthplace into the North Atlantic and South Pacific.

In the North Pacific, the kelps, sea cows, and sea otters reached an accommodation. The sea cows ate mainly the tops of the kelp fronds; the plants, apparently responding to the pressure of sea cow grazing, evolved to bear their reproductive spores low on the fronds, thereby protecting the next generation of kelp from the sea cows. Sea otters protected kelp from urchin grazing. In the South Pacific, where there have never been any carnivores like sea otters, kelps evolved a menu of foul-tasting chemicals to ward off grazers. With otters around, North Pacific kelps have never needed that kind of protection, but if sea otters were to fall on hard times, the northern kelps would be defenseless.

By eating urchins, sea otters guaranteed the sea cows' food supply, and sea cow grazing very likely created more food for the otters. As Steller noted, sea cows sometimes yanked up whole plants, leaving great heaps of kelp on the beach. Opening up the kelp canopy here and there, as a windstorm does in a terrestrial forest, allowed more sunlight to reach the "forest floor," creating a patchwork of shade and sun and homes for many different creatures. It's very likely that when sea cows and sea otters lived together in the North Pacific, it was an even richer tangle of life than it is today with only the otter.

Sea otters and sea cows lived together for millions of years, and the Commander Islands were where the relationship ended, thanks to the Russian fur traders who flocked there after the return of the

American Expedition. For the otters it was local extinction, but for the sea cows it was global and forever.

The first Russian fur venture reached the Commanders in 1743, only a year after Steller left Bering Island. Sea otter commerce was already thriving between Russia and China; Russian fur traders bartered the skins of Asian otters with the Chinese, who transformed them into luxury coats for their nobility, in exchange for tea and silk and other goods. In the business environment of eighteenth-century fur-trade globalism, it was not difficult to finance and outfit an otter-hunting expedition to the islands in the Pacific.

It was, however, much more of a challenge to get from Asia to Bering Island in the boat the first fur hunters used. A soldier named Basov, sponsored by a merchant from Moscow, organized the 1743 voyage. His crew lashed together a pile of wooden planks to make a flimsy, flat-bottomed boat the Russians called a *shitik*. A *shitik* was something Huckleberry Finn might take down the Mississippi, but it was completely out of its depth in the northern ocean, where an average storm could destroy it in a matter of minutes.

Basov was lucky. He came back alive from Bering Island four times, altogether with about 4,000 otter pelts to show for his trouble. From his peak kill of 1,600 otters in one year, the Bering Island otters died off quickly. In 1749, a party that wintered on the island killed a mere 47. By 1756, hunters couldn't find a single otter there.

Meanwhile, Basov and other Russians were busily wiping out the Commander Island sea cows. Dozens of Russian hunting parties after Basov sailed beyond the Commanders searching for new otter islands, but almost unanimously these expeditions stopped first on Bering or Copper Island to lay in stores of sea cow meat.

It was all over very shortly. The Copper Island sea cows were virtually wiped out by 1754, and by the early 1760s the log of a hunting party that wintered at Bering Island describes living on whale meat; their account says nothing about sea cows. Martin Sauer, the recording secretary of a Russian expedition to the American coast at the end of the eighteenth century, claimed that the last sea cow was killed in 1768.

Besides meat hunting, there was likely an ecological angle to the extinction of the Steller's sea cow. The Commander Island sea otters, their numbers severely reduced by the end of the 1740s, probably weren't eating enough urchins to keep the urchins' kelp grazing in check. As odd as it sounds, the local extinction of the sea otter probably put the muffin-size sea urchins and the bus-size sea cows on a collision course, in competition for the same food.

Even a little competition might have been too much for the sea cows; they were in marginal habitat anyway (as Steller had observed, they shrank to skin and bone in winter), and even a small loss of food may have doomed any animals that escaped the hunters. The report of Petr Yakovlev, a Russian mining engineer who wintered on Bering Island in 1754–55, backs this line of reasoning; Yakolev wrote that while he was on the island he saw neither sea cows nor any of the "sea cabbages" the sea cows ate.

So, only a short while after Steller had studied them, the sea cows were gone.

The extermination of the sea otters and sea cows of the Commander Islands was just the beginning. Steller, in a letter to his Russian Academy of Sciences colleague Johann Gmelin after the American Expedition, told Gmelin that a modest amount of otter hunting along the way could easily fund future scientific expeditions to America. But a flood of hunters, not just a handful of scientists, was on the way to the American sea otter grounds.

Russian hunters leapfrogged east through the Aleutians, wiping out the local otters as they went. By the 1780s they had virtually eradicated the otters of the chain. Then, in 1786, a Russian named Gerassim Pribylof discovered the great fur seal rookeries of the Bering Sea, on the specks of land now known as the Pribilof Islands. The Russians shifted their attention to the fur seals, taking two million Pribilof seals over the next thirty-plus years.

With some of the profits from the otters and seals of the Aleutians and Pribilofs, Russian merchants outfitted longer and longer voyages to find new sea-mammal hunting grounds along the American coast. One of them, led by a navigator named Potap Zaikov, anchored off Kayak Island in 1783, in the same anchorage where Steller and the *St. Peter* had come to rest in 1741. The Russians spotted two kayaks traveling by, and Zaikov sent a party after them. The kayakers saw the strangers coming toward them, beached their kayaks, and ran away into the forest, as the people apparently had run from Steller and the watering party from the *St. Peter* forty years earlier.

Zaikov's scouts landed on the island and explored the shoreline. They found a Native camp, but when they approached it, the Americans sprinted into the woods, leaving all their possessions behind. It took the Russians three weeks to find any Native people again. Zaikov's foreman, a fellow named Nagaev, managed to capture a girl and a boy, and brought them to the ship. They told Zaikov the name for their people, which Zaikov wrote down as *Chugach*—the name still in common use for their descendants today.

Nagaev set out to explore the mainland coast around Controller Bay. He met a band of Chugach who told him that Kayak Island was their name for the place where the Russians had first landed. They went there to gather food in the summer, they told him; their main village was two days' paddle to the west. Nagaev and his men then paddled northwest and came across "a good-sized river flowing into the sea, with several shallow mouths." The Russians had discovered the Copper River, south of today's Cordova, the great river that Steller had missed seeing.

Continuing west in his ship, Zaikov searched for a vast, protected bay rumored to be in the vicinity, one that might be full of otters. The Chugach, realizing that Zaikov wanted to poach otters from their hunting territory, fended off his demands for directions. The bay did exist; it is today's Prince William Sound.

Zaikov sent out a party in skin boats to search for the bay, and they passed the eastern gateway between two islands into the Sound without realizing it. Coming across a small Chugach village, they landed, stole food and otter furs, and took several women and children as hostages. A few hours later the village men, who had been away hunting, came back and found the village sacked. Searching the area by boat, they found the Russians camped not far away and waited for nightfall. In the summer semi-darkness the Chugach attacked, killing three Russians and wounding nine more. Most of the hostages escaped during the pandemonium.

Zaikov and his crew spent the winter on an island just outside the Sound, but with the Chugach as sworn enemies and no naturalist like

Steller on the crew to help them, they fell victim to starvation and scurvy. Zaikov left empty-handed in the spring, leaving half his crew behind, dead on Alaska's coast.

Zaikov's disaster hardly slowed the advance of the fur trade. The Russians opened their stay on each new section of the coast with a show of force to subdue the local people before they turned their sights on the local otters. Once established as the overlords of the realm, they ordered fleets of kayaks with Native hunters to join killing drives on the animals. The Russians set up a base of operations on Kodiak Island, where they adopted Kodiak-style double kayaks for the hunting fleets they commanded. The Kodiak kayaks were larger and heavier than the Aleut kayaks Steller described; with space for two paddlers, they better fit the demands of long-distance sea otter hunts. The Kodiak fleets grew to epic proportions, up to 800 boats and 1,600 hunters. In the Aleutians, the short, swift, light Aleut single kayaks began a slide toward extinction, along with the archipelago's sea otters and the traditional sea-hunting ways of the Aleut people.

The hunting fleets hugged the coastline, frequently dividing into smaller parties of five to fifteen kayaks each to scour the otters' favorite haunts—rocky, broken shorelines, rugged coastal points, offshore islands, muddy shellfish shallows, kelp forests, and the entrances to bays—approaching from downwind if they could. The kayaks spread out in a line, each pair of hunters staying in view of the kayaks to the right and left. They moved slowly ahead until one of the hunters spotted an otter; that hunter lifted his paddle as a signal to the next kayak, the next kayak did the same, and the message sped along the line until all the hunters knew an otter was close by.

When the otter sensed the kayaks, it dived. The closest hunter paddled to the spot where the otter had disappeared and floated there, paddle raised, while the others converged into a broad circle around him. An otter can stay submerged for three or four minutes, but eventually it had to surface; when it did, the hunters spotted it, converged on it again, and showered it with darts.

Frightened, maybe wounded, the otter dived again, and the kayakers once again formed their circle around the point where it had disappeared. Each time the otter surfaced, the scene repeated itself, and each time, the animal could hold its breath for a shorter period of time. Finally, wounded, breathless, and exhausted, the animal could dive no more, and the nearest kayaker finished it with a blow from a club or stone. The kayak fleets all but wiped out the otters wherever they went. Only a few—the luckiest, smartest, or swiftest—managed to avoid the hunters.

The Russians continued their otter sweep down the Alaska coastline, eventually extending their reach as far south as Baja California, where they poached otters in Spanish territory. The Spanish otters died quickly; the Russian ships easily outgunned any poorly armed Spanish soldiers who tried to stop the hunters. In 1825 an American ship's captain named Benjamin Morrell sailed past the Farallon Islands, 25 miles out in the Pacific from San Francisco Bay. "On these islands or keys," he wrote in his log, "I expected to find fur-seals; whereas I found them manned with Russians, standing ready with their rifles to shoot every seal or sea-otter that showed his head above water."

Sea lions were never a main quarry, but they did not completely escape the slaughter. The Russians and their Native hunters salted tons of sea lion meat and rendered countless barrels of the animals' oil for food. Sea lion skins, as in indigenous times, became the skins of hunting kayaks. Sea lion intestines became waterproof parkas, their stomachs waterproof containers, and their ligaments and tendons cord and line.

After the United States bought Alaska in 1867, American hunters took the field. In the 1870s and 1880s they killed more than 88,000 otters, wiping out the small population gains the animals had managed in the late stages of the Russian occupation, and pushing the animals back toward oblivion. By the turn of the twentieth century there weren't enough otters left to sustain the commerce in their furs, and the sea otter holocaust ended by default. The Russians and Americans had laid waste to the entire range of the sea otter, from Japan to Baja California, having killed, skinned, and sold somewhere between a half-million and a million animals.

The northern fur seals accounted for most of the profits after the Russians left Alaska. A wild, whiskey-fed slaughter of 300,000 fur seals on the Pribilofs inaugurated the American era. United States authorities finally arrived to protect the rookeries, and the hunters switched to hunting the seals in the ocean, a practice that was unregulated under international law.

Victoria, British Columbia, emerged as the epicenter of the pelagic sealing industry. Sealing schooners sailed out from Victoria in January, and the sealers hunted in seal-wintering waters well off the coasts of California and Oregon until spring. Then they turned north, shooting and harpooning the seals as they migrated along the British Columbia and Southeast Alaska coasts toward their northern rookeries. Sailing west along the Aleutians in June, the sealers then hunted in Russian waters until midsummer, when they entered the Bering Sea, and hunted near the Pribilofs until the seals left in the fall. Then, as winter closed in, the schooners sailed back to Victoria with great loads of furs.

The fur seal's undoing was its habit of feeding at night and sleeping during the day on the surface of the sea. Fur seals are more attuned to sound than smell in picking up danger signals, so hunters approached sleeping seals by quietly sailing or drifting their schooner's catcher boats from upwind rather than by rowing from downwind.

Hunting was especially good after a spell of stormy weather. During a storm the water is too rough for fur seals to sleep, so after a blow they sleep soundly and obliviously in the quiet water. The hunters coined names for seals sleeping in different positions: there were *dog-sleepers,* with their heads partially in the water, the easiest to bag; *jughandles,* seals sleeping on their sides with one fore-flipper over their heads; *breasters,* with crossed flippers resting on their chests; and *finners,* seals with one flipper extended to the side, a position that usually meant the seal was only half-asleep.

The fur seal population plummeted, and by the early 1900s it was so skimpy that some schooner captains took to raiding the rookeries, all of which by then were protected by armed guards. In 1906, on St. Paul Island in the Pribilofs, a spectacular series of shootouts between Aleut rookery guards and Japanese poachers finally spurred international talks on the future of the seals. With the animals hurtling toward extinction, the United States, Japan, Russia, and Great Britain (acting for Canada) signed the North Pacific Sealing Convention in 1911. It was the world's first international conservation agreement. The Convention banned pelagic sealing, allowed a limited seal hunt to continue on land, and prohibited sea otter hunting entirely.

So, by the early twentieth century, the scorecard for Steller's beasts of the sea read like this: the Steller's sea cow extinct; the sea otter almost exterminated; the northern fur seal hanging on despite a close brush with extinction; and the Steller sea lion wounded but holding its own.

The fur seal rookeries Steller studied in the Commander Islands were reduced to a sad fraction of what he had witnessed. By the 1940s the seals had rebounded to about a third of their pre-sealing numbers, but by then St. Paul in the Pribilofs was the only breeding island that supported anything like the masses of fur seals it had before commercial hunting.

The sea otters were in the worst shape of the survivors. When the Sealing Convention went into effect in 1911, there were only one to two thousand otters still alive, compared to the pre-Steller population of about three *hundred* thousand. The surviving otters were scattered along the northern coast among a dozen hidden refuges between the Kuril Islands and Prince William Sound; the southern sea otter survived in only one area: the rugged central California coast near Monterey. Every otter—*every single otter*—that had inhabited today's Baja California, the state of California except for the small central coast population, and all of Oregon, Washington, British Columbia, and Southeast Alaska was gone.

Otter population dynamics limited the speed of their recovery. Sea otters, like all marine mammals, have evolved a cluster of traits such as long lives, low mortality, late sexual maturity, birth of a small number of highly developed offspring, and a long "childhood" for the young. It's a strategy that keeps populations stable, and it works well for a generalist feeder like the sea otter in a rich environment like the North Pacific. (The contrasting life history is that of many of the fish in the otter's habitat: shorter lives, high mortality, early sexual maturity, large numbers of less-developed offspring, and little or no parental care—a strategy born of fluctuating conditions at their level of the food web, which can produce sharp spikes and dips in the populations of any one species.) But the sea otter model crashed in the face of an exotic predator: human fur hunters who destroyed the "low mortality" piece of the otter strategy. The otters would not rebuild quickly from a population collapse of the magnitude the fur hunters caused.

The recovering sea otters also had to overcome the disparity between their homebody habits and big gaps of open ocean between suitable places to live. Swimming between islands across stretches of deep water to find unoccupied habitat was a tough assignment; as Steller recorded, otters prefer to stay close to the territory where they were born, cannot swim as well as other sea mammals, and cannot feed in deep water.

But after 1911, left completely alone by fur hunters for the first time in 170 years, the few remaining sea otters slowly began to multiply and recolonize their old haunts. When their refuges grew too crowded for the food supply, some of them, most likely the younger ones, swam off in search of new coastal homes. The otter-colonists spread along the northern coast, island by island, bay by bay, point by point, finding a beautiful buffet of urchin, crab, and clam in every new place they claimed. Reports began to drift in from fishermen and biologists of sightings of small pods of otters in previously unoccupied territory far from larger known groups.

In the eastern Gulf of Alaska, it was not until the 1950s that fishermen and biologists began noticing otters in numbers again, as the descendants of the fur-trade survivors began a diaspora from a hidden refuge in Prince William Sound. There were sixty miles of open coastline between the Sound and Kayak Island, but the otters negotiated the distance. In 1956 Cordova fishermen reported seeing a group of fifty or sixty otters off Kayak Island, and in 1958 a roving biologist spotted forty in Controller Bay and twenty more off Wingham Island.

It was time for a solid survey of Kayak and Wingham Islands. In 1959 an aerial survey produced a count of 138 otters, which biologists extrapolated to an estimated population of 200 otters at Kayak and Wingham.

Extinguished from Kayak Island in the first sixty years after Steller's visit, exterminated from nearly all of the North Pacific during a century and a half of relentless hunting, the sea otter had ranged back into its old territories and resettled Steller's first landfall.

⁓——⁓——⁓

As the Kayak Island tide pools fill in again, Phil and I break away from the coast and hike back up to the light station, following a set of cedar steps to the station's best-preserved building. Originally the station's boathouse, now an overgrown cabin maintained by a lighthouse preservation group from Cordova, it serves as an overnight shelter for anyone who comes to the island and wants to get out of the weather.

Inside, the cabin is chock-full of bunks, chairs, a barrel stove, a government-gray metal desk, a kitchen table, sink, propane range, and two big sheet-metal lockers stuffed with dried and canned food. The cabin's best feature, other than its roof and walls, is the picture window behind the table, which looks out on the great mass of Pinnacle Rock and the wide ocean.

Leafing through the visitor log, I find Ullrich Wannhoff's entry. A German artist, naturalist, and museum curator from Dresden, Ullrich came to the island in August some years back to find and follow Steller's route. His sketches of the sea lion haulout and an eagle soaring over Pinnacle Rock liven up the log; it seems he had some time to fill, watching it rain from inside the cabin for day after day—"the rain no to end," he writes, with an apologetic footnote that "my english is very bad."

Cape St. Elias is no stranger to bad weather. The log book of the 1916 light station construction crew is especially instructive in that regard, going on in great detail about a dory bouncing down the beach in a gale-force wind, a storm tide ripping out the grade for the crew's cable tramway, rain-soaked landslide slurries tearing out retaining walls and sending a fuel tank sliding down to the beach, and a wind-tossed old-growth spruce flattening their blacksmith shop. A group of biologists, obviously aware of the Kayak Island climate, converted the boathouse into a field cabin in the mid-1990s, when they came to the island to study the Steller sea lions at the cape.

They were the second team of sea lion biologists to visit the island. In the late 1970s a pair of researchers named Walt Cunningham and Susan Stanford spent two seasons studying the sea lions, staying in the half-decayed lightkeeper's house up the hill from the present cabin. Cunningham and Stanford were two of only a handful of biologists since Georg Steller to spend uninterrupted time at a Steller sea lion haulout, and they discovered something significant and strange: the cape's female sea lions were bearing a surprisingly large number of premature, stillborn pups. The Kayak Island stillborns were one of the early signs of trouble for Alaska's sea lions, and in the 1990s, after counts had shown that their population was in free fall, the second group of researchers confirmed the sea lions' reproductive problems. Nosing around on the shelves by the kitchen table, I find, beneath a

Gary Larson castaways-on-a-desert-island cartoon tacked to the wall, a remnant of the later biologists' stay: a list of spontaneously aborted sea lion fetuses they collected at the cape.

The Steller sea lion population between Kayak Island and the Bering Sea, the so-called western stock of the species, fell from a few hundreds of thousands to a few tens of thousands, a drop of 80 percent, between roughly 1970 and 2000. The sharpest plunge took place in little more than a decade, from the late 1970s to the late 1980s. The western Steller sea lion was officially added to the list of endangered species in 1997.

Daylight is fading, and Phil and I decide to set up camp. The weather is cloudy-cool but dry, so we opt for an outdoor evening instead of bunking in the field station. After searching in vain for a tent site among the thickets of salmonberry and spruce seedlings above the rocky beach, we pitch our tent on a planked helicopter-landing pad below the lighthouse. We cook dinner as the sun dives toward the northwest; the low-growing copse of spruce at the edge of the helipad provides a welcome windbreak as an evening breeze begins to pick up. After dinner, we crawl into the tent, nestling into fluffy sleeping bags to the flute-solo songs of hermit thrushes in the brushy forest.

In the morning the air is still, and the sound of the gulls and sea lions carries easily to our camp. Behind us, somewhere in the maze of brush on the hillside, a Steller's jay is cranking out a few raucous notes. We pick some fat, orange-red salmonberries, that new and unknown species of "raspberry" Steller discovered here, pile them on top of our oatmeal, and eat a quick breakfast. Then we're off to explore the outer cape.

We cut across the log-strewn gravel bar that connects the main body of the island to Pinnacle Rock and the sea lions. The bar is high and dry, partially overgrown in cow-parsnip, angelica, yarrow, yellow paintbrush, and dune grass. Clumps of Pacific silverweed, a pioneering cinquefoil, spread bright-yellow, rose-shaped flowers and intensely green foliage over white and black rocks, looking like an untended rock garden. The whistling "three-blind-mice" song of golden-crowned sparrows and the buzzy trills of fox sparrows leak out of the angelica and cow-parsnip. Piles of mossy, bleached logs, tossed here by pre-1964 storms, raised by the earthquake, and now lying above the tangles of

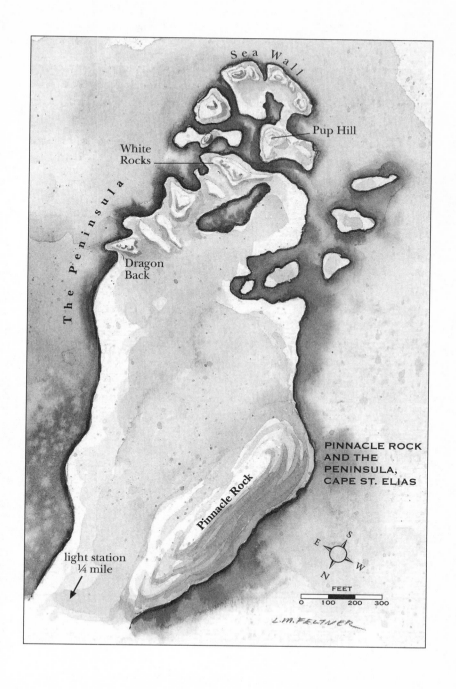

Sea Wall

Pup Hill

White
Rocks

The Peninsula

Dragon
Back

PINNACLE ROCK
AND THE
PENINSULA,
CAPE ST. ELIAS

Pinnacle Rock

light station
¼ mile

S
E   W
N

FEET
0   100   200   300

L.M. FELTNER

upland plants that have invaded the bar, are turning punky as they decompose. Before 1964, low tide was the only time this bar peeked out from under the sea.

Ahead, a jumble of blocky boulders flares out from the base of Pinnacle Rock, the remains of a quake-triggered rockfall that came off the pinnacle during the 1964 shake and killed an unlucky Coast Guard lightkeeper. To our left, east of Pinnacle Rock, is what's called "the Peninsula," the field of boulders and basins where the Steller sea lions congregate. The Peninsula is another new piece of land that emerged from the Pacific in 1964; now the sea floods it only during storms and extreme high tides.

Before the earthquake and the emergence of the Peninsula, Steller sea lions hauled out on the southwest toe of Pinnacle Rock in fairly big numbers. Pre-1964 Cape St. Elias may have been just a winter haulout, a place lions rested between feedings at sea. That would explain why Steller didn't record seeing any of the animals in the summer of 1741; there may not have been any here then. Now, though, the sea lions use the boulders of Pinnacle Rock in winter and the new land of the Peninsula in summer; altogether, the cape is a year-round sea lion haulout.

We skirt Pinnacle Rock, hop boulders to a vantage point a couple of hundred yards from the animals, and pull out the binoculars. There are about a hundred sea lions out on the Sea Wall, a massive chunk of rock that stands several feet above the sea and faces southeast into the open ocean. A narrow tidal cut slices through the wall, splitting the silhouettes of the lions into two throngs. Landward of the wall another rock rises above the sea; the map calls it Pup Hill, but the only two animals we can see look more like juveniles than pups.

Most of the sea lions at St. Elias are juvenile nonbreeders, but the few breeding bulls stand out in the crowd. Within the mass of creatures we easily spot a half-dozen, looking like a handful of bulked-up weightlifters in a crowd of gymnasts. The bulls bellow and growl constantly, lumbering around on their fore-flippers, guarding the perimeters of their hard-won territories. A dozen bachelor bulls are lying among the giant boulders of the White Rocks and the Dragon Back, north and landward of the Sea Wall.

We approach the bachelors warily, and Phil waves me over to one of the Dragon Back boulders. Behind it, one of the sea lions, eight or nine feet long, is lying asleep on his back, belly-up like a dog by a fireplace. His chest is torn, bloody, and raw, apparently hurt in a fight with another bull. We watch him for a moment, and then tiptoe away and leave him to his nap.

Like the fur seals and sea lions Steller observed on Bering Island, the Cape St. Elias bulls haul out on the breeding rocks in the spring—late April or early May here—and immediately begin sorting out territories. Most of the females of breeding age land in June and very shortly give birth to a single pup conceived during the previous year's mating season. A sea lion pup comes out of the womb about the size of a medium-sized dog—say, a border collie. The females then breed again within a few days of giving birth.

Now it's the first of July, and although we can't spot any pups, we can occasionally hear a youngster's sheep-bleat cry. This isn't a major sea lion rookery; biologists guess there are only about twenty pups a year born here these days. But, as is the case with the rest of the western stock's rookeries, there aren't as many sea lions at the cape as there used to be. This haulout's census numbers for June dropped from about 1,600 in the late 1970s to fewer than 400 in the late 1990s, mirroring the plunge in the overall population.

When Susan Stanford and Walt Cunningham were here, they did a thorough job of observing and recording sea lion life. They noted when the animals arrived, how they interacted, and, once spring and all the females had arrived, how their breeding routine went. They also watched for animals biologists had branded with their birth location when they were pups; it turned out that most of the cape's young sea lions had been born on the outer coast of Prince William Sound, on the rookeries of the Kenai Peninsula, and off Kodiak, as much as 400 miles away.

Stanford and Cunningham kept track of individual sea lions by naming them for physical characteristics; Fox Face, Mouse, Arrowhead, Topknot, Pink Pistol, and Killer Bull were the names they gave some of the animals they observed over time. Killer Bull had a huge scar on his hip and was missing his left fore-flipper; both injuries were almost certainly the result of an orca attack, orcas being the only common Steller sea lion predator besides humans.

Susan and Walt kept track of maternal behavior, and they witnessed a few young sea lion dramas. They watched a small, abandoned yearling for a week at Pinnacle Rock as it followed and tried to approach a lactating female without a pup. Finally the female let the yearling nurse, and eventually she let it sleep on top of her back. Another abandoned pup stationed itself behind a nursing mother and her pup, waited until the other pup was suckling, and grabbed a quick squirt of milk from another nipple. When the adult female looked around, the abandoned pup quickly let go of the nipple, lay down, and tried its best to look nonchalant.

One clear message emerges from Stanford and Cunningham's reports: only a very few of the animals they studied survived the journey from fetus to juvenile sea lion. They found twenty-two aborted fetuses that winter, discovering seven of them after a howling March storm that blew in with winds of 50 knots. There were thirty live births that year; of those newborns, only fourteen were still alive by the end of June. In the first week of July another storm roared in, and for five days the wind shrieked again at more than 50 knots, sending waves crashing over the haulout rocks. After the storm was over, only three pups were still alive out of fifty-two known pregnancies that spring.

The biologists weren't on the haulout rocks during the storm, but from earlier observations and the evidence they found after it had passed, they were able to piece together the story of what happened to the sea lion pups. When sea waves swamped the rocks, the sea lions took to the water. In the chaos of abandoning the haulout, adults trampled several pups. Some of the pups apparently made it into the sea but drowned. After the storm, a few of the surviving pups swam around in front of the rocks, apparently looking for their mothers, and they may or may not have found them. One or more of the survivors may have wedged themselves into crevices and hung on while wave after wave broke over them; Cunningham and Stanford had seen two pups lodge themselves among the rocks that way when an earlier high tide had inundated the haulout.

It was serious pup mortality: only 6 percent of the developed fetuses from that spring survived to become two-month-old pups. Biologists consider a 50 percent death rate among young sea lions over the first three years of life to be roughly average mortality, so it was clear that the cape's sea lions could not sustain their population if that year was at all representative.

When the second team of biologists came to Kayak Island in the 1990s, they found the same pattern of premature pupping that Stanford and Cunningham had recorded. They took the remains of twenty-three fetuses off the island for examination at a pathology lab. The lab found no toxins, no disease, no single obvious clue that might explain why they were dying. Kayak Island science alone was not going to solve the biological mystery of the plunging sea lion population.

Rookeries all across the range of the western Steller sea lion were edging toward the deserted and forlorn. For example, on Chowiet Island in the Semidis, the island group where Steller recorded a glut of sea mammals in 1741, the number of pups shrank from 5,500 in 1979 to 234 two decades later. And the sea lion crash was not the only biological mystery in the northern Pacific: populations of harbor seals, sea otters, northern fur seals, and some seabirds were falling as well. In other parts of the world, in less pristine oceans, marine mammal populations were stable or increasing, but signs of serious decline were popping up all over the North Pacific.

Phil and I hear a motor offshore, and in a few minutes we spot a gillnet fishing boat gliding slowly by, just off the Sea Wall. The gillnetter is too close to the sea lion haulout; the colony stirs and a general panic ensues. The sea lions go into a frenzy of caterwauling, a blended chorus of males and females of all ages, revving up like a regiment of small-horsepower outboards dueling the gillnetter. A few of the smaller lions take to the water, and soon it's a movement. Within a few seconds, most of the colony is in the sea. The gillnetter's captain has just violated the laws that protect endangered species and marine mammals, but there is no one out here to enforce them.

We break off from the sea lion haulout and continue around the outside of Pinnacle Rock. Half a dozen harlequin ducks float offshore, and a lone black cormorant sits on an offshore rock, staring out to sea. We circle the pinnacle, maneuvering over and around the enormous earthquake boulders that fan out from the base of the cliff. Crossing the bar back toward the light station, we retreat to our helipad campsite, where we dig into lunch. Sea lion life, we can hear and see from where we sit, has returned to normal on the outer cape, or at least as normal as it can be with only a quarter of the animals the cape used to support.

———— ᴧ ————

We don't know as much as we might think about the life of the oceans. More than 250 years after Steller's visit to the North American coast, the "vast ocean" he described as full of "unknown creatures" is still yielding marine animals new to science. In 2005, for example, scientists identified seventy-eight new species of marine creatures, including a ten-foot jellyfish in arctic waters. The creatures that spend their lives beneath the surface of the sea just don't present themselves easily to biologists, and even the lives of pinnipeds like the Steller sea lion are still a partial mystery, given that they spend only part of their time on land. Although biologists have new tools like telemetry to track sea lions in the ocean, the best way to learn about them, just as in Steller's day, is to study them on their rookeries and haulouts.

So, over several summers in the early 1990s, a small army of marine biologists fanned out to the remote rookeries and haulouts of the western stock of Steller sea lions, looking for clues to what was going wrong for the animals. The leading hypothesis was that something had happened to their prey, that the apex-predator sea lions were the victims of a "bottom-up" disruption in the food web.

The method of choice was collecting scat; digging through sea lion dung was a good way to find out what the animals were eating. (Steller, who was something of a scatologist himself, would surely find some dry humor in the fact that the classic biological odysseys of his day were now devolving into scat-sampling forays.) There was a limited but valuable baseline for comparison. In the 1960s and early 1970s, in the years leading up to the sea lion decline, marine scientists had occasionally shot and dissected sea lions, and their descriptions of the animals' stomach contents provided a snapshot of the pre-decline diet.

The results were clear and compelling. Before the decline, almost anything of the fish, squid, or octopus persuasion could end up in a sea lion's stomach. They ate salmon, groundfish (fish that live on or near the bottom of the sea, such as pollock, cod, mackerel, flounder, and halibut), and small, fatty, smeltlike schooling fish such as herring, capelin, eulachon, sandlance, and lanternfish, all species known for their extremely high oil content.

In the 1990s, however, the average western sea lion diet was far less diverse. In most regions, groundfish made up most of the diet; because these fish have a much lower fat content than the oily schooling fish, the sea lion diet was far less "calorie-dense" than before. However, in the few places where the population had stabilized, Steller sea lions were finding and eating a more diverse diet with at least small amounts of high-fat fish, a pattern much closer to the pre-decline diet. And the diet of these few remaining stable groups was also similar to the diet of the eastern stock of sea lions in Southeast Alaska, which, in contrast to the western stock, was holding at healthy population levels.

It made sense that a lack of the right food (or, perhaps, of the right food at the right time) was central to the decline. The Steller sea lion's cold-water survival plan, worked out over evolutionary time, relies on a high-energy, heat-producing metabolism. The animals have little fur, and for marine mammals they are very lean. As it was for the indigenous people of the Aleutian Islands—the people who identified so strongly with sea lions—their central survival challenge is procuring fat for calories. In the Aleuts' case, whale and seal oil provided the crucial fat and calories; for Steller sea lions, the fatty, schooling fish seemed to be a key. However, the high-fat fish had more or less dropped out of their food universe.

It was this reduced food energy in the sea lion diet that was likely behind the high miscarriage rates at Cape St. Elias and elsewhere. If a pregnant sea lion can't find enough of the right food to sustain a pup, she will, physiologically speaking, give it up before bearing the pup normally and going ahead with lactation, which is the most energy-intensive part of the reproductive cycle. And even after a successful birth, newborn sea lions are vulnerable; they come into the world with only a very thin layer of fat and have to build up their reserves quickly. Without good fish-food nearby, their mothers can't provide them the rich and plentiful milk they need. In addition, after weaning, young sea lions are not proficient at diving and foraging, and they can get into trouble if they aren't able to find good sources of food near the rookeries.

The oily fish that Steller sea lions need were not just missing from the sea lion diet; biologists couldn't find them anywhere. The

1970–1990 population curves for sea lions and the high-fat, school-ing fish in the eastern Bering Sea and the Gulf of Alaska are practi-cally identical: a slight down-slope early in the 1970s, a plunge off a statistical cliff in the late 1970s and through the 1980s, and then back to a gentler decline after about 1990.

Both declines were only part of a greater sea change, a "regime shift" of climate, ocean conditions, and marine species. From the Ber-ing Sea to Prince William Sound, a revolution had come to the food web of the northern seas: the old, diverse assembly of schooling fish, shrimp and crab, and pollock, cod, and other groundfish had morphed into something closer to a near-monoculture of groundfish. Ocean regime shifts were thought to be regular occurrences, but the scale of the shift of the 1970s and 1980s was so dramatic that it raised the question of whether it was outside the norm.

In 1997—coincidentally, the same year the sea lion scat study was published—strong, warm El Niño conditions pushed north into the Gulf of Alaska, the Aleutians, and the Bering Sea. The surface of the eastern Bering Sea turned a milky blue-green, a startling contrast to the usual deep blue, and a color change that was stark and obvious in satellite photos shot from miles above the earth. The milky color was the reflection of sunlight from the scales of alien plankton, calcite scales that piled up on the sea surface and reflected incoming sunlight like billions of tiny mirrors. It was a great bloom of a type of plankton called *coccolithophores,* single-celled creatures that are common in tem-perate seas farther south. Nothing in the sediment record on the bot-tom of the Bering Sea, however, showed that they had ever inhabited northern waters in anything like the densities of 1997.

The guilty party was the warm, peaceful sea that summer. It was a freak, a far cry from the usual summer pattern. Storm winds normally stir up the water column, repeatedly pulling up nutrients from below, feeding multiple blooms of more nutritious plankton, and supporting one of the earth's most productive food webs. The Bering Sea in 1997 was more like a desert. Along with the strange plankton bloom, sea-birds died off in massive numbers and the salmon runs of the Yukon, that great Bering Sea–draining river, essentially disappeared.

The striking changes in the Bering Sea were clearly in line with predictions of how global warming would work its way through the system. Earlier, in the late 1970s and early 1980s, striking warming shifts had occurred in two other large-scale climate patterns in addition to the well-known El Niño cycle: the Pacific Decadal Oscillation, which involves the strength of the winter low pressure center in the Aleutian Islands, and the Arctic Oscillation, which controls sea ice conditions and winter temperatures in the Northern Hemisphere. Coinciding with these changes, temperatures soared, up to 10° F warmer on average in recent winters, putting glaciers on the run and melting sea ice and permafrost at barely believable rates.

Scientists implicated global warming in species shifts and declines of all kinds, from the poles to the tropics, and Steller sea lions were certainly not immune. The warming likely reached them by mutating the flow of ocean currents and the temperature, depth, and location of eddies, pools, and strata of water where nutrients, plankton, and fish larvae come together.

It was disaster for the fatty schooling fish and the creatures that subsisted on them. First, warmer water meant earlier plankton blooms, coinciding with the hatch of walleye pollock (the nondescript, big-eyed fish of fishburger fame); the earlier blooms favored pollock over the fatty, schooling fishes. Second, adult pollock prey on the high-fat fish, and the new mobs of pollock probably ate deeply into their populations. Third, the remaining oily fish seemed to have moved offshore and deeper in the water column to find the cooler temperatures they need, putting them out of reach of the rookery-bound sea lions.

And there was at least one additional factor at work: some biologists maintained that people had killed so many Steller sea lions in the years before the regime shift that the species was primed for a steep plunge when the ocean and prey-fish revolution began. Commercial fishermen shot an unknown but probably very large number because the animals sometime foul fishing gear and take some of the targeted fish. (Until 1990 it was legal to kill Steller sea lions at will.) The military in Kodiak, in one stark example, used to strafe the archipelago's sea lion haulouts before salmon season opened. Thousands more animals died tangled in the trawl nets and gill nets, some of them thirty miles long, deployed from mid-twentieth-century commercial fishing vessels. There were also large legal harvests in the 1960s and early 1970s for sea lion skins and for meat for fox and mink farms—kills that seriously cut into the numbers of animals on some important rookeries.

If there was any doubt that the plunge in the western Steller sea lion population was beyond a natural level of variation, there was the evidence of the sea lions themselves. As a marine mammal, a species with low rates of reproduction and population growth, one that does well only in a relatively rich and constant environment, they are not equipped to rebound quickly from big population drops like those of the late twentieth century. If sea lions had been forced to deal with recurrent, sharp declines over the course of their evolution, they would have evolved a very different reproductive strategy.

Compare, for example, the sea lion strategy with that of the Canada lynx, a northern cat whose populations rise and fall abruptly with swings in populations of its main prey, the snowshoe hare. Lynx take as little as a quarter of the time sea lions take to reach reproductive maturity, they gestate their young a fifth as long, and they wean them far more quickly. Lynx bear litters of one to eight kittens, varying with prey abundance—an average of four or five when hares are abundant, and two or three when they're scarce—while sea lion females essentially always bear a maximum of one pup per year. The lynx is hard-wired to bounce back quickly from large population losses, but Steller sea lions are not; their reproductive setup is good evidence that they did not evolve in a yo-yo environment.

For Steller sea lions, it was a big change in one direction only—down—and any significant bounce back up to their former abundance would take a long time to develop, if it ever did. The prey-fish upheaval, it turned out, was also behind many of the seabird losses. But the sea otter population in western Alaska, which had been plunging since the early 1990s, showed a different pattern. Unlike the decline of sea lions and seabirds, there was no evidence that the otters' decline was related to the climate and ocean regime shift or to any direct interference by *Homo sapiens*. There had to be more to the story of what was happening to Steller's beasts of the sea.

After two nights at Cape St. Elias, Phil and I pack up and hike north along Kayak Island's eastern shoreline. We settle into an ambling pace for the next two days, sinking into the reverie of a twenty-mile backpack toward the north cape of the island. The hike blends into a swirl of images: the tide spreading through cuts in the reef-rock, rising slowly over the flat-as-Iowa tidal shelf like water in a bathtub; scurries of mink tracks and plodding bear prints; skittering sandpipers and plovers; flights of wheeling oystercatchers; and white, bleached tree skeletons at the beach's upper edge, backed by an unbroken, deep-green band of alder. We lounge by driftwood campfires on the shaly beach, climb through one pick-up-sticks logjam after another, wade small creeks and tide channels, and pack up our wet, sandy tent as a fine mist settles over the island.

The only thing that cuts through the island reverie is the beach detritus. We hike past tons of plywood, styrofoam, bottles, buckets, bundles of wire, fishing nets, red plastic hard hats, plastic *everything*, all of it dumped into the ocean by humanity and then regurgitated onto this catch-beach by the Alaska Current. The terra firma of Kayak Island is wild and intact enough, but there's just no escape from the junk the sea is vomiting up onto the beach.

We reach the north end of the island, leave the catch-beach and the detritus behind, and angle across the broad, open marine terrace that forms the northern cape. Miles of beach-strawberry tendrils stretch across the small sand hummocks of the terrace, and all the thin, ground-hugging stems are loaded with tiny, sweet fruit. We have our reward for the hike up the east side of the island.

Satiated on the juicy berries, we round a basalt headland beyond the strawberry terrace and get our first glimpse of the new country on the west side of the island. Wingham Island rises across Kayak Entrance to the west, and the debris-free beaches of Kayak Island's west coast stretch off to the south toward Cape St. Peter. A few yards down the beach we hike under a rock ledge, unaware that we're intruding on a pair of nesting peregrine falcons above us. One of the falcons breaks into a scream from the nest, and then the second takes up the screeching. Both falcons fly off the nest, continuing to shriek at us as we hurry around the next point to get out of their disturbance zone. And there we meet two bald eagles perched in the nearest spruce tree, who chitter nervously at us from atop a nest nearly the size of a small townhouse.

Turning the corner, we've crossed a boundary into a wilder landscape, the domain of falcons and eagles—a welcome change from the washed-up styrofoam and plastic of the catch-beach. With a cool salt breeze in our faces, we hike south along the narrow, sloping strand of beach. In another hour we reach an expansive tidal flat at low tide. The tide-flat mud, covered with a thin film of water, is pleasingly solid under our rubber boots as we tramp toward a pretty, symmetrical bell-curve of a hill that rises behind the forested spit ahead of us.

We're in serious Steller country now. The spit ahead is called Campsite Spit, and the landward edge of the spit is the site of the Chugach campfire Steller saw. The symmetrical green hill is Steller's Hill, where he was standing when he spotted the campfire. It's easy now to imagine the *St. Peter* anchored offshore, out between Campsite Spit and Wingham Island, and a young naturalist standing at the rail, wild with the anticipation of exploring a new world.

After checking the tide tables, we decide to camp on a dry rise a few feet higher than the soppy meadow that lies just above the tide flat. It's a camp with a view, facing Steller's Hill and the lush slopes that rise up to the summit of the island; this is a view, I think, that I'll remember the rest of my life. Then immediate reality reasserts itself in the form of tiny black flies swarming in our faces. The flies convince us to call it a day, and we dive into the tent well before dark, to the loud wing-winnowing of a late-breeding snipe.

We wake up to another wet dawn, but this time the low clouds, drifting fog, and gray drizzle are telegraphing that a real storm is on the way. The halcyon hiking days of light, friendly, misty sprinkles are about to be history; it's time to get on to Cape St. Peter and set up a dry base camp for our last few days on the island.

We cut straight across Campsite Spit, slipping through an outer band of alders into a dark spruce forest. Inside, the forest floor is dry beneath the canopy of big trees, and the soft bed of thick moss underfoot is nothing short of luxury for our feet. As we near the creek on the south side of the spit, the deep woods yield to thickets of alder, salmonberry, and elderberry. The good going of the forest turns into a slow brush-thrash, and the raindrops on the leaves and stems of the plants soak through our raingear and wet us to the skin. Finally we push through a last line of alders and emerge from the forest onto a "fossil beach" set well back from the sea—a beach that was active in the past when the sea was higher relative to the island. We curl around the back of the old beach until we spy, off in the brush, a large cave eroded out of a wall of conglomerate rock, measuring roughly fifty feet wide, deep, and high.

Seacave Rock, it's called, and according to most people who have tried to reconstruct Steller's route on the island, this was his turnaround point, the northernmost spot he reached on his Kayak Island hike. An etched steel plaque mounted on the rock wall outside the cave commemorates the 250th anniversary of Steller's landing and tells us that it was put here during a "Joint Russian-Alaskan Celebration" back in 1991. Exceedingly strange, we find it, to come across a museum-quality plaque on a wall of rock on this lonely seashore.

If Seacave Rock really was Steller's turnaround point, it was lapped by high tides when he was here, according to his description. These days, however, the cave is removed from the ocean by a good five hundred feet and three fossil beach lines. Bering River silt has been building land gradually out into the sea over the centuries, and the ten-foot rise during the 1964 earthquake must have added some acceleration to the build-out of the land. Relative sea level here, geologists say, is about the same now as it was in Steller's day. The pattern for many centuries has been slow subsidence, then a cataclysmic rise in a 1964-like earthquake, followed again by slow subsidence. The '64 quake reversed in an instant the accumulated sinking of several hundred years.

We move along down the beach and reach the deep cut of Fault Creek, the island's longest stream. Peering over the sand berm that divides the sea from the mouth of the creek, we spot four river otters lounging in and around a deep, green pool of fresh water. Two are in the pool, and two are resting on a fallen log angling into the water from the south bank. At first all four freeze when they sense us, but then two swim toward us for a better look. We must not be that interesting; in less than a minute, the otters abruptly end the interview, swim across the pond, climb onto the north bank, and scuttle, otter style, into the forest.

The heavy mist lifts enough for us to catch our first look at Cape St. Peter in the distance, still about two miles away, and Phil spots our first sea otter offshore. South of Fault Creek, we hike beneath the 500-foot cliff face that rises above the beach. The wind has come up, and the rain, falling heavily now, is sending torrents of water down fissures in the cliff rock. The torrents settle into the talus slope at the toe of the cliff, saturating it so completely that globs of talus frequently break away and flow down to the beach like lava from a volcano. Clusters of talus and small rocks slough off the cliffs, and every few minutes a softball-size chunk bounces down onto the beach.

This is a real Pacific storm, and Phil and I are thoroughly wet and ready to find some shelter by the time we get to the south side of Cape St. Peter an hour or so later. We heave off our packs and search for a protected spot to rig up a nylon sanctuary from the storm. After combing the territory between the beach and the brushy woods, we pick a spot against the alders and not far from the creek where the *St. Peter*'s water carriers filled the ship's barrels.

We happily find and retrieve the cache we left in the forest, and then scavenge some flotsam plywood and camp pads from the beach. Seems we're back in a minor beach-accumulation zone; an eddy in the coastal current forms behind the island, like an eddy behind a boulder in a river, depositing some floating debris here, though only a tiny fraction of the garbage the east side of the island collects.

This time we don't complain about a little drift plywood. We put two sheets down on the thoroughly soaked grass and then erect the tent on one and rig up a tarp-covered living room/kitchen on the other. The beach-scavenged camp pads become our living room sofa under the tarp. We set up a second tarp over the tent, double-waterproofing our sleeping quarters against the driving rain, which is blasting in more violently from the north as the afternoon wears on. The alders behind us form a solid wall of protection against the storm.

Time to relax. Our nylon cocoon envelops us, our mugs are full of hot tea, and all is cozy inside as the storm blows wildly outside. Things here are much more comfortable than Steller's sandy, sail-covered pit must have been, but I doubt that spending a winter like this would be much fun. A few millimeters of nylon is very little margin against the pulsing, opaque waves of rain that are now obscuring the green mountainside we could still make out only a few minutes ago. At this moment, Kayak Island seems very wild and very much removed from the human universe, even from the nearby, benign world of Cordova.

As we watch the storm, the contrast between the two sides of the island comes to mind. Schizophrenic is the word—the east side with its collection of human garbage from the sea, the west with its anthology of falcons, eagles, and otters. And, I'm thinking, the disconnect between the two sides of the island is a metaphor for a much larger phenomenon. Kayak Island is on the cusp between two worlds, situated as it is neatly halfway between the heart of one of the world's largest protected wilderness areas—a mosaic of U.S. and Canadian parks and refuges in the coastal mountains bigger than Indiana—and Bligh Reef, the scene of that archetypal marine disaster, the grounding of the *Exxon Valdez*. We've learned to permanently protect landscapes, the lesson seems to be, but we've done nothing comparable in conservation for the oceans, their productivity, or their webs of life.

Consider what was happening in 1964, the year the U.S. Congress passed the Wilderness Act, creating large tracts of protected land and putting them off limits to logging, mining, roads, and motors. During that year of breakthroughs in land protection, the creatures of the North Pacific were being hit harder than at any other time since humans came to this corner of the world.

The middle 1960s was roughly the midpoint of a post–World War II industrial whaling and fishing boom in the North Pacific. Over a period of about twenty-five years from the 1950s to the 1970s, Japanese and Russian whalers took several hundred thousand whales—sperm whales, blues, fins, and seis—with the peak year of the sperm whale kill falling in 1964, the year of the Wilderness Act, when whalers took 30,000 of the great whales. Over the entire bonanza whaling era, whalers may have torn 80 percent or more of the whale biomass out of the North Pacific.

In roughly the same period trawl, seine, and gillnet fishing also claimed massive amounts of the ocean's food web. The fisheries of the era targeted and commercially extinguished, one by one, a number of species, some of which have never completely recovered, such as Pacific ocean perch, yellowfin sole, herring, sablefish, and several species of shrimp and crab. The fishermen of those days took two to three times the biomass of today's North Pacific fisheries (which are huge themselves and certainly hurt marine mammals to some degree). Adding to the bonanza-fishing slaughter was the tremendous "bycatch"—millions of tons of non-target fish and other creatures hauled up and killed in the nets and then dumped overboard.

Altogether, the whaling and fishing of the "take-and-waste" era added up to ocean carnage on a level never seen before or since. And, in the same way sea otter hunting during the fur-trade era cleared the way for urchins to chew down coastal kelp forests, the massive whale and fish removal was sure to have altered the ocean's web of life.

———

At Adak Island in the Aleutians, where Aleksei Chirikov traded Russian knives for Aleut skins of water on the American Expedition, a team of biologists found a clue that solved the case of the disappearing sea otters. During field work in the mid-1990s, they discovered an interesting blip in the otherwise bleak picture of sea otter die-offs throughout the archipelago: although the otters of the outer Adak coast were practically gone, a back bay called Clam Lagoon still had a healthy troop of the animals.

Orcas immediately came to the researchers' minds. Clam Lagoon is the only bay in the area shallow enough to prevent orcas from entering, it was the only place otters were still thriving, and there were no other differences between the bay and the outer coast that could explain the different fates of the resident otters. Nine recent reports of orcas taking otters also had to be considered; they were significant because, before the early 1990s, there were as many recorded sightings of orcas taking moose as there were of orcas taking otters—one sighting each.

Doing the math, the researchers concluded that a single pod of orcas working alone, or a small shift in the regional diet of orcas generally, was enough to account for the entire Aleutian sea otter loss. There was no workable, alternative explanation; the surviving otters were healthy, and there was no evidence of any food problem. Science convicted the orcas; sea otters had a top-down, predator problem, not a bottom-up prey problem like the one apparently behind much of the decline of western Steller sea lions.

But why were orcas hunting otters? The low-fat, furry otters have very little to offer an orca in food value; the tag line for the orca theory of the otters' disappearance was "otters as popcorn," because it would take a lot of otters to make a real meal for such a huge predator. Apparently the depletion of the great whales during the whaling free-for-all of the 1950s–1970s deprived the orcas of their preferred prey, eventually forcing at least some orcas into hunting otters.

Before industrial whaling, the reasoning went, the pods of orcas that feed on marine mammals (other pods feed exclusively on fish) were primarily whale predators (the obsolete name "killer whales" came from the accounts of early whalers, who called orcas "whale killers"). The life histories of some of the great whales are consistent with this interpretation: for example, eastern Pacific gray whales stage epic migrations to shallow bays on the coast of Baja California for calving, and bowhead whales migrate from the rich environs of the Bering Sea to the more barren waters of the Beaufort Sea to bear and raise their young; in both cases, marine scientists think the major benefit of these otherwise "irrational" migrations is avoiding orca predation on the vulnerable calves soon after birth.

So, the theory goes, after whalers whisked away 80 percent or more of their usual food, orcas still had to eat, and with harbor seals and sea lions in decline as well, they were forced to feed on the popcorn-like otters. Then the top-down, orca-predation school of thought focused on the sea lion decline: could orcas be behind that as well? The extended theory held that, after the loss of the great whales, the orcas ate their way through the food web, first preying on harbor seals and sea lions, and when there were no longer enough pinnipeds to eat, they (or some of them) shifted to sea otters. Not everyone agreed with the extended theory, but at the very least orca predation likely played a role in the sea lion decline and kept a lid on the much-diminished population in the 1990s.

Industrial whalers and fishermen of the bonanza era played one more part in the ocean revolution, this one a bottom-up change: they removed so many plankton-eaters (whales, shrimp, crab, herring, and other species) that they opened a "free-food" niche for pollock and other groundfish, which rushed into the breach like seawater into the hole in the *Titanic*. Fishing and whaling probably shoved the food web in the direction of a groundfish takeover, and the climate and ocean regime shift gave it the final push.

Western Alaska's sea otters had one major factor, hungry orcas, working against them, but the western Steller sea lions were not even that lucky. They were being sandwiched from the bottom up, through a prey-fish revolution, and from the top down, through predation. Warming seas, whaling, and fisheries depleted their food supply; gunmen shot them; fishing nets strangled them; and orcas, denied their preferred whale prey, ate them.

In the end, the ocean upheaval that has decimated sea lions, sea otters, and probably northern fur seals as well—Steller's surviving beasts of the sea—is being driven almost entirely by a keystone species from sea mammal hell: humanity.

A cold, steady rain is sheeting across Cape St. Peter from the north. As we look out from under our tarp-covered refuge, guzzling early morning cups of coffee, Phil says that this looks like one of those days when it's really good not to have to go anywhere. It is definitely nasty out, but with our camp nestled into a thick fort of young alders, we are thankfully missing out on the worst of the storm.

Predicting that much tea and coffee will be consumed today, we decide we need more water. I pull on my soggy raingear and step outside, taking a moment to tighten the lines that hold our tarps in place, and then slog out to Steller's watering creek to fill our cooking pots and water bag. As I drop to my knees to reach the water, I see fresh bear prints, *large* bear prints, apparently of a big male, in the sand along the creek bottom. The tracks lead out of the forest and down the creek bed to the tide line, the tracks of a bruin that strolled by our camp in the night on his way to the beach.

Water fetched and tea made, we settle into a lazy routine of reading and writing for the morning. Eventually, after lunch, we decide the storm is not planning to let up today. So, accepting getting wet as a fact of life, we pile on our raingear and rubber boots and set off to explore the route Steller walked.

It took earlier investigators quite a bit of trial and error to figure out Steller's exact route of travel. Recent interpretations favor the stretch of coast from the creek near our camp north to Seacave Rock, and that seems to be the logical choice, given the evidence in Steller's diary and the ship's log and the topography of the island. That will be our route today, more or less retracing the steps of our hike here from the north end of the island, but with more time for exploring Steller's track. The theme for the hike, for me, is to check out what Steller's observations about the indigenous people of the coast may be able to tell us today.

Steller never actually met any of the Chugach people on the island, but he found enough clues here to put together a good picture of how they lived. He found the first of those clues only about a half-mile from our camp, and it takes us only a few minutes to find the approximate spot along a flat, grass-backed beach on the outer cape. Somewhere within a small radius of where we stop to take in the scene, Steller found the remains of a Chugach cookout: a dying campfire, a log trough full of water, several large stones, a scattering of animal bones, a small pile of mussel shells, and a few scraps of dried red salmon. There were still live coals in the campfire, so the people must have left the scene and hidden in the forest only minutes before—probably when they had seen the longboat approaching the island.

Steller guessed, apparently correctly, that a Chugach cook had cut the meat off the bones at the site and boiled the meat in the trough by tossing in hot stones heated in the campfire. He also guessed that they were reindeer bones, but it's most likely that they were the bones of mountain goats. Goats were the only ungulates anywhere in the vicinity in those days, and from other accounts we know the Chugach hunted them. There are no goats on the island today, but there are plenty in the Don Miller Hills on the mainland nearby; goats are good swimmers, so it is possible that they inhabited the island in Steller's day. If the animal remains at the Chugach camp were mountain goats from the island, the hunters were certainly great outdoorsmen; it's a long, hard hump, nearly straight up through practically impenetrable brush, just to get into goat country on Kayak Island.

The mussels were certainly from the island; the Chugach campsite is just a short stroll from a stretch of coast with an expanse of mussel beds along it today. The salmon, though, probably came from the mainland, most likely from one of the salmon rivers of Controller Bay. The food served at this Chugach meal, then, was a combination of mainland and island food.

Our next stop is Pyramid Creek, the creek in the bight north of

Cape St. Peter. Pyramid is about the right distance from the watering creek to be the place where Steller and Lepekhin followed a path into the forest and found the underground cache. The cache was full of dried salmon, cow-parsnip, seaweed, finely made arrows, and rolls of the inner bark of Sitka spruce. The Chugach made a habit of peeling spruce trees; they ate the inner bark and used the outer bark as roofing for their plank houses and smokehouses, and for covering storage cellars like the one Steller found.

Pyramid Creek is the only place on this part of the island where the two Europeans could have walked around for a half-hour, as Steller says they did in his journal, and ended up in an area flat enough for a large Chugach cache. Another piece of evidence pointing to Pyramid Creek as the site of the cache is the protected bay at the mouth of the creek, a beach where the Chugach could have landed, unloaded their skin boats, and set up camp in almost any weather.

We follow the twisting little creek upstream, painfully slowly. The brushy understory of the forest is so thick that a half-hour's thrashing would not get anybody very far into the interior of the island. Too bad, I think, that there's no Chugach trail along the creek anymore. After several minutes of the venerable Alaska sport of brush bashing, we begin to spot, here and there, a few very old spruce trees with large, partially healed-over cuts on their trunks. In archaeology-speak, these are "culturally modified" trees, which people of long ago partially stripped of their bark.

The more we look, the more peeled trees we see. On a low rise above the creek, we find at least a dozen, and more scarred spruces seem to march off into the brushy distance of the valley. Steller says in his journal that he found peeled trees near the underground cache, and these trees, according to a party of historians who cored some of them several years back, are old enough to be the same trees Steller saw. They could also have been the source of the rolls of bark Steller found in the Chugach cache.

From Pyramid Creek, we hike north past the sloughing sea cliffs and Fault Creek, home of river otters, to Seacave Rock. Climbing the slope above the cave, we find, as Steller did, that it would be tough to descend the north side. The grove of trees at the base of Campsite Spit, just visible from a place or two above Seacave Rock, would work for the place where Steller saw the Chugach campfire from his lookout on Steller's Hill. He describes the spot as a "knoll," and although it isn't actually much of a knoll, the location is right, and it could have looked elevated from above. Out beyond the spit we can see Wingham Island, where Khitrovo found a Chugach plank house and camp and in it a whetstone showing traces of copper from sharpening copper blades.

By now our dry camp at Cape St. Peter is calling; we beat a retreat from the steady rain and the wet brush back in the direction of our tarp-covered refuge. Once back in camp, with dry clothes on and nursing cups of hot tea, we settle into our camp-pad couch with books and notebooks.

Steller's journal and Khitrovo's brief report about his trip to Wingham Island are two of only a handful of accounts written at first contact about how the Chugach lived before Europeans arrived in force and changed everything. Combining these scanty, contact-era accounts with the Chugach's own oral traditions and some archaeological evidence and natural history, though, yields a coherent picture of the people Steller came so close to meeting on Kayak Island.

They did not live year-round on the island; from Potap Zaikov's report, we know their main village was two days' paddle to the northwest. The people, at least around the time of European contact, traveled far to the east and south of their village in the summer to trade and to hunt, fish, and gather food. They ascended the Copper River to trade with the Athabaskans of the Interior, mainly trading Chugach sea mammal skins and oil for Athabaskan copper. They stopped along the Copper and Bering Rivers to catch and dry salmon from the enormous runs of those rivers, and they may have hunted mountain goats along the alpine ridges near Controller Bay. Then they crossed in their kayaks and their undecked, dorylike skin boats to Kayak Island.

On Kayak Island, the Chugach had a variety of animals and plants to hunt, fish, and gather. There were shellfish and kelp along the coast, a few silver salmon and Dolly Varden trout in the larger streams, possibly mountain goats in the alpine country, otters and seals offshore, and, as Steller proved, a tremendous array of plants for food and for the Chugach's pharmacopeia. And, as Phil and I were reminded earlier when we found a dead juvenile gray whale on the beach, the main migration route of the eastern Pacific gray whales passes just off the island. If the Chugach ever scavenged whale meat, this would have been the place to do it. In addition, the island's eastern catch-beach would have been a fine place to search for iron. Alaska's coastal people had iron before first contact with Europeans, and there are two hypotheses for the source: trade with Siberian Natives across Bering Strait, and Asian iron carried here by ocean currents on flotsam from wrecked wooden ships.

The best archaeological clues to the people's way of life come from the middens, or garbage heaps, of an ancient village near Cordova, one of the possible locations of the village where the Kayak Island campers lived in the winter. The village middens are a jumble of house posts, slate awls and harpoon heads, bone tools, stone lamps, grinding stones, and, more than anything else, the shells and bones of the creatures the people ate.

Shell and bone lie eight feet deep in the largest midden, which consists mostly of shell fragments but also contains plenty of sea otter, seal, sea lion, porpoise, whale, bear, mountain goat, river otter, bird, and marmot bones. (Zaikov's foreman Nagaev reported that the Chugach trained small dogs to chase marmots out of their burrows.) The midden is set in a massive matrix of salmon, cod, and herring bones, engulfing everything else.

The evidence suggests that fish and shellfish were staple protein foods for the Chugach, probably especially during winter as they were for the Aleut people, and that marine mammals played a crucial role in providing fat and calories in their diet. The Chugach had more land-based food than the people of the Aleutians, but they depended on sea mammals nearly as much as the Aleuts did.

The Chugach are not gone; they still live in Prince William Sound and nearby areas today. The village of Tatitlek, population about a hundred people, on the mainland north of Cordova, is the village closest to Kayak Island. The villagers there still live partially by subsistence fishing, hunting, and gathering. With one foot in the modern world and one in the prehistoric, they use firearms and skiffs these days instead of harpoons and skin boats.

As it is in subsistence villages throughout Alaska, the conspicuous consumption so evident elsewhere is conspicuously absent in Chugach country. Like their ancestors, the Chugach harvest berries and gather intertidal food like clams and octopus. They fish for salmon, halibut, and cod; gather gull and tern eggs; and hunt seals, ducks, geese, bear, mountain goat, moose, and black-tailed deer. (The last two are ungulates that were not here in Steller's day.) Most of the cash in the village comes from the commercial salmon and halibut fisheries, arguably two of the most sustainable and ecologically sound fisheries on the planet. As they say in Tatitlek, "It's God's country."

Living lightly, the Chugach have called the Sound home for at least four thousand years, for the most part harvesting a little here and a little there from the coast's web of life, surviving as a people for centuries because they have lived in a sustainable way. (Those Kayak Island bark-stripped trees were not girdled, so they are still alive many human generations after they were stripped.) Biologically, the people have lived as generalist, opportunistic samplers of their environment, living a human version of the life strategy of Steller sea lions. For all their time in Prince William Sound, the only noticeable traces the Chugach of earlier times have left behind are the well-hidden remains of their camps and villages and a few cliff faces painted with faint red pictographs of whales, hunters in skin boats, and human faces and forms.

The Chugach approach to living along the North Pacific is a colossal contrast to what has happened since Steller visited Kayak Island. For more than two centuries now, the history of this ocean has been the story of serial, species-by-species marine "gold rushes," and the harm to the web of life has escalated with each new rush. First came Steller and his shipmates, who took hundreds of otters, some of them only to use the furs for gambling stakes. Next were the colonial times of sea otter hunting with kayaks in Russian America, and then came the era of pelagic fur sealing. In the last half-century, far more "efficient" technologies of whaling and fishing dominated the oceans. Now we have entered the era of global impact, the greenhouse warming that is transforming the oceans and the atmosphere. The indigenous occupation of the North Pacific may not have been completely benign (the Steller's sea cow might have had something to say about that), but it was nothing compared to what has come since, or what may come in the future.

Subsistence living is a mind-set. The territories indigenous people considered home included (and in many cases still include) the places they hunted, fished, and gathered as well as their seasonal camps, spiritual places, and travel routes. Overall it was, and is, a far broader concept of home than just a dwelling—an expansive concept of the natural world as a place of belonging, with time measured in the cycles of seasons, tides, salmon, whales, and the greening and blooming of plants. In that world, though it may look like the "wilderness" of European imagination, most of the landscape has a human presence, but a presence that has rarely translated into injury to the rest of creation.

The Chugach sites on Kayak Island, the long-abandoned village site near Cordova, and the modern village of Tatitlek all tell us the same thing: humans can coexist with the rest of creation; we can live decently without tearing apart the web of life and threatening the generations who come after us. Subsistence villages like Tatitlek are modern-day equivalents of Irish monasteries after the fall of the Roman Empire—the monasteries where monks salted away records of classical knowledge, preserving them for the time when Europe would be ready to reembrace them and move toward a Renaissance and an Enlightenment. As human as they are, with all the quirks and idiosyncrasies of our species, places like Tatitlek are archives of a *way* of life tied more closely into the *web* of life, preserved for the time when humanity is ready for a rebirth of a healthy relationship with the rest of life on earth.

Three more days at Cape St. Peter drift away in a medley of fog, drizzle, cormorants, sea otters, tides, forests, and wildflowers. It's the evening of the last day of our trip; in the morning, weather permitting, Steve Ranney will be here to pick us up in his Cessna and fly us back to Cordova. After dinner I stroll away from camp toward the beach in the bight south of the cape.

The beach swings in a wide arc around the bay, backed by meadows and forested hills to the north and by a rising wall of black sea cliffs to the east and south. Runners of green descend the black cliffs—ranks of small, determined plants staking out a home on the near-vertical surface of the rock—and a massive pile of black boulders fans out from the base of the cliff.

Directly out from where I stand, there is a gap in Cape St. Peter's ringing reef, a breach filled with smooth water sandwiched between two sets of breakers foaming over the reef on either side. Steller and the water carriers from the *St. Peter* must have rowed through this gap between breakers when they landed here in 1741. Tonight an otter, wrapped in kelp, is snoozing peacefully in this stretch of calm sea.

From here, from the beach where science began in this part of the world, past the sleeping otter, beyond the horizon, the vast ocean stretches for thousands of miles, encompassing a web of life we've barely begun to understand. Steller opened the North Pacific to marine science more than 250 years ago, but the sea still keeps many of its secrets. The greatest challenge for our generation of marine science is to learn enough to help us meet our needs in ways that sustain the wealth and productivity of the oceans. Just as the crew of the American Expedition needed Steller's knowledge to survive, we need scientists and naturalists to help us find the right course.

With my binoculars, I take a closer look at the lone otter floating offshore. For several years, according to otter biologists, an older sea otter male from a bay near Cordova has been doing some un-otterlike traveling: he swims out to Kayak Island in the summer, stays for a month or two, and then swims back home. The otter I'm watching offshore is big, so it's probably a male, and the white fur around its face is the usual tip-off of advancing age in an otter; this could well be the vacationing otter from up north. If it is, I wonder, will he end up as a bite of popcorn for an orca as he swims back to Prince William Sound this year? Or do old sea otters, like old airplane pilots, know some tricks that others of their kind don't?

Since Steller was here, we've stacked the deck heavily against his beasts of the sea. The sea cow is gone, and the sea otter and the northern fur seal barely survived the fur-trade era; now the Steller sea lion and the western Alaska sea otter are in deep trouble, and the fur seal may also be threatened.

The hope for Steller sea lions is that their decline has at least bottomed out and that time, science, a resurgence of their prey, and a new attitude among the people closest to them will eventually clear a path for them to recover. Sea otters will have to wait for a recovery of the orca's preferred prey, the great whales, and deal with anything else lethal that we might throw at them. But if the Steller sea lion, the sea otter, and the northern fur seal survive, it may be a sign that we've learned to live within our means—and that our way of life may survive as well.

Steller's eider *(Polysticta stelleri)*

EPILOGUE: THE LEGACY OF STELLER AND THE EXPEDITION

Pressure of duties does not permit me to spend too much time in perfecting [my papers]. . . . I therefore set out my porridge in carefully made earthen vessels.

If the vessel is an offense to anyone, he will perform for me and others a most friendly service if he will pour it all into a gold or silver urn.

—Steller, *The Beasts of the Sea*

Half a century after Steller landed at Cape St. Peter, the Billings-Sarychev expedition came to Kayak Island as part of a voyage to check and report on Russia's possessions in America. An old Chugach man came aboard the ship and told Sarychev what he recalled about an earlier ship that had anchored off the island:

> *He remembered, that when he was a boy, a ship had come into the bay on the west side of the island, and had sent a boat to shore; but on its approaching land, the natives all ran away. When the ship sailed, they returned to their hut, and found in their subterranean storeroom some glass beads, leaves of tobacco, an iron kettle, and a few other things.*

The old man's account of what the strangers left in the underground cache matched Steller's journal; the ship was the *St. Peter*, and the old man was one of the Chugach people who had hidden in the forest as Steller landed and explored the island.

By the time Sarychev spoke to the old Chugach man, Steller was long dead. He lived only another four years after coming back from America; he never returned to Europe or saw his wife Brigitta again. While trekking through the Siberian winter in 1746, he came down with a sudden illness and died in his sled. He had been traveling toward Irkutsk to defend himself against charges that he had illegally freed some Kamchatka Native prisoners. Apparently Steller was fighting Russian authority to the end.

In the short time left to him after the American Expedition, Steller added to his bundle of discoveries about the North Pacific and Asia. He completed his explorations of Kamchatka, wintered with a Native group on the peninsula's west coast, sailed to the Kuril Islands, and rambled through more of Siberia on botany expeditions. He was already making plans for his next challenge: exploring the vast Asian steppes.

When Carolus Linnaeus heard that Steller had died, his reaction, in a letter to a colleague, was this: "Oh merciful God, that you have taken away such a man!" A great naturalist was gone, and other than his scientific work, there was virtually nothing left to remember him by—not even a single surviving painting or drawing to show what he looked like.

Linnaeus, however, was one of several biologists who kept Steller's work alive, borrowing and blending Steller's material with their own and that of others in pioneering books of biology. In the case of Linnaeus, it was a paper on the botany of Kamchatka, which he coauthored with one of his students in 1750. Science has lost most of the seventy-five or so papers Steller wrote during his travels in Asia and northwestern North America; only *The Beasts of the Sea*, his journal from the voyage of the *St. Peter*, a book about Kamchatka, and a very few of his other papers were ever published. His book on Kamchatka has never been as well known as one that the Academy student assistant, Stepan Krashenninikov, wrote as a combination of his and Steller's observations. For the most part, the world has learned what Steller discovered—for example, the miracle of the Pacific salmon and the hundreds of Asian and American plants Steller described for the first time—from books written by later biologists using the borrow-and-blend approach. Because much of his work has never been published under his name, some of Steller's first descriptions have been mistakenly attributed to other scientists; for example, in some accounts Meriwether Lewis gets the credit for first descriptions of Pacific coastal plants such as the Sitka spruce and the salmonberry, but Steller beat Lewis to those species by sixty-plus years.

Likewise, almost none of Steller's collections from the American Expedition ever made it to Europe for study or exhibit; one item that did, however, is the palate plate from a Bering Island sea cow, which he brought back to Asia on the voyage of the hooker *St. Peter.* The kelp-mashing plate from the extinct sea cow found a home at the Zoological Institute of the Russian Academy of Sciences ("the ZIN") in St. Petersburg, where it remains today.

We remember Steller now mainly for the plants and animals other scientists named for him. The variety reflects his long biological reach: the sea cow and the sea lion, a North Pacific eider and an Asian eagle, and a genus of Asian plants. The common alpine heather of Alaska, the low, aromatic, evergreen mat of the land above the trees, is *Cassiope stelleriana.* The Steller representative in the kelp forest is *Cryptochiton stelleri,* a leathery, retiring, alga-eating invertebrate commonly called the gumboot chiton; often a foot long, it is the largest chiton in the world.

The most familiar reminder of western North America's first scientist is the Steller's jay, the common, black-and-blue jay of conifer forests from Southcentral Alaska through the western states to Nicaragua—the bird that convinced Steller he had landed in America. The jay's bold, self-confident personality and its amazing vocabulary of chats, chuckles, squawks, whistles, and trills are a fair approximation of the personality of the bird's namesake.

As for the other members of the expedition, naval officers Sven Waxell and Sofron Khitrovo went on to long careers in the Russian Navy. The captain of the *St. Paul,* Aleksei Chirikov, never regained his health after his 1741 brush with scurvy and died in 1748. Steller's German friend Friedrich Plenisner became the Russian government's commanding officer at Okhotsk. He kept his connection to science; in the 1760s he drew up a report to the Russian Senate arguing that

Asia and North America must have been joined in the past—an early expression of an idea that has turned out, of course, to be fact.

The hooker *St. Peter* held up remarkably well. The small, single-masted sailing vessel—the one carpenter Sava Starodubtsov and the crew rebuilt from the wreckage of the packet boat of the same name—sailed various Russian parties around the North Pacific and the Sea of Okhotsk for another dozen years, including two return trips to Bering Island carrying sea otter hunters. She ended her seafaring days beached at Okhotsk, where, presumably, the sea eventually claimed her.

In 1991, during the 250th anniversary year of the American Expedition, a joint Russian-Danish archaeological expedition to Bering Island found the forge the crew had used to rework the old ship's iron for the hooker and uncovered a few of the cannon the crew left behind. The archaeologists also located and excavated part of the cemetery where the survivors had buried their dead during the winter of 1741–42, including Bering's grave.

Sven Waxell made one more contribution to the expedition long after the voyage was over. Ten years after his return to Russia, he refuted Joseph-Nicolas de l'Isle's account of what had happened to the crew of the *St. Peter*. De l'Isle's rendition, shown on an "updated" map of the North Pacific he published in 1752, had Bering sailing out from Avacha Bay in 1741 and immediately wrecking on Bering Island. And, incredibly, De Gama Land reappears on the 1752 map; de l'Isle drew Chirikov's course on the *St. Paul* as just missing it to the south. The myth of De Gama Land was slow to die.

Bering today retains his well-deserved credit for leading the first successful European expedition to find and chart the coastline of northwestern North America. The expedition, with the subsequent Russian colonization of Alaska and part of northern California, lives on as proof that the European discovery, conquest, and settlement of North America was no neat, east-to-west process unfolding across the continent from the thirteen colonies to the Pacific.

In the end, Steller's contributions to science, from marine biology to botany to anthropology, were arguably more significant than the expedition's geographic discoveries. Steller was the first of a long line of European naturalists who sailed with voyages of Pacific exploration, a lineage of scientists who gave us a baseline view of the region's plants and animals and Native cultures as Europe began to colonize the Pacific. Their legacy still has value today.

A clue to how precocious the science of Bering's second expedition was pops out of the writing of Thomas Jefferson. More than twenty years before he sent Lewis and Clark west, Jefferson wrote about the hot springs of his native Virginia, comparing them not to other North American geothermal areas but to the hot springs of Kamchatka, which he had read about in Stepan Krashenninikov's book. At that point, courtesy of Krashenninikov, Steller, and Bering, Jefferson knew far more about the distant reaches of Asia than he knew about the rest of his own continent.

There is one last irony to tell, concerning the search for an arctic sea passage, the ultimate reason behind Bering's two expeditions. Bering's search came up empty. There was no such passage; the seas north of Asia were choked off by a perennial ice pack. A passage in summer, however, may be open not long after the three-hundredth anniversary of the American Expedition. Researchers from a number of universities and agencies have computed that at the rate the ice pack is melting, the Arctic Ocean's summer ice cover is on course to disappear completely, possibly as early as the middle of the twenty-first century.

Acknowledgments

The main sources of inspiration for *Steller's Island* were the translations of Steller's writings by O. W. Frost and Margritt Engel, Leonhard Stejneger, and Walter and Jennie Miller; Frank Golder's two-volume account of Vitus Bering's voyages; the Kayak Island slides Dave Blanchett and Ellen Toll shared with me in Anchorage; the work of many of today's marine biologists, some of whom I acknowledge below for specific contributions to the book; and Walt Cunningham and Susan Stanford's Cape St. Elias sea lion biology reports, which Ken Pitcher dug out of his files at the Alaska Department of Fish and Game. I'm especially grateful for the help of O. W. Frost, the leading historian on Steller and Bering, who generously reviewed and pointed out errors in historical passages in the book, and for the faithful good cheer of acquisitions editor Kate Rogers.

Many other people helped in numerous ways. Thanks to them all:

In the realm of biology, sea lion biologist Ken Pitcher, sea lion and fur seal biologist Tom Loughlin, sea otter biologists Jim Estes and Angela Doroff, seabird ecologists Scott Hatch and George Hunt, marine systems ecologist Alan Springer, shark and ocean fisheries biologists Vince Gallucci and Lee Hulbert, ocean fisheries expert Lowell Fritz, statistical biologist Steve Hare, terrestrial wildlife biologist Dan Logan, freshwater fisheries biologist Ken Hodges, terrestrial ecologist Rob DeVelice, and biologists Karen Laing and Mary Cody.

For help with archaeology, anthropology, paleontology, and Native cultures, Aleutian archaeologist Rick Knecht, sea cow paleontologist Daryl Domning, kayak historian George Dyson, archaeologist Linda Yarborough, anthropologist Bill Simeone, Chugach cultural historian John Johnson, and Unangan/Aleut educators Barbara Carlson and Pat Petrivelli and elder Alice Petrivelli.

For reviews of and ideas about the book as a whole, Nancy De-schu, Nancy Barber, Andromeda Romano-Lax, Beth Silverberg, Susan Lamb, Maxine Dunkelman, Melanie Heacox, and copy editor Alice Copp Smith, who contributed much more to the book than her job description implies.

And, in no particular order, Steve and Gail Ranney of Fishing and Flying in Cordova, Bob Behrens of Chugach National Forest, Kim Rivera of the National Marine Fisheries Service, Toni Bocci of the Cape St. Elias Lightkeepers Association, Cordova Historical Society museum staffers Frances Mallory and Judy Fulton, Prince William Sound Science Center staff Penelope Oswalt and Nancy Bird, Earl Krygier of the Alaska Department of Fish and Game, Cindy Pennington of the Alaska Native Heritage Center, Kate Wynne with the University of Alaska Fairbanks, Vladimir Burkanov of the Alaska SeaLife Center, Don McNamee at the Los Angeles County Library and Archives, Santa Barbara Natural History Museum staff, and all the wonderful librarians at Anchorage's Loussac Library, the Alaska Resource Library, Montana State University's Renne Library, and the Bozeman, Montana, Public Library. (How could we keep a civilization going without libraries and librarians?)

The sections on kayaks and indigenous hunting of marine mammals began as research for an exhibit I was contracted to organize for the Anchorage Museum of History and Art by the museum's director, Pat Wolf. That research was greatly aided and abetted by the help and friendship of the former guardians of the museum's library and archives, Diane Brenner and Mina Jacobs. Mina also gave me advice on sorting out the transliterations of Russian names, with the help of Lydia Black's *Russians in Alaska, 1732–1867.*

For geographical names, especially in the fluid world of translit-eration of Asian geographical names, my sources were *Merriam Webster's*

Geographical Dictionary, Third Edition; *National Geographic Atlas of the World,* Seventh Edition; and *The Times Atlas of the World,* Tenth Edition.

This is a book about Steller and marine mammals, so I had to severely limit the story of contemporary marine biology, as amazing and groundbreaking as it is. Since I couldn't begin to credit all the scientists who have made significant contributions to what we know about the seas today, I decided to tell the story without the names of contemporary scientists; I mention only Susan Stanford and Walt Cunningham by name, and I cited them because I included so much of their work in the story and because it was specific to Kayak Island. Please see the headnotes to sections 6 and 7 of the bibliography for references to the scientists whose work is highlighted in the book.

Finally, I consider myself lucky in the extreme to have the help and encouragement of my wife (and archaeology educator), Jeanne Moe, and the companionship of Phil North, with whom I've shared some outstanding outdoor adventures.

Selected Bibliography

This bibliography includes key references I used in writing *Steller's Is-land*. Most subjects are represented by only a few of the sources consulted. I have divided this list by major topic, as follows:

1. Steller, Bering, and the American Expedition
2. North Pacific natural history
3. Enlightenment science
4. Native peoples of Alaska's coast
5. The fur-trade era
6. Biology of sea otters, Steller sea lions, northern fur seals, and Steller's sea cows
7. Contemporary marine science

Key references for specific central subjects treated in the book are listed under each topic.

1. STELLER, BERING, AND THE AMERICAN EXPEDITION

The chief sources for the historical narrative and Steller's place in it were Frost, Golder, Lauridsen, Stejneger, Steller 1899, Steller 1925, Steller 1988, and Waxell.

Bruss, Glen M. *Profiles in Medical History.* Pittsburgh, PA: Dorrance Publishing, 1998.

Catesby, Mark. *Catesby's Birds of Colonial America*. Edited by Alan Feduccia. Chapel Hill: University of North Carolina Press, 1985. First published as *The Natural History of Carolina, Florida and the Bahama Islands*, 1731.

Dampier, William. *A New Voyage Round the World*. New York: Dover Publications, 1968. First published 1697.

Dmytryshyn, Basil, E.A.P. Crownhart-Vaughan, and Thomas Vaughan, editors and translators. *Russian Penetration of the North Pacific Ocean, 1700–1797: A Documentary Record*, vol. 2. Portland: Oregon Historical Society, 1988.

Frost, Orcutt W. *Bering: The Russian Discovery of America*. New Haven, CT: Yale University Press, 2003.

Golder, Frank A., and Leonhard Stejneger. *Bering's Voyages: An Account of the Efforts of the Russians to Determine the Relation of Asia and America*. 2 vols. New York: American Geographical Society, 1925.

Hayes, Derek. *Historical Atlas of the North Pacific Ocean*. Seattle: Sasquatch Books, 2001.

Krasheninnikov, Stepan P. *Explorations of Kamchatka: Report of a Journey Made to Explore Eastern Siberia in 1735–1741.* . . . Translated by E.A.P. Crownhart-Vaughan. Portland: Oregon Historical Society, 1972. First published 1755.

Lauridsen, Peter. *Vitus Bering: The Discoverer of Bering Strait*. Translated by Julius E. Olson. Chicago: S. C. Griggs, 1889. Reprint: Freeport, NY: Books for Libraries Press, 1969. Page reference is to the 1969 reprint.

Miller, Gerard F. *Bering's Voyages: The Reports from Russia*. Translated with commentary by Carol L. Urness. Fairbanks: University of Alaska Press, 1986. First published 1758.

Miller, Gerard F., J. L. Black, and Dieter K. Buse. *G.F. Müller and Siberia, 1733–1743*. Kingston, Ont., Canada: Limestone Press, 1989.

Miller, Gerard Fridrikh, Sven Waxell, and Arthur Dobbs. "A Letter from a Russian Sea-Officer . . . Containing His Remarks upon Mr. De L'Isle's Chart and Memoir, Relative to the New Discoveries Northward and Eastward from Kamtschatka: Together with some observations on that letter." First printed 1754. In *Western*

Americana, Frontier History of the Trans-Mississippi West, 1550–1900, edited by Archibald Hanna. New Haven, CT: Research Publications, 1975. Microform: Reel 383, no. 3780.

Mull, Gil, and George Plafker. "The First Russian Landings in Alaska." *Alaska Journal* 6 (1976): 135–45.

Murphy, Robert. *The Haunted Journey.* New York: Farrar, Straus & Giroux, 1969.

Smith, Barbara Sweetland. *Science Under Sail: Russia's Great Voyages to America, 1728–1867.* Anchorage: Anchorage Museum of History and Art, 2000.

Stejneger, Leonhard. *Georg Wilhelm Steller: The Pioneer of Alaskan Natural History.* Cambridge, MA: Harvard University Press, 1936.

Steller, Georg W. *The Beasts of the Sea.* Translated by Walter Miller and Jennie E. Miller. In Jordan, David S., *The Fur Seals and Fur Seal Islands of the North Pacific Ocean,* 179–218. Washington, DC: U.S. Government Printing Office, 1899. First published 1751.

———. *Catalogus Plantarum Intra Sex Horas in Parti Americae Septemtrionalis Iuxta Promontorium Eliae Observatarum Anno 1741 Die 21 Iulii Sub Gradu Latitudinus 59.* In Stejneger, Leonhard, *Georg Wilhelm Steller: The Pioneer of Alaska Natural History,* 554–61. Cambridge, MA: Harvard University Press, 1936.

———. *Journal of a Voyage with Bering, 1741–1742.* Edited by O. W. Frost and translated by Margritt A. Engel and O.W. Frost. Stanford, CA: Stanford University Press, 1988.

———. *Steller's Journal of the Sea Voyage from Kamchatka to America and Return on the Second Expedition, 1741–1742.* Translated by Leonhard Stejneger. Vol. 2 in Frank A. Golder and Leonhard Stejneger, *Bering's Voyages: An Account of the Efforts of the Russians to Determine the Relation of Asia and America.* New York: American Geographical Society, 1925.

Thilenius, John F. "Steller's Journey on Kayak Island, Alaska, July 20, 1741: Where and How Far Did He Travel?" In *Transportation in Alaska's Past,* edited by Michael S. Kennedy, 50–70. Anchorage: Alaska Historical Society, 1982.

Waxell, Sven. *The American Expedition.* Translated by M. A. Michael. London: William Hodge and Company, 1952.

2. NORTH PACIFIC NATURAL HISTORY

Field, Carmen M., and Conrad J. Field. *Alaska's Seashore Creatures.* Anchorage: Alaska Northwest Books, 1999.

Hitchcock, C. Leo, and Arthur Cronquist. *Flora of the Pacific Northwest: An Illustrated Manual.* Seattle: University of Washington Press, 1973.

Hultén, Eric. *Flora of Alaska and Neighboring Territories: A Manual of the Vascular Plants.* Stanford, CA: Stanford University Press, 1968.

MacKinnon, Andy, Jim Pojar, and Paul B. Alaback. *Plants of the Pacific Northwest Coast: Washington, Oregon, British Columbia, and Alaska,* 2nd ed. Vancouver, B.C., Canada: Lone Pine Publishing, 2004.

O'Clair, Rita M., and Sandra C. Lindstrom. *North Pacific Seaweeds.* Auke Bay, AK: Plant Press, 2000.

O'Clair, Rita M., and Charles E. O'Clair. *Southeast Alaska's Rocky Shores: Animals.* Auke Bay, AK: Plant Press, 1998.

Plafker, George. *Preliminary Geologic Map of Kayak and Wingham Islands, Alaska.* Washington, DC: U.S. Geological Survey, 1974.

Ricketts, Edward F., and Jack Calvin. *Between Pacific Tides,* 4th ed. Stanford, CA: Stanford University Press, 1985.

Winkler, G. W., and George Plafker. *Geologic Map of the Cordova and Middleton Island Quadrangles, Alaska.* Washington, DC: U.S. Geological Survey, 1993.

3. ENLIGHTENMENT SCIENCE

Frängsmyr, Tore, Sten Lindroth, Gunnar Eriksson, and Gunnar Broberg. *Linnaeus: The Man and His Work.* Berkeley: University of California Press, 1983.

Gould, Stephen Jay. "The First Unmasking of Nature." *Natural History* 102, no. 4 (1993): 14–21.

Hankins, Thomas L. *Science and the Enlightenment.* Cambridge, UK: Cambridge University Press, 1985.

Koerner, Lisbet. *Linnaeus: Nature and Nation.* Cambridge, MA: Harvard University Press, 1999.

Linnaeus, Carolus (Linné, Carl von). *Caroli Linnaei Systema Naturae,* 2 vols. A facsimile of the tenth edition, 1758–59. London: British Museum, 1956.

———. *Species Plantarum.* A facsimile of the first edition, 1753. London: Ray Society, 1957.

Mayr, Ernst. *The Growth of Biological Thought: Diversity, Evolution and Inheritance.* Cambridge, MA: Belknap Press, Harvard University, 1982.

Stearn, William T. *Botanical Latin: History, Grammar, Syntax, Terminology, and Vocabulary,* 4th ed. Newton Abbot, Devon, UK: David and Charles, 1983.

Wilson, Edward O. *Consilience.* New York: Alfred A. Knopf, 1998.

4. NATIVE PEOPLES OF ALASKA'S COAST

The main sources for the sections on the people and kayaks of the Aleutians were Black and Pierce, Dyson 1986, Dyson 2000, Liapunova, Zimmerley, and my earlier research involving dozens of other sources. Waldemar Jochelson recorded the traditional Aleut sea lion story paraphrased in the book (Jochelson 1990, recorded in the early 1900s). For the Chugach and Tatitlek, the chief sources were DeLaguna, Hassen, Johnson et al., Spaan et al., and Taylor et al.

Birket-Smith, Kaj. *The Chugach Eskimo.* Copenhagen, Denmark: Nationalmuseets publikationsfond, 1953.

Black, Lydia T., and Richard A. Pierce. *The History and Ethnohistory of the Aleutians East Borough.* Kingston, Ont., Canada: Limestone Press, 1999.

DeLaguna, Frederica. *Chugach Prehistory: The Archaeology of Prince William Sound, Alaska.* Seattle: University of Washington Press, 1956.

Dyson, George. *Baidarka: The Kayak.* Anchorage: Alaska Northwest Books, 1986.

———. "The Aleutian Kayak." *Scientific American* 282:4 (2000), 84–91.

Hassen, Harold. "The Effect of European and American Contact on the Chugach Eskimo of Prince William Sound, Alaska, 1741–1930." PhD diss., University of Wisconsin–Milwaukee, 1978.

Jochelson, Waldemar. *History, Ethnology, and Anthropology of the Aleut.* Washington, DC: Carnegie Institution, 1933.

———. *Unangam ungiikangin kayux tunusangin: Aleut Tales and Narratives Collected 1909–1910 by Waldemar Jochelson.* Edited by Knut Bergsland and Moses L. Dirks. Fairbanks: Alaska Native Language Center, University of Alaska, 1990.

Johnson, John F.C., Denise Caldwell, and Candace Totemoff. *Chugach Cultural CD*. CD-ROM. Anchorage: Chugach Heritage Foundation, 2001.

Laughlin, William S. *Aleuts: Survivors of the Bering Land Bridge*. New York: Holt, Rinehart, and Winston, 1980.

Liapunova, Roza G. *Essays on the Ethnography of the Aleuts: At the End of the Eighteenth and the First Half of the Nineteenth Century*. Translated by Jerry Shelest. Fairbanks: University of Alaska Press, 1996.

Spaan, Laura B., Russ Weston, and Vanessa Norman. *Nourished by Our Food, Sustained by Our Traditions*. Video. Anchorage: Chugachmiut Inc., 2001.

Stratton, Lee. *Resource Harvest and Use in Tatitlek, Alaska*. Division of Subsistence Technical Paper No. 181. Anchorage: Alaska Department of Fish and Game, 1990.

Taylor, Francine Lastufka, Jonathan Butzke, and William E. Simeone. *Tatitlek: Changing Tides*. Video. Anchorage: Alaska Department of Fish and Game, 1999.

Zimmerley, David. *Qajaq: The Kayaks of Siberia and Alaska*. Juneau: Alaska State Museum, 1986.

5. THE FUR-TRADE ERA

Bancroft, Hubert H. *History of Alaska, 1730–1885*. Darien, CT: Hafner Publishing Co., 1970. First published 1886.

Berkh, Vasilii N. *A Chronological History of the Discovery of the Aleutian Islands*. Translated by Richard A. Pierce. Kingston, Ont., Canada: Limestone Press, 1974.

Busch, Briton Cooper. *The War Against the Seals: A History of the North American Seal Fishery*. Kingston, Ont., Canada: McGill–Queen's University Press, 1985.

Chevigny, Hector. *Russian America: The Great Alaskan Venture, 1741–1867*. New York: Viking Press, 1965.

Elliott, Henry Wood. *The Seal-Islands of Alaska*. Washington, DC: U.S. Government Printing Office, 1881. Reprint: Kingston, Ont., Canada: Limestone Press, 1976. Page reference is to the 1976 reprint.

———. *Our Arctic Province: Alaska and the Seal Islands*. New York: Charles Scribner's Sons, 1887.

Essig, E. O., Adele Ogden, Clarence J. DuFour, and Richard A. Pierce. *Fort Ross: California Outpost of Russian Alaska, 1812–1841.* Kingston, Ont., Canada: Limestone Press, 1991.

Khlebnikov, Kiril T. *Notes on Russian America.* Edited by Richard A. Pierce and translated by Serge LeComte and Richard A. Pierce. Kingston, Ont., Canada: Limestone Press, 1994.

Martin, Fredericka I. *Sea Bears: The Story of the Fur Seal.* Philadelphia: Chilton, 1960.

National Oceanic and Atmospheric Administration (NOAA). *The Story of the Pribilof Fur Seals.* Washington, DC: NOAA, 1977.

Roppel, Alton Y. *Management of Northern Fur Seals on the Pribilof Islands, Alaska, 1786–1981.* Washington, DC: National Marine Fisheries Service, 1984.

Sims, Edwin W., and Walter I. Lembkey. *Report on the Alaska Fur-Seal Fisheries.* Washington, DC: U.S. Government Printing Office, 1906.

Tikhmenev, P.A. *A History of the Russian American Company.* Edited and translated by Richard A. Pierce and Alton S. Donnelly. Seattle: University of Washington Press, 1978. First published 1861.

Sauer, Martin. *An Account of a Geographical and Astronomical Expedition to the Northern Parts of Russia . . .* London: T. Cadell and W. Davies, 1802. Reprinted as *Expedition to the Northern Parts of Russia.* Richmond, Surrey, UK: Richmond Pub. Co., 1972. Page references are to the 1972 reprint.

Williams, Gerald O. *The Bering Sea Fur Seal Dispute: A Monograph on the Maritime History of Alaska.* Eugene, OR: Alaska Maritime Publications, 1984.

6. BIOLOGY OF SEA OTTERS, STELLER SEA LIONS, NORTHERN FUR SEALS, AND STELLER'S SEA COWS

These were the key references for topics presented in detail:

- Role of sea otters in kelp forest: Estes 1996, Estes and Steinberg, Riedman and Estes, VanBlaricom and Estes
- Biology of pinnipeds: Reeves et al., Riedman
- Evolution of Steller's sea cow: Anderson, Domning 1978, Domning 1987
- Steller's sea cow habitat: Stejneger
- Kayak Island sea otter recovery: Lensink

Alaska Geographic Society. *Seals, Sea Lions, and Sea Otters.* Anchorage: Alaska Geographic Society, 2000.

Anderson, P. K. "Competition, Predation, and the Evolution and Extinction of Steller's Sea Cow, *Hydrodamalis gigas.*" *Marine Mammal Science* 11 (1995): 391–94.

Berta, A., and A. R. Wyss. "Pinniped Phylogeny." In *Contributions in Marine Mammal Paleontology Honoring Frank C. Whitmore, Jr.,* edited by Annalisa Berta and Thomas A. Deméré, 33–56. San Diego: San Diego Society of Natural History, 1994.

Berta, Annalisa, and James L. Sumich. *Marine Mammals: Evolutionary Biology.* San Diego: Academic Press, 1999.

Chanin, Paul. *The Natural History of Otters.* London: Croom Helm, 1985.

Domning, Daryl P. *Sirenian Evolution in the North Pacific Ocean.* Berkeley: University of California Publications in Geological Science vol. 118, University of California Press, 1978.

———. "Sea Cow Family Reunion." *Natural History* 96 (1987): 64–71.

Estes, J. A. "The Influence of Large, Mobile Predators in Aquatic Food Webs: Examples from Sea Otters and Kelp Forests." In *Aquatic Predators and Their Prey,* edited by Simon P.R. Greenstreet and Mark L. Tasker, 65–72. Oxford, UK: Fishing News Books, 1996.

Estes, James A., David O. Duggins, and Galen B. Rathbun. "The Ecology of Extinctions in Kelp Forest Communities." *Conservation Biology* 3 (1989): 252–64.

Estes, James A., and Peter D. Steinberg. "Predation, Herbivory, and Kelp Evolution." *Paleobiology* 14 (1988): 19–36.

Haley, Delphine. "The Saga of Steller's Sea Cow." *Natural History* 87, no. 9 (1978): 9–17.

Kenyon, Karl W., *The Sea Otter in the Eastern Pacific Ocean.* New York: Dover Publications, 1975.

Lensink, Calvin J. *The History and Status of Sea Otters in Alaska.* PhD diss., Purdue University, 1962.

Love, John A., *Sea Otters.* Golden, CO: Fulcrum Publishing, 1992.

Levin, Simon A., ed. *Encyclopedia of Biodiversity.* San Diego: Academic Press, 2001.

Reeves, Randall R., Brent R. Stewart, and Stephen Leatherwood. *The Sierra Club Handbook of Seals and Sirenians.* San Francisco: Sierra Club Books, 1992.

Riedman, Marianne L. *The Pinnipeds: Seals, Sea Lions, and Walruses.* Berkeley: University of California Press, 1990.

Riedman, Marianne L., and James A. Estes. *The Sea Otter* (Enhydra lutris) *: Behavior, Ecology, and Natural History.* Washington, DC: U.S. Fish and Wildlife Service Biological Report 90 (14): 1990.

Stejneger, Leonhard. "How the Great Northern Sea-Cow (*Rytina*) Became Exterminated." *American Naturalist* 21 (1887): 1047–54.

VanBlaricom, Glenn R., and James A. Estes, eds. *The Community Ecology of Sea Otters.* Berlin: Springer-Verlag, 1988.

Wilson, Don E., and Sue Ruff, eds. *The Smithsonian Book of North American Mammals.* Washington, DC: Smithsonian Institution Press, 1999.

7. CONTEMPORARY MARINE SCIENCE

Key sources for the recent studies described in the "Kayak Island" chapter are as follows:

- Kayak Island sea lions: Cunningham 1977, Cunningham and Stanford 1978
- Steller sea lion diet study: Merrick et al. 1997
- Sea lion energetics and reproduction: Calkins et al., Pitcher and Calkins, Pitcher et al. 1998
- The regime shift in the North Pacific and global warming: Anderson and Piatt, Benson and Trites, Conners et al., Hare and Mantua, Kennedy et al., McGowan et al., Otterson et al., Root et al., Schumacher et al., Thompson and Wallace, Walther et al.
- Orca predation on sea otters and other sea mammals: Estes et al., Springer et al. 2003
- Suggested reading for an overview of the ecological revolution in the North Pacific: DeMaster and Atkinson, Mercy et al., National Research Council 2003, Trites 1998, Trites et al. 1999

A few suggested websites for more information on North Pacific marine biology:

- Alaska Fisheries Science Center: *www.afsc.noaa.gov*
- Alaska SeaLife Center: *www.alaskasealife.org*
- National Marine Fisheries Service Steller Sea Lion Program: *www.stellersealions.noaa.gov/*
- North Pacific Universities Marine Mammal Research Consortium: *www.marinemammal.org*

- U.S. Geological Survey Alaska Science Center: *www.absc.usgs.gov*
- University of Alaska Institute of Marine Science: *www.ims.uaf.edu*

Anderson, Paul J., and John F. Piatt. "Community Reorganization in the Gulf of Alaska Following Ocean Climate Regime Shift." *Marine Ecology Progress Series* 189 (1999): 117–23.

Andrews, Russel D. "The Population Decline of Steller Sea Lions: Testing the Nutritional Stress Hypothesis." In *Experimental Approaches to Conservation Biology,* edited by Malcolm S. Gordon and Soraya M. Bartol, 132–46. Berkeley: University of California Press, 2003.

Benson, Ashleen J., and Andrew W. Trites. "Ecological Effects of Regime Shifts in the Bering Sea and Eastern North Pacific Ocean." *Fish and Fisheries* 3 (2002): 95–113.

Calkins, D. G., E. F. Becker, and K. W. Pitcher. "Reduced Body Size of Female Steller Sea Lions from a Declining Population in the Gulf of Alaska." *Marine Mammal Science* 14 (1998): 232–44.

Conners, M. E., A. B. Hollowed, and E. Brown. "Retrospective Analysis of Bering Sea Bottom Trawl Surveys: Regime Shift and Ecosystem Reorganization." *Progress in Oceanography* 55 (2002): 209–22.

Cunningham, Walt. "Observations on Steller Sea Lions at Cape St. Elias." Field report, Alaska Department of Fish and Game, Anchorage, 1977.

Cunningham, Walt, and Susan Stanford. "Steller Sea Lion Investigations at Cape St. Elias: March 22 through July 5, 1978." Field report, Alaska Department of Fish and Game, Anchorage, 1978.

DeMaster, Douglas, and Shannon Atkinson, eds. *Steller Sea Lion Decline: Is It Food II.* Fairbanks: University of Alaska Sea Grant Program, 2002.

Estes, J. A., M. T. Tinker, T. M. Williams, and D. F. Doak. "Killer Whale Predation on Sea Otters Linking Oceanic and Nearshore Ecosystems." *Science* 282 (1998): 473–76.

Francis, Robert C., Steven R. Hare, Anne B. Hollowed, and Warren S. Wooster. "Effects of Interdecadal Climate Variability on the Oceanic Ecosystems of the Northeast Pacific Ocean." *Fisheries Oceanography* 7 (1998): 1–21.

Gay, Joel. *Commercial Fishing in Alaska.* Anchorage: Alaska Geographic Society, 1997.

Grebmeier, Jacqueline M., James E. Overland, Sue E. Moore, Ed V. Farley, Eddy C. Carmack, Lee W. Cooper, Karen E. Frey, John M. Helle, Fiona A. McLaughlin, and S. Lyn McNutt. "A Major Ecosystem Shift in the Northern Bering Sea." *Science* 311 (2006): 1461–64.

Hare, Steven R., and Nathan J. Mantua. "Empirical Evidence for North Pacific Regime Shifts in 1977 and 1989." *Progress in Oceanography* 47 (2000): 103–45.

Jackson, Jeremy B.C., Michael X. Kirby, Wolfgang H. Berger, Karen A. Bjorndal, Louis W. Botsford, Bruce J. Bourque, Roger H. Bradbury, Richard Cooke, Jon Erlandson, James A. Estes, Terence P. Hughes, Susan Kidwell, Carina B. Lange, Hunter S. Lenihan, John M. Pandolfi, Charles H. Peterson, Robert S. Steneck, Mia J. Tegner, and Robert R. Warner. "Historical Overfishing and the Recent Collapse of Coastal Ecosystems." *Science* 293 (2001): 629–37.

Kennedy, Victor S., Robert R. Twilley, Joan A. Kleypas, James H. Cowan, and Steven R. Hare. *Coastal and Marine Ecosystems and Global Climate Change: Potential Effects on U.S. Resources.* Arlington, VA: Pew Center on Global Climate Change, 2002. Primarily available online: *www.pewclimate.org/global-warming-in-depth/all_reports /coastal_and_marine_ecosystems/index.cfm*

Loughlin, Thomas R. "The Steller Sea Lion: A Declining Species." *Biosphere Conservation* 1 (1988): 91–98.

Loughlin, Thomas R., and Kiyotaka Ohtani, eds. *Dynamics of the Bering Sea.* Fairbanks: University of Alaska Sea Grant Program, 1999.

McGowan, John A., Daniel R. Cayan, and Le Roy M. Dorman. "Climate-Ocean Variability and Ecosystem Response in the Northeast Pacific." *Science* 281 (1998): 210–17.

Mercy, Deborah, John Hyde, and Susan Reilly. *Steller Sea Lions in Jeopardy.* Video. Anchorage: Alaska Department of Fish and Game, 1998.

Merrick, Richard L., M. Kathryn Chumbley, and G. Vernon Byrd. "Diet Diversity of Steller Sea Lions (*Eumetopias jubatus*) and Their Population Decline in Alaska: A Potential Relationship." *Canadian Journal of Fisheries and Aquatic Science* 54 (1997): 1342–48.

Merrick, Richard L., and Thomas R. Loughlin. "Foraging Behavior of Adult Female and Young-of-the-Year Steller Sea Lions in Alaskan Waters." *Canadian Journal of Zoology* 75 (1997): 776–86.

National Marine Fisheries Service. *Alaska Groundfish Fisheries: Final Programmatic Supplemental Environmental Impact Statement.* Juneau, AK: National Oceanic and Atmospheric Administration, 2004.

National Marine Fisheries Service. *Steller Sea Lion Protection Measures: Final Supplemental Environmental Impact Statement.* Juneau, AK: National Oceanic and Atmospheric Administration, 2001.

National Research Council. *The Bering Sea Ecosystem.* Washington, DC: National Academies Press, 1996.

———. *The Decline of the Steller Sea Lion in Alaskan Waters: Untangling Food Webs and Fishing Nets.* Washington, DC: National Academies Press, 2003.

Otterson, G., B. Planque, A. Belgrano, E. Post, P. C. Reid, and N. C. Stenseth. "Ecological Effects of the North Atlantic Oscillation." *Oecologia* 128 (2001): 1–14.

Pitcher, Kenneth W., and Donald G. Calkins. "Reproductive Biology of Steller Sea Lions in the Gulf of Alaska." *Journal of Mammalogy* 62 (1981): 599–605.

Pitcher, Kenneth W., Donald G. Calkins, and Grey W. Pendleton. "Reproductive Performance of Female Steller Sea Lions: An Energetics-Based Reproductive Strategy?" *Canadian Journal of Zoology* 76 (1998): 2075–83.

Root, Terry L., Jeff T. Price, Kimberly R. Hall, Stephen H. Schneider, Cynthia Rosenzweig, and J. Alan Pounds. "Fingerprints of Global Warming on Wild Animals and Plants." *Nature* 421 (2003): 57–60.

Rosen, David A. S., and Andrew W. Trites. "Pollock and the Decline of Steller Sea Lions: Testing the Junk-Food Hypothesis." *Canadian Journal of Zoology* 78 (2000): 1243–50.

———. "Examining the Potential for Nutritional Stress in Young Steller Sea Lions: Physiological Effects of Prey Composition." *Journal of Comparative Physiology* 175 (2005): 265–73.

Schumacher, J. D., N. A. Bond, R. D. Brodeur, P. A. Livingston, J. M. Napp, and P. J. Stabeno. "Climate Change in the Southeastern Bering Sea and Some Consequences for Biota." In *Large Marine*

Ecosystems of the World: Trends in Exploitation, Protection, and Research, edited by Gotthilf Hempel and Kenneth Sherman, 17–40. Amsterdam: Elsevier Science, 2003.

Shima, Michiyo, Anne Babcock Hollowed, and Glenn R. VanBlaricom. "Response of Pinniped Populations to Directed Harvest, Climate Variability, and Commercial Fishery Activity: A Comparative Analysis." *Reviews in Fisheries Science* 8 (2000): 89–124.

Springer, Alan M. "Is It All Climate Change? Why Marine Bird and Mammal Populations Fluctuate in the North Pacific." In *Biotic Impacts of Extratropical Climate Variability in the Pacific,* edited by Greg Holloway, Peter Muller, and Diane Henderson, 109–20. Honolulu: University of Hawaii, 1998.

Springer, A. M., J. A. Estes, G. B. van Vliet, T. M. Williams, D. F. Doak, E. M. Danner, K. A. Forney, and B. Pfister. "Sequential Megafauna Collapse in the North Pacific Ocean: An Ongoing Legacy of Commercial Whaling?" *Proceedings of the National Academy of Sciences* 100 (2003): 12223–28.

Springer, A. M., J. F. Piatt, V. P. Shuntov, G. B. Van Vliet, V. L. Vladimirov, A. E. Kuzin, A. S. Perlov. "Marine Birds and Mammals of the Pacific Subarctic Gyres." *Progress in Oceanography* 43 (1999): 443–87.

Springer, Alan M., John F. Piatt, and Gus Van Vliet. "Sea Birds as Proxies of Marine Habitats and Food Webs in the Western Aleutian Arc." *Fisheries Oceanography* 5 (1996): 45–55.

Thompson, David W. J., and John M. Wallace. "Regional Climate Impacts of the Northern Hemisphere Annual Mode." *Science* 293 (2001): 85–89.

Trites, A. W., and C. P. Donnelly. "The Decline of Steller Sea Lions (*Eumetopias jubatus*) in Alaska: A Review of the Nutritional Stress Hypothesis." *Mammal Review* 33 (2003): 3–28.

Trites, Andrew W. *Steller Sea Lions* (Eumetopias jubatus): *Causes for Their Decline and Factors Limiting Their Restoration.* Vancouver: University of British Columbia Fisheries Centre, 1998.

Trites, Andrew W., and Peter A. Larkin. *The Status of Steller Sea Lion Populations and the Development of Fisheries in the Gulf of Alaska and Aleutian Islands.* Vancouver: University of British Columbia Fisheries Centre, 1992.

————. "Changes in the Abundance of Steller Sea Lions (*Eumetopias jubatus*) in Alaska from 1956 to 1992: How Many Were There?" *Aquatic Mammals* 22 (1996): 153–66.

Trites, Andrew W., Patricia A. Livingston, Steven Mackinson, Marcelo C. Vasconcellos, Alan M. Springer, and Daniel Pauly. *Ecosystem Change and the Decline of Marine Mammals in the Eastern Bering Sea: Testing the Ecosystem Shift and Commercial Whaling Hypotheses.* Vancouver: University of British Columbia Fisheries Centre, 1999.

University of Alaska. *International Symposium on the Role of Forage Fishes in Marine Ecosystems.* Fairbanks: University of Alaska Sea Grant Program, 1996.

Walther, Gian-Reto, Eric Post, Peter Convey, Annette Menzel, Camille Parmesan, Trevor J.C. Beebee, Jean-Marc Fromentin, Ove Hoegh-Guldberg, and Franz Bairlein. "Ecological Responses to Recent Climate Change." *Nature* 416 (2002): 389–95.

Quotation Sources

Sources of quotations in the book are given below, referenced to the text by page number and the first words of the quotation. The numeral following the author citation refers to the section of the bibliography where the full reference is cited.

For excerpts from Steller's 1741–42 journal, page references are given for both the Stejneger (1925) and Engel/Frost (1988) translations. Apart from introductory material and annotation, the translations themselves are equivalent, differing in only minor ways.

EPIGRAPH
Steller, 1742 letter to Johann Gmelin, in Golder (1), vol. 2, 245.

PROLOGUE: OUT OF CORDOVA
21 "No one who has studied. . . . ": Steller 1899 (1), 179.

CAPE ST. ELIAS
31 "The mountains were so lofty. . . . ": Steller 1925 (1), 33–34 and Steller 1988 (1), 60.

39 "This bird. . . . ": Steller 1925 (1), 59–60 and Steller 1988 (1), 78.

43 "They had at their disposal. . . . ": Lauridsen (1), 63.

48 "I have entirely forgotten. . . . ": Steller, quoted in Stejneger (1), 135.

57 "a large land . . . " ff.: "A Statement from the Cossack Ilia Skurikh Concerning the Voyage of the *Sv. Gavriil* to the Shores of Bolshaia Zemlia (America) in 1732," in Dmytryshyn et al. (1), 132.

58 "We were all led astray. . . . ": Waxell 1952 (1), 103.

63 " . . . if we continued our initial course. . . . ": Steller 1925 (1), 23 and Steller 1988 (1), 54.

64 "shore duck": Golder (1), vol. 1, 290.

65 "curtly and sarcastically. . . . " ff.: Steller 1925 (1), 26 and Steller 1988 (1), 56.

65 "it was, as usual. . . . ": Steller 1925 (1), 33 and Steller 1988 (1), 60.

69 "pregnant windbags": Steller 1925 (1), 34 and Steller 1988 (1), 61.

69 "a petty quarrel": Steller 1925 (1), 35.

70 "To get ashore. . . . ": Steller 1925 (1), 37 and Steller 1988 (1), 64.

70 "in the spirit. . . . ": Steller 1925 (1), 40 and Steller 1988 (1), 64.

71 "sweet grass": Steller 1925 (1), 44 and Steller 1988 (1), 65.

73 "Concerning the animals. . . . ": Steller 1925 (1), 58-59 and Steller 1988 (1), 77.

74 "Of fruit-bearing bushes. . . . ": Steller 1925 (1), 57 and Steller 1988 (1), 77.

76 "Luck, thanks to my hunter. . . . ": Steller 1925 (1), 59 and Steller 1988 (1), 78.

AUTUMN IN THE ISLANDS

79 "We were as well accustomed. . . . ": Steller 1925 (1), 117 and Steller 1988 (1), 115.

82 "a very unusual . . . ": Steller 1925 (1), 64 and Steller 1988 (1), 82.

83 "the berry. . . . ": Steller 1936, in Stejneger (1), 560 (translation by author).

84 "Generic names. . . . ": Linnaeus, quoted in Stearn (3), 285.

84 "a born collector . . . ": Linnaeus, quoted in Stejneger (1), 543.

85 "the West's greatest. . . . ": Wilson (3), 14.

85 "confidence, optimism . . . " ff.: Wilson (3), 21.

87 "The water is good. . . . ": Steller 1925 (1), 78 and Steller 1988 (1), 89.

93 "Gale." ff: Golder (1), vol. 1, 143.

96 "he put [it] to his lips. . . . ": Waxell 1952 (1), 115.

96 "tried to make up. . . . ": Steller 1925 (1), 94 and Steller 1988 (1), 100.

99–100, "The American boats. . . . ": Steller 1925 (1), 95-96 and Steller 1988 (1), 102–3.

101 "sporting about. . . . ": Sauer (5), 157–58.

105 "for, thanks to God. . . . ": "Chirikov's Report on the Voyage of the *St. Paul*," in Golder (1), vol. 1, 322.

106 "sea parrots" ff.: Steller 1925 (1), 105-6 and Steller 1988 (1), 107–8.

107 "By the will. . . . ": Golder (1), vol. 1, 167.

107 " . . . we heard the wind. . . . ": Steller 1925 (1), 115 and Steller 1988 (1), 113.

107–108 "On September 30. . . . ": Steller 1925 (1), 115 and Steller 1988 (1), 114.

111 "as customary . . . ": Steller 1925 (1), 135 and Steller 1988 (1), 125.

111 "as if death. . . . ": Steller 1925 (1), 136 and Steller 1988 (1), 126.

SEA OTTERS, BEARS, LIONS, AND COWS

113 "These sea animals. . . . ": Steller, 1742 letter to Johann Gmelin, in Golder (1), vol. 2, 245.

115 "From the continual pounding. . . . ": Steller 1925 (1), 200 and Steller 1988 (1), 177.

116 "We later realized. . . . ": Waxell 1952 (1), 126.

118 "excellent and wholesome" ff.: Steller 1925 (1), 208-9.

119 "You have in me. . . . ": Steller 1925 (1), 141 and Steller 1988 (1), 129.

121 "grave": Steller 1925 (1), 144 and Steller 1988 (1), 131.

122 "May God spare us. . . . ": Steller 1925 (1), 144 and Steller 1988 (1), 130.

122 "Even before. . . . ": Steller 1925 (1), 146 and Steller 1988 (1), 134.

122 "The foxes. . . . ": Steller 1925 (1), 147 and Steller 1988 (1), 134.

122 "Every morning. . . . ": Steller 1925 (1), 212.

123 "want, lack of clothing, cold. . . . ": Steller 1925 (1), 153 and Steller 1988 (1), 136.

124 "5 AM. . . . ": Golder (1), vol. 1, 230.

124 "died more from hunger. . . . ": Steller 1925 (1), 158 and Steller 1988 (1), 141.

125 "He might well not. . . . ": Steller 1925 (1), 159 and Steller 1988 (1), 141.

128 "[T]he officers themselves. . . . ": Steller 1925 (1), 161 and Steller 1988 (1), 144.

129 "These animals. . . . ": Steller 1899 (1), 210.

129 "never shine . . . ": Steller 1899 (1), 210.

130 "As they come out. . . . ": Steller 1899 (1), 215.

130 " . . . they fall down. . . . ": Steller 1899 (1), 215–16.

130–131 "When they sleep. . . . ": Steller 1899 (1), 216.

131 "When she caught sight. . . . ": Steller 1899 (1), 217.

131 "are not naturally . . . ": Steller 1899 (1), 213.

131 "hold out. . . . ": Steller 1899 (1), 212.

131 "a genuine American . . . ": Steller 1925 (1), 217 and Steller 1988 (1), 146.

131–132 "always give birth. . . . ": Steller 1899 (1), 216.

132 "tender and savory" ff.: Steller 1899 (1), 217.

132 "the greatest reverence": Steller 1925 (1), 221 and Steller 1988 (1), 148.

134 "caused a severe defeat . . . ": Steller 1925 (1), 170 and Steller 1988 (1), 152.

135 "joyful news" ff.: Steller 1925 (1), 173 and Steller 1988 (1), 154.

135 "believing that we . . . ": Steller 1925 (1), 171.

136 "Doctor Georg Steller": Golder (1), vol. 1, 233.

139 "is sickening. . . . ": Elliott 1881 (5), 75.

141 "Adjunct Steller. . . . ": Waxell 1952 (1), 142.

141 "looked as if they. . . . ": Steller 1925 (1), 213.

142 "Although at different times. . . . ": Steller 1899 (1), 205.

143 "a careless observer. . . . ": Steller 1899 (1), 203.

143 "There is no doubt. . . . ": Steller 1899 (1), 206.

144 "attacked me. . . . ": Steller 1899 (1), 205.

144 "For many years. . . . ": Steller 1899 (1), 202.

146 "[Sea lions] far surpass the sea bear. . . . ": Steller 1899 (1), 208.

147 "If I had to say. . . . ": Steller 1899 (1), 206.

149 "half swim and half walk": Steller 1899 (1), 198.

151 "The boiled fat. . . . ": Steller 1925 (1), 234 and Steller 1988 (1), 163.

151 " . . . they have an uncommon. . . . ": Steller 1925 (1), 232-33 and Steller 1988 (1), 162.

151 "each cooked. . . . ": Waxell 1952 (1), 151.

152 "the bark of an ancient oak.": Steller 1899 (1), 183.

153 "The stomach . . . : Steller 1899 (1), 191.

153 "If only a very slight. . . . ": Steller 1899 (1), 192.

154 "The final product. . . . ": Steller 1899 (1), 192.

154 "When the animals. . . . ": Steller 1899 (1), 187.

156 "constant efforts. . . . ": Steller 1925 (1), 181 and Steller 1988 (1), 165.

158 " . . . one and all. . . . ": Steller 1925 (1), 182-83 and Steller 1988 (1), 166.

158–159 "We lay one on top. . . . ": Steller 1925 (1), 183 and Steller 1988 (1), 166–67.

159 "The more we gazed. . . . ": Steller 1925 (1), 184 and Steller 1988 (1), 167.

159 "everyone was in. . . . ": Steller 1988 (1), 168.

161 "We were all by this time. . . . ": Steller 1925 (1), 186–87 and Steller 1988 (1), 169.

KAYAK ISLAND

163 "I do not doubt. . . . ": Steller 1899 (1), 181.

168 "sea cabbages": Petr Yakovlev, quoted in Domning 1978 (6), 164.

169 "a good-sized river. . . . ": "Journal of Navigator Potap Zaikov. . . . ", in Tikhmenev (5), vol. 2, 5.

171 "On these islands. . . . ": Benjamin Morrell, quoted in Essig et al. (5), 48.

199 "It's God's country." Kelly Kompkoff, in Taylor and Simeone (4).

EPILOGUE

203 "Pressure of duties. . . . ": Steller 1899 (1), 208.

203 "He remembered. . . . ": Sauer (5), 194–95.

204 "Oh merciful God. . . . ": Linnaeus, quoted in Stejneger (1), 489.

Permissions

Grateful acknowledgment is made to the following sources, for allowing me to use excerpts of previously published translations of Georg Steller's 1741–42 journal:

American Geographical Society: *Steller's Journal of the Sea Voyage from Kamchatka to America and Return on the Second Expedition, 1741–1742*, translated by Leonhard Stejneger. Vol. 2 of *Bering's Voyages: An Account of the Efforts of the Russians to Determine the Relation of Asia and America* by Frank A. Golder and Leonhard Stejneger. Copyright © 1925 by the American Geographical Society.

Stanford University Press: *Journal of a Voyage with Bering, 1741–1742.* Edited and with an introduction by O. W. Frost, translated by Margritt A. Engel and O. W. Frost. Copyright © 1988 by the Board of Trustees of the Leland Stanford Jr. University.

Index

dead reckoning, 62, 105, 108
Dementiev, Avraam, 66–67, 75
Diomede Islands, 42
Don Miller Hills, 195
Dragon Back (Kayak Island), 178, 179
dugong, 155
Dzhugdzur Range (Siberia), 49

earthquake, 1964 Alaska, 34, 176, 178, 189
East Cape (Siberia), 42
eider, Steller's, 137, 202
El Niño, 184–85
Enhydra lutris, 113. *See also* sea otter
Enlightenment, 84–85
Eumotopias jubatus, 162. *See also* sea lion, Steller
Exxon Valdez, 191

Fairweather, Mount, 103
Farallon Islands, 171
Fault Creek (Kayak Island), 189, 196
fireweed, 141
fishing, commercial, 185, 191–92, 193
fox, arctic: in Bering Island camp, 118, 119, 120, 121, 122; on Nagai Island, 90; predation by sea-eagle, 141; in Steller's cave, 135–36
Fritillaria camschatcensis, 140
fur seal, Juan Fernández, 145
fur seal, northern: behavior, 139, 141–44; Commander Island rookeries, 142–45, 147, 173; evolution, 34, 146, 147; as food, 139; fur, 147; fur trade hunting of, 171–72; range/migration, 144–46, 172; physical traits, 82, 143, 147; Pribilof Island rookeries, 145, 168; recent decline, 181, 194; "sea ape," 81–83

gentian, 90
Glacier Bay National Park, 103
global warming, 185, 207
Gmelin, Johann, 44, 48–49, 50
Good Hope, Cape of (Africa), 41
Greenland, 100, 150
groundfish, 182, 193
guillemot, pigeon, 90, 106
Gulf of Alaska, 26, 174, 184
Gvozdef, Mikhail, 57

Haliaeetus pelagicus, 20. *See also* sea-eagle, Steller's
halibut (fishery), 199
harbor seal. *See* seal, harbor
harpoon, Aleut, 101
Harrison, John, 61
heather, alpine, 205
hemlock-parsley (wild carrot), 140
Heracleum lanatum, 51. *See also* cow-parsnip
herring, 182, 191
Hesselberg, Andreas, 59, 86, 87, 107, 123
Hoffman, Friedrich, 46, 47
Hokkaido (Japan), 55
Honshu (Japan), 55
Hydrodamalis gigas, 149. *See also* sea cow, Steller's

iqyan, 89, 101. *See also* kayak: Aleutian
Irkutsk, Siberia, 44, 46
iron (in pre-European America), 198

Irtysh River (Siberia), 40
Itelmen (Siberian Natives), 52, 53, 91
Ivanov, Aleksei, 111, 133–34, 136

Jansen, Nils, 133
Japan, 41, 49, 55, 144
jay, blue (eastern), 76
jay, Steller's, 33, 76, 176, 205
Jefferson, Thomas, 31, 44, 207
Juan Fernández Islands, 145

Kamchatka, 41, 53, 115, 119, 144, 207
kayak: Aleutian, 94–95, 96, 97, 98–102, 105, 170; Chugach, 27, 197; history and use, 98, 100; Kodiak, 170
Kayak Entrance, 69, 187
Kayak Island: catch-beach, 31, 34–36, 187, 190; Chugach sites, 33, 71–73, 188, 195–97; climate, 23, 175; geography, 27, 34, 36–37, 69, 187; name, 27, 169; plant life, 22, 197; sea lion haulout, 37, 178–81; Steller's route, 194–97; tidal zone, 164–65. *See also* St. Elias, Cape; St. Peter, Cape
kelp, 72, 148–49, 164–66
Ket' River (Siberia), 40
Ketchikan, Alaska, 65
Khitrovo, Sofron: later years, 205; as officer, 53–54, 59, 110, 111, 123; as pilot, 50–52, 61, 114; in Shumagin Islands, 86–87, 92, 93; Wingham Island landfall, 70, 75
Kodiak Island, 170, 185
Koryak (Siberian Natives), 100, 157–58
Koryak interpreter, 60, 95, 96
Krashenninikov, Stepan, 44, 52–53, 204, 207
Krasilnikov, Andrei, 54
Kronotski, Cape (Kamchatka), 115, 160
Kuril Islands, 49, 55, 108
Kyakhta, Siberia, 48

Latin (language of science), 83–84
Lauridsen, Peter, 43, 54
Lena River (Siberia), 40, 49, 61
Lepekhin, Thomas: on Bering Island, 116, 118–20, 121, 135–36; on Kayak Island, 60, 70–72; on Nagai Island, 87, 90, 91, 92; on *St. Peter*, 82, 109
Lewis, Meriwether, 31, 33, 84, 205
Lewis and Clark Expedition, 31, 33, 34
lily, Kamchatka (chocolate), 140
Lind, James, 91
Linnaean hierarchy, 84
Linnaeus, Carolus, 84, 146, 204
longboat, 60
Lopatka, Cape (Kamchatka), 41, 51, 52
lynx, 186

manatee, 150. *See also* sea cow, Steller's
Manati, Cape (Bering Island), 159
Mendocino, Cape, 55
Messerschmidt, Daniel, 48
mica (as preservation medium), 45–46
monkshood, 101
Morrell, Benjamin, 171
Moscow, Russia, 41, 48
mountain goat, 195
Muir, John, 32
Müller, Gerhard, 44

dation on, 185–86, 193; recent decline, 175–76, 179, 181, 194; skin, 147, 171, 185; western stock, 176, 183; young animals, 175–76, 180–81, 183
seal, Baikal, 46
seal, eared, 81, 82, 138, 146
seal, earless (true), 81, 138
seal, fur. *See* fur seal
seal, harbor: as food on Bering Island, 118, 125; recent decline, 181, 193; Steller's observations, 65, 72, 81
Sea of Okhotsk, 32–33, 41, 51
sea otter: behavior, 130, 131, 132; Bering Island population, 116, 127, 132; diet/metabolism, 129–30; evolution/adaptation, 34, 81, 131, 132, 138, 173; as food, 122, 132; fur, 129, 132; habitat/range, 131, 170, 171; hunting of, fur trade, 166–68, 170–71; hunting of, indigenous, 101; Kayak Island population, 73, 165, 174, 201; as keystone species, 165–66; "otters as popcorn" theory, 192–93; physical traits, 147; recent decline, 181, 186, 192–94; recovery after fur trade, 173–74; southern, 173
sea urchin, 130, 165, 166, 167–68
Sea Wall (Kayak Island), 178, 181
Second Kamchatka Expedition, 32, 43–44
Semichi Islands, 108
Semidi Islands, 81, 82, 181
Senate, Russian, 49, 70, 205
Seward Peninsula, 57
shitik (Russian boat), 167
shore boats, 60
Shumagin Islands, 90
Shumagin, Nikita, 90
Sind, Johan, 59, 121, 134
sirenians, 34, 138, 150. *See also* sea cow, Steller's
skin boats, 57, 197, 199
sole, yellowfin, 191
South Pacific Ocean, 81, 166
Spangberg, Martin, 42, 49–50
Species Plantarum, 84
spruce, Sitka, 72, 196, 205
Stanford, Susan, 175, 178–80
Starodubtsov, Sava, 135, 136, 159–60
Steller, Georg: as anthropologist, 33, 71, 99–100, 150, 195; and Bering, 50, 53–54, 65, 70, 75, 122, 125; Bering Island landfall, 116–21; off Bird Island, 94–95, 106; as botanist, 22, 84, 140; collections, 48–49, 151, 158, 205; death, 204; fur seal studies, 141–48; Germany, early years in, 46–47; Kayak Island landfall, 33, 70–76, 194–97; as leader, 121, 136, 150, 161; legacy, 23, 33–34, 161, 204–5, 206–7; marriage and separation, 48; Nagai Island landfall, 86–87, 91–92; naval officers, tensions with, 51, 53–54, 63, 65, 85, 87, 90–91, 110, 125, 128; papers, 33, 46, 74, 83, 204 (*see also Beasts of the Sea, The*); as physician, 47, 58, 59, 85, 87, 90–91, 123, 141; in St. Petersburg, 47–48; sea cow studies, 148–150, 151–54; sea lion studies, 146–47; sea otter studies, 128–32; in Siberia, 44–46, 48–54, 204
Steller Glacier, 26
Steller, Mount, 26

Steller sea lion. *See* sea lion, Steller
Steller's eider. *See* eider, Steller's
Steller's Hill (Kayak Island), 188
Steller's jay. *See* jay, Steller's
Steller's sea cow. *See* sea cow, Steller's
Steller's sea-eagle. *See* sea-eagle, Steller's
Subarctic Current, 35

Tatitlek, Alaska, 198–99, 200
throwing board, Aleut, 101
Tlingit (Alaska Native people), 67–68
tobacco, 75, 96
Tobol River (Siberia), 40
Tobol'sk, Siberia, 40
Tretyakov, Andrei, 107
Turner Island, 86, 87, 92

Unalaska Island, 102
Unangan, 94, 98. *See also* Aleuts
University of Halle, 46
University of Wittenberg, 46
Urak River (Siberia), 40–41
Ural Mountains (Russia), 40

Vancouver, George, 81
Vaua (Kamchatka), 62, 105
Veniaminov, Ioann, 101
Victoria, British Columbia, 172
visor, Aleut sea hunting, 97
vodka, 59, 96, 108, 109

walrus, 81, 138
Wannhoff, Ullrich, 175
War of the Polish Succession, 47
Waxell, Laurentz, 59, 116, 158
Waxell Ridge, 26
Waxell, Sven: at Avacha Bay sea council, 54, 58; illness, 118, 123, 127; later years, 205, 206; as mariner, 60, 80–81, 107, 108; as officer, 59, 87, 90–91, 96, 110, 111, 128, 156
whale: blue, 191; bowhead, 193; humpback, 101; gray, 101, 193, 197–98; fin, 191; minke, 191; northern right, 137; orca, 192–93; sperm, 191
whaling, commercial, 191–92, 193
whaling, indigenous, 101–2, 150
wheatgrass, 45
White Rocks (Kayak Island), 178
Wilderness Act, 191
Wilson, Edward O., 85
Wingham Island, 26, 75, 174, 197
wintergreen, 141
Wood Creek (Bering Island), 134
Wrangell, Mount, 26

Yakobi Island, 66
Yakovlev, Petr, 168
Yakutsk, Siberia, 40, 41, 44, 49
yawl, 60
Yelagin, Ivan, 105, 106
Yenisey River (Siberia), 40, 44
Yeniseysk, Siberia, 44
Yudoma River (Siberia), 40
Yukon River, 184
Yushin, Kharlam, 59, 109, 133, 134, 139
Yushin's Valley (Bering Island), 139

Zaikov, Potap, 168–70, 197

About the Author

Dean Littlepage—a writer, interpretive planner, naturalist, and historian—has been exploring Alaska's remote corners for more than twenty years, covering thousands of miles on foot and skis and by sea kayak and canoe. He served as a special exhibit curator for the Anchorage Museum of History and Art, the largest museum in the state, and has written and produced numerous interpretive exhibits and programs for other groups and agencies. He is the author of the guidebook *Hiking Alaska*, co-author of an interpretive guide to the middle Yukon River, and author of two popular history chapbooks, and his writing has appeared in several regional and national periodicals.

Following academic days in the social sciences, Littlepage took to the woods as a trail builder, youth work-crew leader, and environmental education instructor. He was the manager of the Iditarod National Historic Trail for several years, and he lived in a cabin in Southcentral Alaska for a decade with more moose, bears, wolves, coyotes, and beavers as neighbors than humans.

Littlepage also co-founded an Alaska land trust and had a hand in the creation of Anchorage's Campbell Creek Science Center, Alaska's first environmental education center. He has served on the boards of directors of several conservation and education groups and has been involved in wilderness preservation for more than thirty years in Alaska and the West.

He recently moved from Alaska to southwest Montana, where he lives with his wife, archaeologist Jeanne Moe.

THE MOUNTAINEERS, founded in 1906, is a nonprofit outdoor activity and conservation club, whose mission is "to explore, study, preserve, and enjoy the natural beauty of the outdoors. . . . " Based in Seattle, Washington, the club is now the third-largest such organization in the United States, with seven branches throughout Washington State.

The Mountaineers sponsors both classes and year-round outdoor activities in the Pacific Northwest, which include hiking, mountain climbing, ski-touring, snowshoeing, bicycling, camping, kayaking, nature study, sailing, and adventure travel. The club's conservation division supports environmental causes through educational activities, sponsoring legislation, and presenting informational programs.

All club activities are led by skilled, experienced instructors, who are dedicated to promoting safe and responsible enjoyment and preservation of the outdoors.

If you would like to participate in these organized outdoor activities or the club's programs, consider a membership in The Mountaineers. For information and an application, write or call The Mountaineers, Club Headquarters, 300 Third Avenue West, Seattle, WA 98119; 206-284-6310. You can also visit the club's website at *www.mountaineers.org* or contact The Mountaineers via email at *clubmail@mountaineers.org.*

The Mountaineers Books, an active, nonprofit publishing program of the club, produces guidebooks, instructional texts, historical works, natural history guides, and works on environmental conservation. All books produced by The Mountaineers Books fulfill the club's mission.

Send or call for our catalog of more than 500 outdoor titles:

The Mountaineers Books
1001 SW Klickitat Way, Suite 201
Seattle, WA 98134
800-553-4453
mbooks@mountaineersbooks.org
www.mountaineersbooks.org

The Mountaineers Books is proud to be a corporate sponsor of The Leave No Trace Center for Outdoor Ethics, whose mission is to promote and inspire responsible outdoor recreation through education, research, and partnerships. The Leave No Trace program is focused specifically on human-powered (nonmotorized) recreation.

Leave No Trace strives to educate visitors about the nature of their recreational impacts, as well as offer techniques to prevent and minimize such impacts. Leave No Trace is best understood as an educational and ethical program, not as a set of rules and regulations.

For more information, visit *www.LNT.org,* or call 800-332-4100.

OTHER TITLES YOU MIGHT ENJOY FROM
THE MOUNTAINEERS BOOKS

Strange and Dangerous Dreams:
The Fine Line Between Adventure and Madness
Geoff Powter
Adventurers are among our greatest heroes, but cross a line and the pursuit of fame can lead to derision, madness, and death.

The Art of Rough Travel:
From the Peculiar to the
Practical, Advice from a 19th
Century Explorer
*Sir Francis Galton; Edited by
Katharine Harmon*
A fun re-editing of the classic 19th century adventure manual—retaining advice both deliciously bizarre and surprisingly relevant for 21st century adventurers.

Being Caribou
Karsten Heuer
Newlyweds spend five months following the Arctic caribou herd to their breeding grounds and back!

Everest:
The West Ridge
Thomas Hornbein
One of the great mountaineering adventure books of all time.

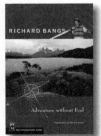

Richard Bangs:
Adventure Without End
Richard Bangs
Sixteen globe-spanning adventure tales from a guide extraordinaire.